Annie W. Chieves.

American S. S. Union
   Published by Union Press — small
copies of Peter Janssen's "Madonna
& Child" (Mary with a book & Child
looking up in her face)
   2 Henrich Hofmann's Christ in Temple
(the Boy picture alone)

The Historical Series for Bible Students.

EDITED BY

PROFESSOR CHARLES F. KENT, PH.D., *of Yale University,*

AND

PROFESSOR FRANK K. SANDERS, PH.D., *formerly of Yale University.*

Volume VIII.

CHRISTIANITY

IN

THE APOSTOLIC AGE.

The Historical Series for Bible Students

*Edited by Professor CHARLES F. KENT, Ph.D., of Yale University, and
Professor FRANK K. SANDERS, Ph.D., formerly of Yale University*

IN response to a wide-spread demand for non-technical yet scholarly and reliable guides to the study of the history, literature, and teaching of the Old and New Testaments, and of the contemporary history and literature, this series aims to present in concise and attractive form the results of investigation and exploration in these broad fields. Based upon thoroughly critical scholarship, it will emphasize assured and positive rather than transitional positions. The series as a whole is intended to present a complete and connected picture of the social, political, and religious life of the men and peoples who figure most prominently in the biblical records.

Each volume is complete in itself, treating comprehensively a given subject or period. It also refers freely to the biblical and monumental sources, and to the standard authorities. Convenience of size, clearness of presentation, and helpfulness to the student make the series particularly well adapted for (1) practical text-books for college, seminary, and university classes; (2) handbooks for the use of Bible classes, clubs, and guilds; (3) guides for individual study; and (4) books for general reference.

Vols.

I. HISTORY OF THE HEBREW PEOPLE.

1. The United Kingdom. Sixth edition.   CHARLES F. KENT, Ph.D., Professor of Biblical Literature, Yale University.
2. The Divided Kingdom. Sixth edition.

II. HISTORY OF THE JEWISH PEOPLE.

3. The Babylonian, Persian, and Greek Periods.   CHARLES F. KENT, Ph.D., Professor of Biblical Literature, Yale University.
4. The Maccabean and Roman Period (including New Testament Times).   JAMES S. RIGGS, D.D., Professor of Biblical Criticism, Auburn Theological Seminary.

III. CONTEMPORARY OLD TESTAMENT HISTORY.

5. History of the Ancient Egyptians.   JAMES H. BREASTED, Ph.D., Professor of Egyptology and Oriental History, The University of Chicago.
6. History of the Babylonians and Assyrians.   GEORGE S. GOODSPEED, Ph.D., Professor of Ancient History, The University of Chicago.

IV. NEW TESTAMENT HISTORIES.

7. The Life of Jesus.   RUSH RHEES, President of the University of Rochester.
8. The Apostolic Age.   GEORGE T. PURVES, Ph.D., D.D., late Professor of New Testament Literature and Exegesis, Princeton Theological Seminary.

V. OUTLINES FOR THE STUDY OF BIBLICAL HISTORY AND LITERATURE.

9. From Earliest Times to 200 A. D.   FRANK K. SANDERS, Ph.D., Professor of Biblical Literature, Yale University, and HENRY T. FOWLER, Ph.D., Professor of Biblical Literature and History, Brown University.

CHRISTIANITY

IN

THE APOSTOLIC AGE

BY

GEORGE T. PURVES, D.D., LL.D.

RECENTLY PROFESSOR OF NEW TESTAMENT LITERATURE AND EXEGESIS
IN PRINCETON THEOLOGICAL SEMINARY

WITH MAPS

NEW YORK
CHARLES SCRIBNER'S SONS
1923

To my Colleagues

IN THE FACULTY OF

PRINCETON THEOLOGICAL SEMINARY

WITH WHOM I HAVE SPENT EIGHT HAPPY YEARS DEVOTED TO
THE STUDY OF GOD'S WORD
AND WHOSE FRIENDSHIP WILL NOT CEASE ALTHOUGH
WE MAY NO LONGER TOIL TOGETHER

THIS VOLUME

IS AFFECTIONATELY DEDICATED

PREFACE

A HISTORY of Christianity in the Apostolic Age should begin with an account of the life and teachings of our Lord. In the series, however, to which the present work belongs a separate volume has been assigned to "The Life of Jesus," and intrusted to the competent hand of Professor Rhees. I have therefore only touched upon the post-resurrection period, so far as it was necessary to set forth the immediate origin of apostolic Christianity.

The purpose of this volume, like the others in the series, is strictly historical. At the same time brief accounts of the New Testament books, with occasionally a defence of their right to be classed with apostolic literature, have been introduced, both because they constitute practically our only sources for the history and because an examination of them is the best means of illustrating the history itself. It is hoped, also, that this feature will make the volume serviceable to a larger number of readers.

I have not, except in a few instances, attempted to mention the many works by which my own studies have been guided and enlightened. To have done so would have compelled me to exceed by a copious use of foot-notes the narrow limits within which I have been confined. The bibliography at the end of the volume will, however, indicate the principal books bearing upon the subject.

In writing upon a theme so vital to the interests of our religion, and upon which a vast amount of literature, representing all shades of opinion, has been produced during this century, I have, of course, often taken positions which readers of different schools will condemn. The positions, however, have been taken only after careful and candid investigation; and, if the result is to uphold in all essential points the traditional conception of apostolic Christianity, it has been because such appears to me to be the inevitable issue of unprejudiced inquiry. An account of the course which the criticism of the New Testament and the consequent constructions of the history of the apostolic age have taken in modern times would show that there has been a steady return on the part of most investigators towards the acceptance, in the main, of the dates to which tradition has assigned the origin of the books out of which apostolic history must be ascertained. This, indeed, does not prevent the most widely different theories both of the interpretation of the books and of the forces which entered into the formation of Christianity. But, in the opinion of the author, it does not appear possible, if the dates of the origin of the books be thus established, to account for the rise and course of apostolic Christianity except by the recognition of those supernatural facts and forces to which the books themselves testify. The frank acknowledgment of the supernatural, together with the perception of the no less truly genetic way in which the original faith in Jesus as Messiah was unfolded and extended, would seem to be required of the historian who wishes to be faithful to his sources of information and to present apostolic Christianity as it really was.

GEORGE T. PURVES.

NEW YORK

THE ROMAN EMPIRE

at its widest extent

Milliaria 50 0 50 100 200 350 Romana
Milliaria 50 0 50 100 200 350 Anglica

B. Sandos & J. Krumholz, del

Russell & Struthers, Eng's, N.Y.

CONTENTS

—◆—

PART I

RISE OF CHRISTIANITY IN JERUSALEM

I

HISTORICAL SOURCES

II

THE ORIGIN OF CHRISTIANITY

III

THE INAUGURATION OF CHRISTIANITY IN JERUSALEM

SECTIONS 22–35. PAGES 21–34

IV

INTERNAL PROGRESS OF THE CHURCH IN JERUSALEM AFTER PENTECOST

SECTIONS 36–48. PAGES 35–46

V

EXTERNAL HISTORY OF THE CHURCH IN JERUSALEM AFTER PENTECOST

SECTIONS 49–61. PAGES 47–55

PART II

EARLY EXPANSION OF CHRISTIANITY

I

HISTORICAL SOURCES

II

THE DISPERSION

III

THE CONVERSION OF PAUL

IV

PROGRESS OF THE MOTHER CHURCH

Sections 98–107. Pages 91–100

V

RISE OF GENTILE CHRISTIANITY IN ANTIOCH

Sections 108–116. Pages 101–110

VI

THE MISSIONARY JOURNEY OF PAUL AND BARNABAS

Sections 117–131. Pages 111–122

PART III

JUDAIC CHRISTIANITY

I

HISTORICAL SOURCES

II

THE CHARACTER OF JUDAIC CHRISTIANITY

III

THE COUNCIL AT JERUSALEM

IV

JUDAIC CHRISTIANITY AFTER THE COUNCIL

Sections 167–173. Pages 160–166

PART IV

EXPANSION OF CHRISTIANITY UNDER PAUL

I

HISTORICAL SOURCES

Sections 174–180. Pages 169–176

II

ENTRANCE OF CHRISTIANITY INTO EUROPE

Sections 181–197. Pages 177–193

III

PAUL IN CORINTH

SECTIONS 198–208. PAGES 194–203

IV

PAUL IN EPHESUS

SECTIONS 209–227. PAGES 204–223

V

FROM EPHESUS TO ROME

SECTIONS 228–245. PAGES 224–237

VI

PAUL IN ROME

SECTIONS 246–261. PAGES 238–251

VII

THE LAST YEARS OF PAUL

SECTIONS 262–271. PAGES 252–261

PART V

PROGRESS OF CHRISTIANITY TO THE CLOSE OF THE APOSTOLIC AGE

I

HISTORICAL SOURCES

II

THE LAST YEARS OF THE APOSTLE PETER

III

THE FINAL TRANSITION FROM JUDAISM TO CHRISTIANITY

SECTIONS 296–300   PAGES 286–289

SECTION 296. Occasion of the Epistle to the Hebrews.   297. Importance of the epistle in the statement of apostolic Christianity.   298. Its leading ideas.   299. Argument of the epistle. 300 Historical value of its teaching.

IV

RISE OF HISTORICAL NARRATIVES

SECTIONS 301–304.   PAGES 290–293

SECTION 301. The apostolic preaching about Jesus.   302. Tendency of the recital to acquire fixity of form; its general contents.   303. Appearance of written gospels.   304. The historical consciousness of the church.

V

THE JOHANNEAN PERIOD

SECTIONS 305–321.   PAGES 294–312

SECTION 305. Transitional character of the last third of the first century.   306 Continued spread of Christianity.   307. Variety of classes in the church.   308. Christian worship. 309. Development of organization.   310 Spread of false teaching.   311. Enmity of the world.   Persecution.   312. Influence of the age on the church.   313. The last years of John.   314. John in Ephesus.   315. The gospel according to John.   Significance of its prologue.   316. Relation of John's first epistle to his gospel   317. The Second and Third Epistles of John.   318. The Revelation.   319. Historical implications of the Revelation.   320. The world-consciousness of Christianity.   321. *Conclusion;* the unity of the apostolic age.

PART I

RISE OF CHRISTIANITY IN JERUSALEM

HISTORICAL SOURCES

1. WE are dependent practically for our knowledge of Christianity in the apostolic age upon the books which compose the New Testament. The Jewish historian Josephus furnishes little, if any, information. He gives, indeed, a brief account of John the Baptist (Antiq. xviii. 5. 2), relates the death of "James the brother of Jesus who is called Christ" (Antiq. xx. 9. 1), and, at the close of the famous paragraph in which he speaks of Jesus, adds, "the tribe of Christians so named from him are not extinct at this day" (Antiq. xviii. 3. 3). The latter passage, however, has probably been largely interpolated by a Christian hand (see *Gieseler*, Eccles. Hist. I. 48; *Schürer*, HJP. I., II. 143), and even the two other passages, though with much less reason, have been questioned. At the most, Josephus furnishes nothing that is of special value. Of Roman writers, likewise, only Tacitus (*Annals*, xv. 44) and Suetonius (*Nero*, 16) mention the Christians, and this in connection with Nero's persecution. The former states that "Christ, the author of this name, when Tiberius was emperor, was put to death by the procurator Pontius Pilate. Though repressed for a while, the deadly superstition again broke forth, not only throughout Judea, the original home of this evil, but

throughout the city [Rome] also, whither all atrocious
and shameful things flow and are practised." While
thus from pagan sources glimpses may be caught of the
new religion, no real account is obtained of its beginnings and development. Neither is there in the Christian writings of the second century anything which adds
substantially to the New Testament records. The historian must depend, therefore, upon the critical study
and careful interpretation of the apostolic literature
itself.

2. For the earliest period, covering the rise of Christianity in Jerusalem, the authorities are the closing
chapters of the four gospels and the opening chapters
of the Acts. None of the so-called apocryphal gospels
are worthy of consideration, even the lately recovered
Gospel of Peter being built on the canonical ones and
adding nothing of historical value (*Swete*, Gosp. of P. p.
xv). Still more valueless are the apocryphal Acts of
Peter, of John, of Thomas, of Andrew, which circulated,
chiefly among heretical sects, in the second and third
centuries. The canonical gospels, however, came from
the apostolic age, and contain the testimony of original
witnesses to the life of Christ (sects. 277–281). We
are only concerned with their closing chapters. These
accounts of the Lord's resurrection and post-resurrection
life are obviously fragmentary. The last twelve verses
of Mark, moreover, are now generally recognized as
an addition to the gospel, having taken the place of the
original conclusion, and cannot be considered of equal
authority with the rest (see *Westcott and Hort*, N. T.
in Greek. Notes on select readings, p. 28). Luke's
last chapter is, from verse forty-four, a condensed summary of Christ's final instructions, and is transitional to

the account with which the Acts begins. Yet in spite of their fragmentary character, and however difficult it may be to construct a chronological narrative from the material contained in them, these brief apostolic records are of the highest value, not only as testimony to the fact of Christ's resurrection, but also as disclosing the state of mind in which the disciples entered on their independent career.

3. Still more important for our purposes is the book commonly entitled the Acts of the Apostles. Its historical value has been warmly disputed in modern times, although upon it rests the whole traditional idea of the greater part of apostolic history. Evidence of many kinds, however, has accumulated to support its accuracy. That it was written in the first century must certainly be admitted (so *Harnack*, Chronologie, I. p. 246; *Ramsay*, St. Paul the Trav. p. 386). In fact, after the middle of the second century it appears as a recognized canonical book, and traces of its use in the churches may be found still earlier. The author was a companion of Paul, for he significantly uses at times in his narrative of the apostle's travels the first person plural (xvi. 10–16; xx. 5 to xxi. 18; xxvii. 1 to xxviii. 16); and that this is not an instance of the use by a later writer of an earlier source is demonstrable, first, by the general similarity of the style of the " we sections " with the rest of the book, and, secondly, by the fact that for the author to have allowed the " we " of his source to have remained unchanged in his narrative would have been to pursue a method entirely different from that which he follows elsewhere when using earlier sources. Furthermore, the tradition, which appears the accepted one in the second century, that the author was Luke,

harmonizes with the notices in Paul's epistles of Luke's movements, as the latter do with no other of the apostle's prominent associates. The objection that a companion of Paul ought to have given fuller information, and that he even shows ignorance of much that such a man would have known (*McGiffert*, Ap. Age, p. 237), proceeds on an arbitrary assumption concerning what Luke would be likely to record, and a failure to appreciate the plan and purpose of his book.

4. What, then, is the value of Acts as an historical source ? That Luke carefully gathered his material is expressly stated by him in the beginning of his gospel (Luke i. 1-4), — an earlier book to which he plainly refers (Acts i. 1, 2). It is highly probable that he collected his matter not only from oral but also from written sources. He had his own notes on Paul's travels. Then the speeches of Peter and others were probably preserved among the Jewish Christians in writing. Other historical records may have been used. Yet Luke does not copy his material slavishly. He weaves it into his narrative, giving much of it in language which is characteristically his own, while at the same time he reproduces in great part the equally characteristic phrases and follows the thought of the original speakers in a way which gives remarkable variety and verisimilitude to his reports. Certainly his opportunities for gathering information were of the best. A companion of Paul, he was acquainted also with some of the leading actors in the earlier history (Acts xxi. 8, 18; Col. iv. 14, compared with 10). He appears to have remained in Palestine during the two years of Paul's imprisonment at Cæsarea, at which time his materials may have been, at least in part, collected.

5. His value as an historian, however, is to be estimated in two ways: first, by comparison with other sources; secondly, by an examination of his method. So far as concerns the first, he may be tested by the epistles of Paul and by archæological evidence relating to the condition of the places in which his narrative moves. His harmony with the epistles, when both are fairly interpreted, has become more and more manifest with the progress of modern exegetical study. Opinions still differ on details, but in the main the trustworthiness of Acts in these matters is certain. Numerous proofs of this will appear in the following pages. Archæology, likewise, has notably confirmed his record. Here the student is specially indebted to the recent works of Prof. W. H. Ramsay (Ch. in Rom. Emp.; St. Paul the Trav.). Luke moves through the varied and changing political relations of the cities of Asia Minor and Europe with perfect accuracy. He reproduces the local coloring of events and repeats the common parlance of the people about whom he writes. It may be safely said that his accuracy has stood the test of fair investigation.

6. It is often said, however, that in the earlier parts of Acts he is not as trustworthy as elsewhere. He cannot be here tested directly by epistles or archæology. But he can be tested as to his method. Does it show an intelligent grasp of the situation and a perception of real progress in the history? The answer to this is also favorable. His whole book is arranged on an artistic, but not artificial, plan, to show the establishment by the Spirit through the apostles of universal Christianity. In his account of the early church in Jerusalem (i. 1 to viii. 3) he follows a

method which shows intelligent comprehension of the course of events and corresponds to what is inherently probable. After describing Christ's last instructions and ascension, and the company which formed the original nucleus of the church, he relates six events (ii. 1–47; iii. 1 to iv. 37; v. 1–16; v. 17–42; vi. 1–8; vi. 9 to viii. 3) which pertain alternately to the internal and external life of the community, and set forth in a representative way the development of the church and its changing relation to Judaism. He thus conceived the history in its logical relations and understood the movement with manifest intelligence. The book of Acts may therefore be used as an authority of the first order. In Luke is to be found the first Christian historian. It may be added that in using Acts we follow the usually received critical Greek text. The theory of Professor Blass of Halle that Luke issued two editions of his books does not seem to have been verified; and the interesting facts occasionally introduced into the narrative by the alleged first edition of Acts, which Professor Blass obtains from certain Greek and Latin manuscripts, are not sufficiently attested.

II

THE ORIGIN OF CHRISTIANITY

7. CHRISTIANITY originated in the appearance among the Jews of Jesus Christ, and specifically from the belief in his Messiahship created by the events of his career, his teaching, and his unique personality. It did not, however, become an independent movement until shortly after its Founder's death. The gospels show that the immediate object of Jesus during his life was twofold. On the one hand, he offered himself to the Jews as one who had come from God to establish the kingdom of heaven, inveighed against current Judaism as a false interpretation of God's commands, and summoned the people to accept him as the revealer of the true religious life. On the other hand, foreseeing from the start their rejection of him (see John ii. 19; iii. 11, 14, 19; Luke iv. 24–27; Matt. viii. 10–12; xii. 39, 41; Luke xi. 49–51; Matt. ix. 15; John vi. 51–56; Matt. xvi. 21–23, etc.), he addressed himself to the task of attaching to himself and his teaching a nucleus of believers who should carry on, after his death, the establishment of the kingdom. But he did not organize them into a separate society, save by the appointment of the twelve apostles. These he constituted his personal representatives and the official heads of the new Israel (Matt. x. 40; Mark iii. 14, 15; Matt. xvii. 19; xviii. 18; xix. 28, cf. Mark x.

37; Luke xxii. 29, 30); but he attempted no further organization. Nor is it difficult to see the reason. It would have interfered with his offer of himself as the Messiah of the nation. It would also have been premature; for he clearly realized (see Matt. xvii. 9; John xvii. 12, 13, etc.) that their activity could proceed successfully only after his own career on earth had been finished. While, therefore, Jesus was the founder of Christianity, the history of the latter as an organized movement may be said properly to have begun with the little company of disciples who believed in him after his rejection by the Jews and crucifixion by Pilate.

8. It is the unanimous testimony of all our sources of information that these disciples, dismayed by the death of Jesus, were re-established in their faith by his resurrection, his subsequent appearances to them, and the instructions which then he gave them. It is beyond question that *belief* in his resurrection was suddenly created among them shortly after his death. Nothing will explain the confidence with which they proclaimed him as Messiah, except the conviction in all of them that he not only still lived, but had been clothed by God with power; and that this conviction took the specific form of belief in the resurrection of his dead body is equally certain from their express testimonies (Acts ii. 24–32; iii. 15; iv. 10, etc.; I. Thess. iv. 14; I. Cor. xv. 4–8, etc.).

9. In considering the grounds upon which this belief rested, the following facts should be borne in mind. (a) The belief appears as strong and universal at the beginning of the history of the church as afterwards. This is attested in the Acts not only by

Luke's own narrative, but by the speeches of Peter which he reports. In the earliest epistle of Paul, also, Christ's resurrection is mentioned as one of the commonplaces of Christian faith (I. Thess. iv. 14), while in I. Corinthians (xv. 1–8) it is presented as a basal fact on which all Christianity reposes. There is thus no indication that the belief formed gradually, even during the earliest period of the apostolic age. It is to be observed also that in the speeches of Peter (Acts ii. 31; x. 41) as much stress is laid on the corporeal reality of the resurrection as is done in the later gospels; nor did Paul conceive of the future bodies of believers, which are to be like the Lord's (I. Cor. xv. 49), as any the less material because they will be also " spiritual " or perfect organs of the Spirit. As, therefore, the belief in Christ's resurrection did not form gradually, so neither is there any trace of a modification of the belief in the interest of a more literal representation. The apostolic description of it is essentially the same throughout.

10. (b) The appeal in support of the fact was made publicly and to well-known and accredited witnesses. The apostles were the official witnesses (Acts i. 22; x. 41; I. Cor. ix. 1; xv. 5–8; John xxi. 14), though their testimony was confirmed by that of James and many others. A large number of persons, therefore, must have received together or at different times evidence of its reality. There is no indication that it was accepted by a majority of these witnesses on the report of a few. Peter, the most conspicuous witness in Acts, — the appearance of Jesus to whom is specifically mentioned by Luke (Luke xxiv. 34) and Paul (I. Cor. xv. 7), — never represents it as resting on his own testimony or on that

of any other individual, but on that of all the apostles
(see *e. g.* Acts ii. 32; iii. 15; x. 41). A belief produced
in so many minds of very different temperaments must
have had a firm foundation.

11. (*c*) The accounts of the resurrection period
given in the gospels were evidently not framed for the
purpose of presenting the evidence on which the church
rested its belief. Such a view of them would be inconsistent with the method of proof illustrated by Paul
(I. Cor. xv. 3–8), which summarizes the evidence, from
the apologetic point of view, current in the churches.
The gospels were written for believers, and give incidents to confirm faith or to serve other religious purposes. This is in accordance with the general character
of those books. Comparison with the kind of evidence
to which appeal is made elsewhere clearly shows that
they give but fragments of the proof by which the belief
in the resurrection was created. It would be wrong,
therefore, to rest the case, affirmatively or negatively,
on them alone.

12. (*d*) At the same time the incidents related in
the gospels or referred to elsewhere (Acts i. 4, 6–8; x.
41; I. Cor. xv. 5–7), however difficult a precise harmony of them may be, exhibit a sobriety and variety of
testimony which lends a strong confirmation to the
formal apostolic witness. There is a notable absence
from them of extravagant elaboration of details, in
regard to either the appearance, actions, or teaching of
the risen Lord, such as are found in later apocryphal
works (see *e. g. Gospel of Peter, Gospel of Nicodemus*).
We learn from them that Jesus appeared both to individual disciples and to companies of them, both by day
(Matt. xxviii. 9, 16–18; Luke xxiv. 29; John xx.

16; xxi. 4; Acts i. 4) and by night (Luke xxiv. 36; John xx. 19), that he conversed and ate with them, and that they handled (Matt. xxviii. 9; Luke xxiv. 39; John xx. 27) and walked with him. The testimony is not merely that his body disappeared from the tomb, or that a few persons, who might have had inflamed imaginations, professed to have seen him, but that a considerable company of people on many occasions and under a variety of conditions received what they believed to be sensible proofs of his appearance to them in the same body which had expired upon the cross. Judging from these fragments of the evidence, the apostolic testimony as a whole must have been based on abundant proof.

13. Nor can the universality and persistence of the disciples' belief be explained on any theory which denies its objective reality. The Jews charged them with having stolen the body and fabricated the story of the resurrection (Matt. xxviii. 11–15). But the honesty of their belief is attested irrefragably by the pure and unselfish character of their lives and preaching, and of the Christian movement as a whole. The Jewish charge also implies a deliberate conspiracy, in which many were induced to unite, and which was carried out so successfully that not only were Pilate's guards circumvented, but no one of the conspirators ever betrayed the plot; and the mental condition of the disciples after the crucifixion, as well as their moral character, absolutely forbids such an hypothesis. No critic, however sceptical, is now disposed to question seriously the honesty of the disciples' belief.

14. Neither can their belief be attributed to illusion. Apart from the evidence already mentioned, and which of itself makes illusion quite impossible, this hypoth-

esis, which would account for the belief by vision
which the disciples supposed they had had of their
Lord, requires the assumption that an expectation of
the resurrection existed among them.   Only thus
would there be a psychological basis for the false
belief.   It is certain, however, that such an expectation did not exist.   It is true that Jesus on at least
three occasions (Mark viii. 31; ix. 31; x. 34) had predicted his death and resurrection.   But the testimony
is equally explicit that under the distress and dis-
appointment of his death the prediction as well as the
command to meet him in Galilee (Mark xiv. 28) was
either forgotten or entirely without influence on the
disciples.   Even the women prepared spices for his
burial.   The first reports of the resurrection were received with incredulity.   There is only one intimation
that any remembered the prediction (Luke xxiv. 21),
and that was after the report of the women had been
heard.   All the information, therefore, which we can
gather concerning the mental condition of the disciples forbids the hypothesis of illusion by eliminat-
ing the element of expectation which is its necessary
psychological basis.   Add to this the large number of
witnesses and the variety of occasions on which their
belief was created, and the hypothesis becomes doubly
incredible.

15. Finally, the evidence likewise forbids even the
mediating opinion that Jesus did show himself to his
disciples in some form, but not in the body which had
been laid in the grave.   This theory is a purely speculative one, and rests on no historical evidence whatever.
It is incontestable that the grave was empty, as the
charge of the Jews clearly proves.   It is equally

certain that the disciples received evidence, and that, too, in spite of a strong indisposition to believe it, that the body in which their Lord appeared to them, though changed in some respects, was identical with that which had been crucified (Acts ii. 31; I. Cor. xv. 15, 20). They particularly narrate the physical proofs given of this identity (Luke xxiv. 40, 43; John xx. 27). The recital of these physical proofs of identity cannot be regarded as the result of a later and legendary tendency, for, as we have already remarked, equal stress is laid on the physical reality of Christ's resurrection body by Peter in the Acts. All views, therefore, which deny the objective reality of the event are beset by insuperable difficulties. If we add to these considerations the ethical and rational character of the Christian life manifested by the apostles, the supposition of either dishonesty or mistake in their belief must certainly be rejected. Criticism itself, if not swayed by philosophical prejudice, must accept the resurrection of Jesus as a supernatural fact lying at the foundation of apostolic history.

16. While, however, the resurrection of their Lord reanimated the faith and hopes of the disciples, his subsequent appearances to them and the instructions which he gave them determined the particular form of their renewed life. He did not live with them habitually as he had done before, but "manifested himself" (John xxi. 1, 14) on repeated occasions and often under altered conditions (Matt. xxviii. 17; Luke xxiv. 16, 31, 36; John xx. 9, 26; xxi. 4). They thus were led to realize that a new order of things had begun. He now plainly appeared a supernatural being, clothed with heavenly power. This could not have appeared

to them unnatural, since they had previously seen
abundant evidence of his celestial origin and power.
It was even more in accord with their Jewish ideas of
a Messiah than the lowly man of Nazareth had been.
But the point to be observed is that the new order,
with its periods of withdrawal and reappearance, accustomed them to the thought of an invisible and yet
active Lord, and prepared them to believe in his continued power after his final departure. His instructions also gave definite direction to their faith. While
dealing in general, as before, with " the things pertaining to the kingdom of God " (Acts i. 3), it consisted
largely in the explanation of the Hebrew Scriptures
with regard to himself (Luke xxiv. 27, 44–47), and
thus pointed to the instrument by which they were
to advance further in the understanding of his mission
and message. They were, moreover, formally directed
to proclaim him to the world, and baptism was appointed as the rite, significant of repentance and faith,
to be used for the admission of new members to the
community (Matt. xxviii. 18–23 ; Luke xxiv. 47). The
faith itself was defined as faith in the Father, Son, and
Holy Spirit (Matt. xxviii. 19), a statement which sum-
marized the teaching of Jesus. He had proclaimed the
fatherhood of God, had represented himself as the Son
of God, and had promised the Spirit of God to his disciples. While, therefore, this summary of his teaching
may not have been at once regarded as a liturgical
formula, there is no reason to doubt that it was used
by Jesus (sect. 36). Finally, on the apostles a special
gift of the Spirit was bestowed whereby they were
authorized to be the spiritual heads of the whole community of believers (John xx. 22, 23).

17. The disciples were thus prepared to begin their independent career, not as a body of mere enthusiasts, but as a society organized by certain definite beliefs. Certainly they had no thought of separating themselves from the existing religious institutions of their nation. They were all the more enthusiastic Hebrews for believing that Israel's Messiah had come. Yet they formed a distinct community. The bond which united them was their faith in Jesus as the divinely sent and now victorious Messiah, the Saviour of all believers, the sure restorer of Israel's glory, the revealer of the Father, the source of power, and the lawful Lord of all mankind. Around this gathered an apprehension of his teaching about God, himself, the kingdom, and the future, which probably varied in degree and extent with different individuals. This faith compacted and energized them. It contained Christianity in the germ. For it the teaching and career of Jesus had prepared. He had always made himself, equally with the Father, the object of their religious trust (see *e. g.* John iii. 14–18; Matt. iv. 19; Mark i. 40; ii. 5; John v. 23; Luke vii. 9, 47; viii. 25; Matt. ix. 28; xi. 28–30; xvi. 16–18; John vi. 47–57, 69; Mark ix. 23; Luke x. 22, etc.). Now, with his career before them as a whole, the object was fully presented on which their faith and love might be fixed so as to be fruitful in a new religion.

18. It is affirmed by Luke that the disciples began their history, as an organized society, in Jerusalem, and he relates only appearances of the risen Lord in or near that city (xxiv. 1–43). The first gospel, on the other hand, while narrating the Lord's appearance to the women near the sepulchre, represents the apostles

2

as receiving the great commission in Galilee (xxviii.
16–20), and the fourth gospel records appearances of
Jesus to them in both Judea and Galilee (xx., xxi.).
The concluding verses added to Mark (xvi. 9–20) apparently have in mind only appearances in and near
Jerusalem, but do not mention the locality. The
supposition of some critics that these differences disclose two originally divergent traditions is, however,
gratuitous. That Jerusalem was, in fact, the place
from which the new religion radiated is attested not
only by Luke, but by the speeches of others which he
incorporated in his narrative (Acts ii. 14; iii. 13–15;
iv. 10; xiii. 31; xxii. 5, 17–20; xxvi. 10), and by
the epistles of Paul (I. Thess. ii. 14; Gal. i. 17–19,
22; ii. 1–10; Rom. xv. 19, 26, 27); and the third
evangelist was content to confine himself to appearances of Jesus at that place because of his interest
in the history of the formation of the church as
such. He does not, however, deny appearances elsewhere.

19. It is to be inferred, therefore, that the disciples,
incredulous of the first reports of their Master's resurrection, and not yet recovered from the shock caused
by his death, lingered in Jerusalem, and there his first
appearances were made to them. Then, however, the
original command (Matt. xxvi. 32; Mark xiv. 28) to
meet him in Galilee was obeyed. There he frequently
appeared to them and gave them most of his instructions. In Galilee they were in safety. Being without
fear of interruption, and even resuming on occasion
their former occupations (John xxi. 3), calmness and
courage were restored. The associations of Galilee
with the earlier ministry of Jesus doubtless served

also to preserve the continuity of their faith with his former teaching.

20. When the time drew near for their mission to begin, Jesus sent them back to Jerusalem. Their message must not appear as a Galilean faith. It must link itself with the centre of Judaism. They must proclaim the Messiah in the sacred city. He himself, though most of his ministry had been in Galilee, had always regarded Jerusalem as the place where alone a national acceptance or rejection of him was possible. It was, therefore, in full accord with his previous declarations that he sent his disciples forth in his name from the capital itself. There he again appeared to them. He directed them to wait for the enduement of spiritual power which he had promised, and which, he said, would not be long delayed (Acts i. 4–8). For he was no more to appear to them as he had been doing. He finally led the eleven out over the Mount of Olives until Bethany was in sight (Luke xxiv. 50). They were expectant of some, perhaps miraculous, manifestation of his power in the near future by which he would overwhelm his enemies and establish his kingdom (Acts i. 6). Instead of this, he repeated their commission and then visibly ascended into the skies. While they gazed upon his vanishing form, two angels appeared by their side who declared that he would return in like manner as he had gone (Acts i. 8–11).

21. The ascension of their Lord thus completed the preparation of the disciples. While Luke alone relates the event, belief in it is implied in the words of Peter, " For David is not ascended into the heavens " (Acts ii. 34), and again, " Whom the heavens must receive "

(Acts iii. 21), in the vision of Stephen (Acts vii. 56), and in the doctrine of the exaltation of Christ and his enthronement at the right hand of God, which is repeatedly adjoined to that of his resurrection (*e. g.* I. Thess. i. 10; iv. 16; II. Thess. i. 7; Eph. i. 20, 21; Phil. i. 9; Col. iii. 1). We are here concerned, however, to note its significance for the first disciples at the time of its occurrence. It completed their preparation for service by making definite their idea of the relation which the Lord was to occupy to them. They were not to look for any more visible appearances until he should come, after their mission was concluded, to establish finally his kingdom. But they henceforth thought of him as not only risen, but as enthroned in heaven and possessed of all power. Trusting in his invisible aid, they were to proclaim him to the world. He was henceforth to them the exalted and reigning Lord and King of the universe. The ascension, added to the resurrection, explains the form which, as we shall see, the first preaching of the apostles took. Luke rightly placed it at the beginning of the Acts. It completed the origin of Christianity and the introduction of apostolic history.

III

THE INAUGURATION OF CHRISTIANITY IN JERUSALEM

22. THE apostles returned to Jerusalem from their
Lord's ascension to wait for the promised Spirit, by
whose power they were to be enabled to do their appointed work (Acts i. 12–14). They met constantly
in a private house, the upper room of which was at
their disposal. It belonged, doubtless, to some fellow-
disciple, and may have been the same in which Jesus
had observed with them the last passover. The company, however, comprised more than the eleven apostles.
Mention is made of certain women, who were perhaps
wives of disciples or others mentioned as witnesses of
the resurrection, with perhaps still others who, like
Mary and Martha of Bethany, had been followers of
Jesus. Their presence was a significant fact. It was
quite in accord with the example set by Jesus in his
ministry (e. g. Luke viii. 2, 3), and indicated the free
individualism of the new movement and the equal participation in its benefits on the part of every believer.
The mother of Jesus also belonged to the company,
and with her were his brethren. The latter had not
believed in his Messiahship even toward the close of
his life (John vii. 5). But to one of them, James, he
had appeared after his resurrection (I. Cor. xv. 7); and
doubtless this, with the other evidence, had secured
their faith. The total number assembled in the upper
room was about one hundred and twenty (Acts i. 15).

By far the majority were Galileans (Acts ii. 7). Two
of them, Joseph Barsabbas and Matthias, had been, like
the apostles, disciples of Jesus from the beginning of
his Galilean ministry. It is clear that his command to
assemble in Jerusalem had caused a considerable ex-
odus of his followers from Galilee. The approach of
Pentecost also made such a pilgrimage the more natural,
and new-comers joined the first band. Amid the general preparation for the festival, their coming attracted
no attention.

23. The disciples, thus assembled, were in a state of
intense expectation. Jesus had promised them "the
baptism of the Holy Spirit," and for it they were to wait.
By it they were to be enabled to proclaim him as
the triumphant Messiah. Belief in the Holy Spirit, or
the Spirit of Jehovah, was thoroughly Jewish, and had
required no special revelation by Jesus. The doctrine
was furnished by the Old Testament, where the Spirit's
work in the divine kingdom is that of endowing God's
agents with the gifts required for their calling (*Oehler*,
O. T. Theol. § 65). By the Spirit of Jehovah the
heroes of Israel had been qualified for service (*e. g.*
Judg. iii. 10; vi. 34; I. Sam. xi. 6, etc.) and the prophets inspired (Hos. ix. 7; Is. xlviii. 16; Mic. iii. 8;
Zech. vii. 12). Isaiah, Ezekiel, Joel, and Zechariah had
described the age of the Messiah as one in which the
Spirit of the Lord would be poured out abundantly upon
his people. This Spirit, they had said, would impart
wisdom, knowledge, power, and devotion (Is. xi. 2;
Joel ii. 28, 29), give fruitfulness to Israel (Is. xxxii.
15), prompt the offer of salvation to all nations (Is.
xlii. 1), and bring the comfort of salvation to all saints
(Is. lxi. 1–3). It would be the pre-eminent possession

of the true Israel (Is. lix. 21), the fulness of the divine
blessing (Is. xliv. 3 ; Ezek. xxxix. 29), the source of a
holy (Ezek. xxxvi. 37) and renewed (Ezek. xxxvii. 14)
life, and the power by which alone the kingdom would
be erected (Zech. iv. 6). John the Baptist, assuming
that he would be understood, had likewise declared
that Messiah would come with the power of the Spirit
(Matt. iii. 11; Mark i. 8; Luke iii. 16; John i. 33).
Jesus had added nothing to this expectation beyond
assuring his disciples that the Spirit would descend
upon them after his departure, would reveal him fully
to their minds, guide them into the truth, and enable
them to testify of him ; in short, would give them sev-
erally the power needed for their appointed tasks. It
is not to be supposed that all these elements of the
Spirit's work were as yet present to the disciples' minds.
But, relying on the promises, they expected such a
bestowment of the Spirit of God as would qualify them
for whatever service they might be called upon to perform. They were thus sensible of their dependence
upon a power from on high which they did not yet
possess. Their ardent desire for this found expression
in " the prayer " in which with one accord they were
constant (Acts i. 14).

24. In only one respect did they further prepare for
their expected mission. The treachery of Judas had
left a vacancy in the original number of the apostles.
Peter proposed that one of those who had been disciples of Jesus from the beginning of his Galilean ministry and who had seen him after his resurrection should
fill the vacant place. Two satisfied the conditions ;
and, after prayer to Christ to indicate his choice, the
lot was cast, and Matthias, on whom it fell, was num-

bered with the apostles (Acts i. 15–26). This incident reveals and implies much. Peter justified his proposal by appealing to the language of the Old Testament. This implies that the Old Testament was not only recognized as authoritative, just as it was by all Jews, but was already interpreted in the light of the new faith, for which it was believed to be a preparation. At the same time the proposal originated in Peter's own reflection. His conduct, therefore, shows that it was recognized by all that the new community had been organized by Christ under the direction of a body of apostles. Peter's prominence indicates neither that he occupied a position of primacy, nor that the authority of the apostolic body as a whole did not yet exist. His words imply quite the contrary. He was simply the most active leader of the governing body. The power of further organization had also, it is clear, been left by Christ with his disciples. This alone explains why the action was taken when the Lord himself had not filled the vacant place. As yet, however, no need was felt of more organization than the restoration of the original number of apostles, whose special duty of witnessing officially to the resurrection was, as all believed, soon to be called into exercise.

25. This incident throws light on the primitive conception of the apostolic office itself. Peter describes the function of an apostle as that of witnessing to the Lord's resurrection. Since any one who had seen the risen Christ could do this, it is clear that a distinction was intended between official and private testimony, and that on the former, as has already been shown, the faith of the world was expected to rest. But the qualifications for the office mentioned by Peter imply still

more. An apostle must have been a disciple of Jesus throughout his ministry from the close of that of the Baptist. This evidently assumes that he was to teach Christ's whole message, life, and work, which alone, indeed, made the resurrection of unique importance. With this accords Peter's subsequent speeches (Acts ii. 22; x. 39–42), and the actual position of the apostles as teachers in the early church (Acts ii. 42; vi. 4; Matt. xxviii. 20; I. Cor. ix. 1; II. Cor. x. 5) as well as their testimony about Christ found in the gospels (see Luke i. 2). Moreover, the language of the psalm, quoted by Peter (Acts i. 20), " his overseership let another take," implies that the office was regarded as charged with the management of the church. It is thus evident not only from Luke's narrative, but from the language of others quoted by him, that the body of apostles were recognized from the beginning as the authoritative heads of the Christian community. To the world they were the official witnesses of the resurrection; to the church, its official instructors and overseers. This agrees with their original appointment by Jesus (sect. 7), nor can the special promise of the Spirit (John xiv. 26; xv. 26, 27; xvi. 13) to qualify them for their office have been forgotten. The actual selection of Matthias was, moreover, accomplished, as in no other case, by the use of the lot, since an apostle had to be chosen by the Lord himself (comp. Acts i. 2; x. 41; I. Cor. ix. 1; Gal. i. 12, etc.); and Luke evidently intends us to understand that Matthias became a recognized member of the apostolic body.

26. We conclude, therefore, that the apostolate, thus defined, was an original institution. The subsequent addition of Paul, since he was qualified in an excep-

tional manner, did not alter the primitive conception
(I. Cor. ix. 1; xv. 8–10; Gal. i. 1, 11–15). Still less
does the occasional use of the term in a broader sense
(Acts xiv. 4, 14; II. Cor. viii. 23; Phil. ii. 25; and according to some Acts ix. 27; Gal. i. 19; I. Cor. xv. 7;
Rom. xvi. 7), or the special prominence of some of the
twelve, or the use of the term in the "Teaching of
the Apostles" (about A.D. 100) to denote travelling
missionaries, conflict with the representation here
given.

27. The feast of Pentecost was the second of the
three chief Mosaic festivals. It fell on the fiftieth day
after the second day (Nisan 16th) of the passover. It
celebrated the completion of the grain harvest. In the
Old Testament it is called the feast of harvest (Ex.
xxiii. 16) or of weeks (Ex. xxxiv. 22) and the day of the
first fruits (Num. xxviii. 26). Special offerings were
made, and two leavened loaves of wheat bread, significant of the finished harvest, together with two lambs
as peace-offerings, were waved before the Lord. It was
a popular and joyful festival. Multitudes of Jews, not
only from Palestine but from abroad, attended the
celebration. If passover reminded them of their redemption from the land of bondage, Pentecost celebrated their possession of the land of promise. Among
the later Jews it also celebrated the giving of the law
at Sinai; but that idea apparently did not attach to it
at the time of which we are writing. Gladness and
gratitude were the keynotes of the festival.

28. According to Acts, it was on the day of Pentecost that the promised Spirit descended on the disciples and the career of the Christian community
was inaugurated. The expression "when the day of

Pentecost was being fulfilled" (Acts ii. 1, R. V. marg.) is to be understood as distinctly affirming that the event occurred during that day. We learn from Peter's words (Acts ii. 15) that it was early in the morning, soon after the temple ritual had been concluded. The determination of the day of the week depends on the date assigned to the crucifixion of Jesus. If he died on Nisan 14th, the resurrection was on the 16th, and Pentecost likewise fell on Sunday. If, however, he died on Nisan 15th, Pentecost fell on Saturday. It is sometimes said that the Jews would not observe Pentecost on the third, fifth, or seventh days of the week, but there is no evidence of this rule at the time of which we are treating (comp. *Ideler*, Handb. der Chronol. I. p. 537). We think it most probable that this Pentecost was on Saturday, and that the later custom of commemorating it on Sunday arose from considerations of ecclesiastical convenience, especially from the wish to observe it fifty days after Easter (comp. *Wieseler*, Chron. d. Apost. Zeitalters, pp. 19–21). Nine days, therefore, after the Lord's ascension his promise was fulfilled.

29. On that day the disciples, having doubtless returned from the temple services, were assembled in the upper room. Suddenly they heard a roaring sound, like that of a rushing wind, coming from above. It filled the whole house where they were gathered. Immediately also a small tongue, having the semblance of fire, appeared resting upon the head of each disciple. At the same time their minds were filled with joyous exultation and spiritual enlightenment; and, realizing that the promise had begun to be fulfilled, they broke forth with one impulse into ecstatic praise of God.

But the noise from heaven had been heard by others in the crowded streets, and a number soon gathered before the house. We may suppose, also, that the disciples, confident that the time to proclaim the Messiah had arrived, willingly went out from the upper room into the street, and finally, perhaps, into one of the outer courts or porches of the temple. Their praises continued and the audience increased. The latter was composed of such varied elements as might be found always in Jerusalem and especially at a festival (see *Josephus*, Antiq. xvii. 10. 2; B. J. II. 3. 1). That many foreign-born Jews had taken up permanent residence in the holy city is attested by the synagogues which they had established there (Acts vi. 9; *Schürer*, HJP. II. 1. p. 49). A graphic portrayal of the variety of countries represented is given by Luke in the summary of expressions of astonishment which he puts into the lips of the assembled crowd (Acts ii. 7–11). This astonishment was caused by the fact that the Galileans uttered their praises of God in the languages of the various countries from which the listeners came. Such is clearly Luke's statement (Acts ii. 8, 11). We are doubtless to understand that some spoke in one language and others in others, so that each foreigner found himself in the presence of one or more using his native tongue. This miracle served to increase the number and wonder of the audience. Some, indeed, mocked at the confusion of sounds and said, "These men are full of new wine." But the majority took the matter more seriously. The praises of the disciples do not appear to have ceased until Peter, standing forth with the other apostles, addressed the assemblage.

30. The apostle's address consisted first of an explanation of the phenomenon. It was, he said, the fulfilment of Joel's prediction of the outpouring of the Spirit upon Israel before the Messianic judgment should take place. It denoted the renewal of Israel, the arrival of the day of salvation, and the impending retribution which Messiah would visit on unbelievers (Acts ii. 15–21). Thereupon Peter proclaimed Jesus to be Messiah. He rehearsed God's attestation of him by miracles, and described his crucifixion as a crime which, nevertheless, God had intended to come to pass. Then he declared his resurrection (22–24). He next entered on an argument to prove that a dying and risen Messiah had been foretold in Scripture. David had foreseen such (Ps. xvi. 8–11), and his words of hope after death had referred to his promised Seed (25–31). Hence the apostle concluded by a renewed declaration of the resurrection of Jesus and of his exaltation to the right hand of God. He, being now enthroned, as had also been predicted of him (Ps. cx.), had given the promised Spirit to his disciples. All Israel should therefore know that the one whom they had crucified was their Messiah and Lord (32–36). This noble address, which was followed by other exhortations, made a profound impression. The conditions of salvation which the apostle announced — repentance for sin and baptism in the name of Jesus as the Christ — were simple and natural, and involved no rupture with the existing state or church. So faith was awakened in many minds, and the close of the day of Pentecost saw the little band of one hundred and twenty expanded into a company of about three thousand (Acts ii. 41).

31. This account of the formal inauguration of Christianity in Jerusalem has, of course, been the subject of criticism. It is evident, however, that some great spiritual quickening must have occurred, if we are to account for the subsequent activity of the disciples and for the large number of Jews who, by all reports, speedily accepted the new faith (see *e. g.* Acts v. 28; viii. 1–3; Gal. i. 22, etc.). Furthermore, while the speeches of Peter do not describe the external events of Pentecost, they do refer to the outpouring of the Spirit as a fact which was manifest to the eyes and ears of spectators (Acts ii. 17, 33; iii. 19; x. 46, 47). That the presence of the Spirit was usually evidenced in the apostolic churches not only by the quickening of faith and by boldness and devotion in service, but also by miraculous powers and by inspired utterances of various kinds, is amply attested by the epistles of Paul (*e. g.* I. Cor. xii., xiv.; Gal. iii. 5), and this makes it probable that the beginnings of Christianity in Jerusalem were attended by similar phenomena; while the established observance of Pentecost in the second century (comp. also Acts xx. 16) as a Christian festival must have been based on some momentous fact which occurred on that day.

32. Nor need the large number of converts cause surprise, if the whole situation be realized. The death of Jesus was recent, and the consciousness that a national crime had been committed in his crucifixion was easily aroused (Acts ii. 23; iii. 13; iv. 9; v. 30). The remembrance of his teaching and miracles was still fresh, and to it appeal was constantly made by the apostles (Acts ii. 22; iii. 14; x. 38). The nation had long been in a fever of excitement and was re-

sponsive, especially at the feasts, to every appeal made
on patriotic or religious grounds (comp. Acts v. 34–39).
The confident testimony of the disciples to the resurrection of Jesus would be the more readily believed
because of the remembrance of his former miracles.
Their exultant praises, with the strange phenomena
which attended them, deepened the impression. Their
appeal to prophecy made their faith seem genuinely
Hebrew.   Possibly also the new converts numbered
not a few from both Galilee and Judea who had previously been followers or admirers of Jesus. If we add
the quickening of conscience under the power of the
Spirit, it is not difficult to comprehend the motives
which led so many to yield obedience to the apostle's
summons.

33. Finally, the miraculous incidents of this event
will not appear incredible to one who accepts the miracles and resurrection of Jesus. The account of "the
tongues" at Pentecost has indeed been thought by
some, who are not otherwise opposed to the miraculous,
to betray legendary embellishment. There should be
no doubt that Luke affirms that the utterances were
in foreign languages. The view that the miracle lay
in the minds of the hearers (see *Wendt*, Kommentar)
is opposed by his express statements (Acts ii. 4, 8, 11).
But of such speaking in foreign languages there is no
description elsewhere in the New Testament. Paul,
on the other hand, speaks of the "gift of tongues" as
a frequent possession of believers when under the
power of the Spirit. He gives (I. Cor. x. 12; xiv.)
directions for its regulation in public assemblies, and
it would appear from his language that the gift manifested itself in unintelligible ejaculations of praise or

prayer. He distinguishes it from prophecy, which was the inspired utterance of truth in the language of the hearers. The gift of " tongues " needed the correlative gift of " interpretation," if it was to be profitable to any but the speaker himself. It does not seem possible, however, to believe that the unintelligibility of the " tongue " was due to its utterances being in a foreign language. Paul uses languages as an illustration of the gift (I. Cor. xiv. 10, 11), which must, therefore, have been different from the thing used to illustrate it; and he regards it by no means as a possible instrument of missionary work, but as a spiritual exercise profitable only to the speaker (I. Cor. xiv. 14, 28). It is possible that in his quotation (I. Cor. xiv. 21) from Isaiah, " By men of strange tongues and by the lips of strangers will I speak unto this people," he betrays a reminiscence of Pentecost; but his description of the " tongues " in Corinth is hardly consistent with the idea that they were utterances in foreign languages.

34. Now the Pentecostal " tongues " present in many respects similar characteristics to those described by Paul. Their utterances were not preaching but praise. They were the expression of a highly exalted state of mind. Neither is it likely that two gifts so nearly alike should have existed and yet have been fundamentally different. Both Peter at Pentecost and Paul to the Corinthians explain the utterances as warnings to unbelievers. Moreover, Luke himself elsewhere refers to " speaking with tongues " in a way which shows that he was acquainted with the gift which Paul describes; yet in one place he seems clearly to identify it with the tongues of Pentecost (Acts x. 46; xix.

6). The very term "tongue" to describe the gift would seem also to point to some such event as that of Pentecost. It is altogether probable, therefore, that the Pentecostal tongues were the introduction of this "gift." But, if so, then the utterances at Pentecost differed in form from the gift as we find it at Corinth. This, however, should by no means be regarded as improbable or as impeaching Luke's accuracy. It is quite possible that on other occasions the gift took a different form from that in Corinth, and there were certainly special reasons why it should at Pentecost take the form which Luke reports. It had been the express command of Jesus that his disciples should carry his message to all nations, and the expectation of doing this lay already in their minds. What more natural than that the Spirit, in inaugurating the church, should indicate the universality of the Messianic reign, which was to find ultimate expression in the praises to God of all mankind? Moreover, Peter himself (Acts ii. 18) regarded the utterances as a form of prophecy, so that they must on that occasion have been intelligible; and this inference is rendered the more cogent by the fact that the words, "they shall prophesy," are not found in Joel, but are an addition by the apostle himself.

35. The statements, therefore, of so careful an historian as Luke should not be doubted. The praises of the disciples not only uttered their own lofty joy at the coming of the promise, but expressed in the very forms of their utterances the universal reign of the true Messiah. The symbolism of the sound-like wind from heaven was manifestly appropriate to denote the coming of the Spirit. It indicated his source, his

3

power, his mysterious, invisible operation. The fire-like appearance of the tongues emblemized the purifying character of his influence (comp. Matt. iii. 11). The tongues themselves, distributed on the heads of the disciples, indicated the universal possession of the Spirit by all believers, and that boldness of access to God was now their privilege. So, as we have seen, the form of the inspired utterances expressed the truth that not a Jewish but a universal kingdom of God had been established. All this had been done by the power of the risen and exalted Christ. Christianity, therefore, was not a natural evolution out of the teachings and career of Jesus. The human agents acted in full accordance with their natural dispositions and under the immediate influence of the historical situation in which they were placed. But in its deepest essence, Christianity was inaugurated by the supernatural operation of the Spirit of Christ. This is the testimony of the documents; and of such an operation the miraculous incidents of Pentecost were appropriate emblems.

IV

INTERNAL PROGRESS OF THE CHURCH IN JERUSALEM AFTER PENTECOST

36. THE enlarged and increasing (Acts ii. 47) body of believers continued to form a closely united company. They were not only bound together by their common faith in Jesus, but they constituted an actual society under the direction and instruction of the apostles (Acts ii. 42). They met daily for "the prayers" (*ibid.*) which as Jews they had been accustomed to offer but which had now obtained new import and value. They also had together, probably in the evening (Acts xx. 7), daily meals at their homes (Acts ii. 42, 46), — the "love feasts" of a later time (Jude 12), — which were concluded by the observance of the memorial rite which Jesus had instituted on the night of his betrayal (I. Cor. xi. 18–29). In their assemblies they constantly received instruction from the apostles (Acts ii. 42; vi. 2), who were recognized as the Spirit-taught guides of the rest. The instruction consisted, doubtless, of the recital of Jesus' life and teaching and the exposition of the Old Testament. New members were received, after repentance and the confession of faith in Jesus, by the rite of baptism. This was in accordance with the express command of Christ (Matt. xxviii. 19). The administration of it was

not always performed by the apostles (Acts viii. 16, 38). Probably any disciple felt himself at liberty thus to welcome a new believer. Nor is it clear what formula, or whether any unvarying one, was used. In Acts and the epistles, baptism is said to have been in or on the name of Christ, or as into Christ (Acts ii. 38; viii. 16; x. 48; xix. 5; Rom. vi. 3; Gal. iii. 27). Possibly, however, these phrases do not describe a formula, but the truth which the baptized professed and the relationship into which he entered. On the other hand, it is possible that the words of Christ (Matt. xxviii. 19) were not at first regarded as a liturgical formula. They are primarily a statement of the threefold faith which summarizes the teaching of Jesus (sect. 16). The first record of their use in baptism is in the "Teaching of the Apostles" (ab. A.D. 100). But, whatever the formula employed, the recipients of baptism penitently accepted Jesus as their Messiah, and expected to obtain from the Father and his Son remission of sins and the gift of the Holy Spirit.

37. Meanwhile the Spirit continued to manifest his power among them. The apostles wrought many miracles, chiefly of healing, in the name of Jesus (Acts ii. 43; iii. 6, 7; v. 12–16), which were regarded as God's attestation of their teaching and office (iv. 29, 30) ; and "with great power they gave witness of the resurrection of the Lord Jesus" (iv. 33). Others of the disciples also, as Joseph Barnabas (iv. 36) and Stephen (vi. 8, 9), were conspicuous in word or miracle or both. No doubt, too, though Luke does not mention it, the company as a whole enjoyed such "spiritual gifts" as we read of later in the church of Corinth (comp. Heb. ii. 4). But still

more impressive was the spectacle of their intense religious joy. This also was the Spirit's work. The sense of salvation already attained broke the hard shell of formal Judaism and revived the genuine life of Israel, as psalmists and prophets had described it. The faith in a living and reigning Messiah ended the doubt and feebleness which had long fallen on the nation's hope. Joy and love were the most marked features of the disciples' life (Acts ii. 46), and only increased with the rise of peril from the civil authorities (Acts iv. 23–37). What the future might be, and how long Jesus would remain in heaven, they did not know. But they knew that their present task was to convince the nation of his Messiahship. They believed that the great crisis, for weal or woe, had come to Israel; that salvation for nation and individual lay in repentance and faith toward Jesus; and for some time they evidently hoped that the nation would be converted to their belief.

38. One feature of the movement calls for special notice. The disciples considered all their worldly property to be at the service of the community and freely parted with it to supply the needs of the brethren. At first this seems to have been done only when special cases of need arose (Acts ii. 45). But there must have been many such occasions. The majority were probably from the poorer classes. Others, like the Galileans, had left their homes and occupations. The service of the cause, no doubt, often entailed pecuniary loss. At any rate the occasions for such beneficence seem for a while to have increased, so that the sale of property became general. The proceeds were given to the apostles and distribution made

to those in need (Acts iv. 34, 35). We read also of
a "daily ministration" of supplies to the widows of
the community. These were probably not the only
ones thus cared for. They are mentioned because in
their case a difficulty arose (vi. 1). At the same time
there is no indication in the descriptions given of this
liberality that it was imposed as a law, or that the
possession of private property was considered improper.
On the contrary, Ananias was reminded that his
property was wholly in his own power. Neither can
the liberality be traced to any other motive than love.
It is possible that belief in the near approach of the
second advent may have operated with some. It is
possible that others may have been moved by the
remembrance of certain teachings of Jesus (*e. g.* Matt.
xix. 21 ; Luke xi. 33), or by the common purse which
the Master and his disciples had. But the dominant
motive was clearly love, born of the joy of their great
salvation. It is quite gratuitous also to see in this
practical communism a sign of Essenic influence, since
the most characteristic features of the Essene mode
of life do not appear among the disciples (comp.
Schürer, HJP. II. 2. p. 188), and since the causes
lying within the Christian life itself are abundantly
sufficient to account for the result. Indeed we cannot suppose that the sale of property was absolutely
universal, nor that it continued to the extent to which
it was at first practised ; for we afterwards read that
Mary, the mother of Mark, owned a house in Jerusalem
(Acts xii. 12), and distinctions between rich and poor
are known to have continued among Jewish Christians
generally (Jas. ii. 2, 3 ; Gal. ii. 10). We may believe
rather that the enthusiasm was checked, or at least

regulated, when experience proved the injurious consequences to which its abuse might lead. Nevertheless this feature of early Jerusalem Christianity powerfully exhibited the entire devotion and the unbounded brotherly love which the Spirit of Jesus produced in the disciples.

39. In spite, however, of the strong bonds by which they were united, there was as yet no rupture with the national worship. On the contrary, the temple services, which they frequented (Luke xxiv. 53; Acts ii. 46; iii. 1), must have been filled with fresh meaning to the disciples, and the outer courts and porches of the temple were the places where the apostles commonly preached (Acts iii. 11; v. 12, 20). The new movement, in fact, seemed a genuine revival of Hebrew faith, and none as yet imagined, however much it involved a condemnation of the rulers for the crucifixion of Jesus, that it involved a breach with Judaism itself. It appeared rather a spiritual interpretation of Judaism. This gave it the more favor with the people. The apostles stood forth as the leaders of a movement which honored above all the God of Israel (Acts v. 12–14). Hence even the Pharisees do not seem to have actively opposed them; and in course of time many priests, the number of which in Jerusalem was very large, accepted the new faith (Acts vi. 7). Thus, in spite of the opposition of the Sadducees, to be mentioned presently, the outlook was favorable, and the impression was strengthened among the disciples that Israel's golden age had at last dawned.

40. Yet all was not ideal even within the Christian community itself. Two incidents broke the harmony. One was the attempt of Ananias and Sapphira to pose before the brethren as having devoted their entire

property to the cause, when in reality they gave only a portion (Acts v. 1–11). It was an offence against the very spirit by which the community was organized; for it exhibited falsehood, worldliness, and essential unbelief. Hence their sin, detected by Peter, was visited by God with awful punishment. This was intended to be a solemn warning to others of the sincerity which the Lord demanded. It enhanced also the authority of the apostles. The incident further shows that the spiritual life of the disciples, even in the freshness of its first days, was not exempt from commonplace temptation and was liable to fall before it. Neither was it a life of fanatical enthusiasm. It was as sensible of ethical duty as it was exuberant with spiritual hope.

41. Later on, complaints arose on the part of the Greek-speaking Jews that the widows belonging to their part of the community were being neglected in the daily ministration of supplies (Acts vi. 1). Thus, as in the case of Ananias, the attempt to put in operation a practically common life proved liable to produce spiritual dangers. The complaint of the Hellenists, moreover, touched a phase of the situation which was likely to become serious, and led to the first step in the further organization of the new community.

42. Thus far the apostles had been the only officials of the infant church. They had, doubtless, with the increase of converts and duties, used subordinates in the administration of affairs, and " the young men " who carried away the bodies of Ananias and Sapphira (Acts v. 6, 10) may indicate the class oftenest employed. The terms used of them, however, show that they did not constitute an office; and as the disciples still retained their connection with the synagogues (vi. 9), no

need of special organization of their own was felt. In fact it would have implied a breach with Judaism which as yet was foreign to their thoughts. The complaint of the Hellenists, however, suggested to the apostles the necessity of some arrangement to meet the difficulty; and this was accomplished in a way which satisfied all parties and harmonized with both the supremacy of the apostles and the rights of the community. Seven men were chosen by the brethren and were set apart to the work by the imposition of the hands of the apostles. Thus the apostles again appear as the authoritative founders of the church, whose special function, however, was teaching. The advance in organization, it should be noted, was brought about by the pressure of practical needs and without reference to any previous program. The whole congregation were recognized as having the right to choose their officials. But the step was a most important one, for it was the first in the solidification of the disciples into a society separate from the synagogue.

43. All the seven men chosen for the new office had, singularly enough, Greek names. It would be too much to infer that all were Hellenists. But some of them were, and one was even a proselyte. The choice of them manifests, therefore, the spirit of love and unity which prevailed. They had for their work specifically the distribution of the common funds. No title is given to their office by Luke, nor can it be shown that it was modelled after any in the synagogue. Since, however, we afterwards find in the Pauline churches the office of deacon (Phil. i. 1; I. Tim. iii. 8), the function of which was the care of the poor, and since the Pauline churches were modelled naturally

after the Jewish-Christian, it is not improbable that
among the latter the office of "the seven" developed
into one which had the care of the poor generally, and
obtained by pre-eminence the title of deacon or minister.
This supposition may seem to be opposed by the silence
of Acts on the subject of "deacons" and by the fact
that the gifts from Antioch for the poor in Judea are
said to have been sent to the *elders* (Acts xi. 30); but
it may be said in reply that the author of Acts has little
interest in organization for its own sake, and that the
gifts from Antioch would naturally be sent to the elders,
even though there were deacons to distribute them.
Neither can the silence of the Epistle of James on the
subject of deacons be pressed as an argument either way.
At the same time the appointment of "the seven" was
an arrangement to meet a specific need arising from a
particular situation. There is nothing to show that
the apostles were at the time conscious that they were
establishing a permanent office. It remained for the
progress of events to perpetuate or modify the new arrangement. None the less does the event exhibit the
principle of self-organization, under the direction of the
apostles, inherent in the community, and containing
the power by which the disciples were destined eventually to separate themselves from the Jewish church.

44. Meanwhile the apostles had been constantly
occupied in giving instruction to the disciples (Acts
ii. 42; vi. 2, 4) and in preaching to the populace (iii.
12–26; iv. 2, 20; v. 28, 42). We can hardly be wrong
in supposing that the former consisted mainly in the
recital of the deeds and teaching of Jesus as well as in
pointing out the fulfilment of prophecy in him. Thus
the beginnings were made of that stream of evangelic

narrative which ultimately was embodied in our synoptic gospels. The story would naturally be repeated again and again. Perhaps portions of it were already reduced to writing. We may infer from the contents of the synoptics that the apostles recited especially the events of the Lord's ministry in Galilee, in which he had trained them in his doctrines, and the thrilling story of the last week of his life. This, however, was not done in the interest of biography, but to guide the converts into those religious ideas in which the apostles had themselves been instructed by the Master, and to fix their faith and love on his person and on his work in their behalf.

45. To obtain an idea of the forms in which the truth as yet lay in the apostles' minds, we are dependent on the speeches of Peter recorded in the Acts. These indeed must be used for this purpose with caution. It would be unfair to suppose that they express all that the apostles believed or taught. Being public addresses to unbelievers, they only contain such truths as might induce belief. Yet the very simplicity of their statements assures us of their genuineness, and enables us partly to understand the progress of theological thought. They certainly show that from the beginning Christianity embodied thought as well as zeal. It gave a rational account of itself. It based itself on the known facts of Jesus' life and teaching, and began to interpret these by the aid of the Old Testament and the spiritual illumination which since Pentecost had been granted to the apostles and in some measure to all. It assumed, of course, Hebrew monotheism and the authority of the Old Testament. The new faith arose out of the soil of the Hebrew religion. All its presup-

positions were those of Moses and the prophets. To them the apostles constantly appealed and to no others. But the facts of Jesus' life and teaching threw a new light on the older revelation, even as the latter did on the former; and out of the adjustment of the two, under the Spirit's guidance, Christian theology began.

46. Yet the statement of the new faith advanced slowly from the nature of the situation. The fundamental truth was that Jesus was the Messiah. His crucifixion is not further explained by Peter than that it had been in accordance with God's purpose (ii. 23) and had been predicted by the prophets (iii. 18). His resurrection and exaltation to the right hand of God proved that by his work on earth he had secured the right to grant to all believers remission of sins (ii. 38; iii. 19) and the gift of the Spirit, which was the seal of their acceptance and the promised sign of the Messianic salvation (ii. 16–18, 33; iii. 19; v. 32). Jesus himself was called the " Servant " of God (iii. 13; iv. 27; comp. Is. lii. 13, etc.), the Holy One and the Just (iii. 14). By his exaltation he had become Lord of all (iii. 36), and the giver, as he was the possessor, of spiritual life (iii. 15; v. 31). In short, he was the Saviour (iv. 12; v. 31). He would remain in heaven, clothed with authority, until the spiritual restoration of Israel be accomplished (iii. 21), when he will return in glory (iii. 20) and usher in the judgment (ii. 19, 20; iii. 23; x. 42). Meanwhile the call to salvation was addressed first to Israel (iii. 25, 26), though whosoever (ii. 21), even of those afar off (ii. 39), should call upon his name would be saved.

47. The apostle's teaching, meagre as this report of it is, is notable both for its omissions and its contents.

It evinces no effort to define the nature of Christ nor to adjust his dignity to that of Jehovah; nor is there any reference to his pre-existence. No explanation of his death is given beyond the declaration that God had appointed and predicted it. The work of the Spirit likewise is not presented in its regenerating aspect, but as it appears in the subsequent experience of the believer. Moreover, faith in Jesus and enjoyment of life from him lay side by side with the observance of the Mosaic ritual, without the latter, so far as appears, being used to interpret the work of the Christ. Yet, as has been said, much more must have been believed than these discourses disclose; for, on the other hand, Jesus is represented as possessing in his exaltation divine prerogatives. He can grant remission of sin and the gift of the Spirit. To him prayer was made (i. 24), and he will be the Judge of all. His work on earth was one of obedience (iii. 14; iv. 27) and revelation (iii. 23), and his exaltation was the reward which he merited (ii. 33; iii. 13). The Christian life is represented as a purely religious one, and Christ is the object on which saving faith rests in the same way as upon God (comp. ii. 21 and iv. 12). Belief in the pre-existence of Jesus is probably to be assumed both because Jesus had so habitually represented himself as having come from heaven, that the disciples, especially with their now exalted view of him, could hardly have forgotten his words, and because belief in Messiah's pre-existence was by no means unfamiliar to the Jews (see *The Book of Enoch*, xlvi. 1, 2; xlviii. 3, 6; lxii. 6, 7, etc. *Fourth Esdras*, xii. 32. So John the Baptist, John i. 30).

48. In Peter's speeches we may thus see Christian

thought beginning to express itself along those lines which the situation made necessary. The issues and the motives were very practical. The popular ideas of Messiah were so various and some of them so exalted that no need was felt of adjusting in popular discourse the glory of Jesus with belief in monotheism. The fulfilment of prophecy was the most natural and forcible argument to employ, and seemed to many to provide of itself a sufficient explanation of what had happened to him. The new movement was not primarily theological. Yet neither was it without definite beliefs. These, however, attained expression in accordance with the progress of the history. The truths proclaimed by Peter were, as far as they went, an interpretation of Jesus' life and personality. They were sufficient for the time, and evidence the power of apostolic Christianity to give a rational statement of its faith.

EXTERNAL HISTORY OF THE CHURCH AFTER
PENTECOST

49. THE external growth of the new community was
certainly rapid. The believers, including doubtless
those converted at Pentecost, soon numbered about
five thousand (Acts iv. 4). It is safe to say, from
various expressions used in Acts (v. 14; vi. 7), that in
the three or four years following Pentecost the number
converted on that day was trebled. Perhaps even a
larger estimate may be allowed. On the other hand,
in a large city like Jerusalem the disciples formed a
small fraction of the population. Their activity, however, made their progress very impressive. Nor need
we suppose that believers were confined to Jerusalem.
The movement naturally spread into Judea and Galilee,
and it is probable that it penetrated farther. A little
latter we hear of disciples in Damascus (Acts ix. 2,
10) and other foreign cities (xxvi. 11), and this diffusion of the faith must have begun early. It would
appear that at least the Jews in Syria were affected,
and it is not impossible that the new gospel was carried still more widely throughout "the dispersion" by
visitors to the feasts and by other Jewish travellers.

50. But, as already explained, the loyalty of the
disciples to the national worship prevented inter-
ference by the Jewish authorities, while, of course,
there was nothing in their practices to call for inter-

ference by the Romans. It was too common for sects and parties to rise among the excited population of Palestine for this peaceful one to attract the attention of the government (comp. Acts v. 36, 37; *Jos.* Antiq. xvii. 10). The first opposition emanated from the Sadducees. To that party most of the nobility belonged, and especially the branches of the high-priestly family (Acts iv. 6; *Schürer*, HJP. II. 2. p. 29, etc.). The new sect offended them for several reasons. The chief priests had been active in securing the crucifixion of Jesus. They also opposed belief in a future life, and especially ridiculed belief in a resurrection (Mark xii. 18–27, etc.). Still further, they were engrossed in the maintenance of their political power, so that such religious enthusiasm as that of the disciples was specially obnoxious to them. Yet even the opposition of the Sadducees arose quite incidentally. The healing of the lame man by Peter at the gate of the temple called " Beautiful " (Acts iii. 1, 2; *Jos.* Antiq. xv. 11. 5; B. J. v. 5. 3) led to a great concourse of people in Solomon's porch, — a portico on the east side of the temple area (*Jos.* Antiq. xx. 9. 7), — where Peter addressed them. The temple guard, at the command of the Sadducees, arrested Peter and John, probably on the charge of fomenting tumult. The next day the Sanhedrim was convoked. Peter made a brave address, proclaiming to them Jesus as the Christ and only Saviour, and reproaching them for his crucifixion (Acts iv. 8–12). The presence of the man who had been healed, the boldness of the apostles, whom the rulers recognized as former companions of Jesus, and the well-known sympathy of the people, prevented any further consequence than a command to discontinue their teaching. But while the arrest was unpremeditated and the issue favorable, the event boded ill for the future. The disciples realized this (Acts iv. 23–30), and prepared for the conflict which their Lord had faced and which evidently lay before them.

51. So, in time, more active measures were taken by the high-priestly party to put down the growing sect. By their orders all the apostles were arrested and imprisoned (Acts v. 17, 18). But when, on the next day, the Sanhedrim assembled, the prisoners were not to be found. During the night an angel had liberated them, and by his instructions they had boldly resumed in the morning their preaching in the temple. This was plainly inviting conflict. When news of it was taken to the council, officers were sent to bring the apostles without violence ; for the rulers, doubtless attributing the escape of the prisoners to treachery, were awed by the popularity and fearlessness of the Galileans. Their plans were thus unsettled. They upbraided the apostles for disobedience and sedition (v. 28). When the latter again proclaimed their faith, the rage of the rulers was unbounded, and they consulted how they might put the men to death.

52. A fatal issue was, however, prevented by the speech of Gamaliel. He was the leading Pharisee and Rabbi of his day, and is said by some to have been the grandson of the still more famous Hillel (but comp. *Schürer*, HJP. II. 2. p. 363). He exerted influence also, not only because of his personal reputation, but because he represented the numerous and popular Pharisaic party. As such, he was disposed to look with indulgence on men who were strict ob-

4

servers of the law, preached the resurrection of the
dead, and represented a religious, rather than a political, movement. He had, of course, no real sympathy
with the apostles' views, and probably did not even
understand them. But he was opposed to religious
persecution. He seems to have felt also that they were
living in unusual times, and that an outburst of religious zeal, with whatever errors it might be combined,
ought not to be summarily condemned. God might be
back of it. He pointed out two former movements,
those of Theudas [1] and Judas the Galilean, which had
been suppressed by Roman arms. So would this one
be, if it became dangerous. If, on the other hand, it
was purely religious, why should the Sanhedrim persecute it? It should be allowed to run its course, and
reveal in due time its worth or weakness.

53. The speech of Gamaliel was a shrewd and timely
argument. It was the speech of a politician and a philosopher. It held the Sadducees in check; it pleased
the people; it showed some breadth of view; while it
committed the speaker to nothing, and indicates no
real interest on his part in the merits of the controversy. It is not strange that it determined the action
of the Sanhedrim. To placate the Sadducees, the
apostles were beaten and commanded not to teach.

[1] It is unnecessary to identify the Theudas mentioned by Gamaliel,
in Luke's report of his speech, with the one mentioned by Josephus
(Antiq. xx. 5. 1), who appeared some years later. The descriptions of
the number of adherents of the two men, as given by Gamaliel and
Josephus, do not agree; it is unlikely that the writer of Luke iii. 1, 2,
who also relates with accuracy the complicated political arrangements
of the cities which Paul visited, would have made such a blunder as this
identification supposes; and the account of Josephus (Antiq. xviii. 10)
shows that there were many seditions prior to that of Judas the
Galilean.

But they were set at liberty, and the spread of the movement proceeded with unabated vigor.

54. The whole situation, however, was suddenly changed by an event which roused the anger of the Pharisees even more than of the Sadducees, and thus brought upon the disciples the hostility of the whole Sanhedrim. Stephen, one of " the seven," rivalled the apostles in both deed and word (Acts vi. 8). Himself evidently a Hellenist, he labored among the Greek-speaking Jews in Jerusalem. These were often, just because they had returned to the sacred city, especially zealous for the honor of the Mosaic law ; and they, for the first time, brought against Stephen the charge of disloyalty to Judaism. Those most active against him belonged to the synagogue of " the Libertines [Freedmen] and the Cyrenians and the Alexandrians," with whom others from Cilicia and Asia joined (Acts vi. 9). They produced witnesses who accused him of blasphemy against Moses and God. This was a wholly new charge against a disciple. It moved the Pharisees and affected the disposition of the people. Stephen was arraigned before the council, and his defence was so unconciliatory that he was immediately stoned to death.

55. We are not told what Stephen had said in the synagogue, but his defence before the council (Acts vii.) furnishes some explanation of the charge made against him. It consisted of a recital of Hebrew history, from the call of Abraham to Solomon's dedication of the temple. It emphasized God's special guidance of Abraham and his descendants with a view to the fulfilment of the original promise ; then, the repeated resistance of the Hebrews to their divinely sent leaders, and

especially to Moses; finally, the typical character, according to the Old Testament itself, of both tabernacle and temple. Then the speaker closed with a terrible denunciation of the rulers before him, as the children of those who had slain the prophets, as murderers of Messiah, and as violators of the law of God. As his doom was certain, he broke out into an ecstatic description of "the Son of man standing at the right hand of God." Christianity had found its first martyr.

56. The significance of Stephen's address is very great. His ideas went much beyond those expressed by Peter. His point of view was historical rather than prophetic. It presented Christianity as the intended goal of the whole history of the Hebrews. Just because Stephen contemplated the history rather than the prophecies of Israel, he inferred that in the present, as had been the case in the past, God's purpose would be opposed by the existing church and state. So had it ever been, and so would it continue to be. Judaism, in fact, had ever belittled its own system and lost the substance in attachment to the form. It hated the ideal of whose image it was proud. It substituted the material for the spiritual, and regarded as its own peculiar possession what had been given as a trust for the world (vii. 44-50).

57. It is interesting to inquire how Stephen was led to these views. No doubt further study of the Old Testament had much to do with them. Stephen betrays acquaintance with Jewish traditions (Acts vii. 14, 16, 22, 23, 30) as well as with the Scriptures; but the biblical history had evidently been illuminated by the Messianic idea, as the prophecies had been to Peter. It would seem, also, that certain of the teachings of

Jesus had made a deep impression on his mind. Not only did he describe Jesus by the term "Son of man," which was the Lord's favorite description of himself, but Jesus had denounced the rulers and current Judaism in quite the same way that Stephen did (*e. g.* Matt. xxi. 33–41 ; xxiii. 34–36). Thus Christ's teaching was working among the disciples toward a rupture with Judaism as well as toward a spiritual interpretation of the Mosaic law ; and this was doubtless accentuated, as had been the case also with Jesus, by the rise of opposition from the authorities.

58. Stephen's address thus indicates a growing discontent of the new faith with its primitive environment. It was realizing its self-sufficiency. It was beginning to feel that it must absorb Judaism or break with it; that it was the true goal of Hebrew history. Yet this took place by its own development, through the appropriation of the teaching of Jesus and the more profound interpretation of the older revelation. The expansion was that of its own original idea. Faith in Jesus had been proclaimed from the commencement as the only condition of salvation. Stephen was the first to intimate that this involved more than a revived Jewish religion. It might involve the condemnation of Judaism and the substitution of forms of service that would be commensurate with the universal worship of Christ. It is not impossible that he took ground where many of the disciples could not as yet follow him. But he embodied the irresistible logic of the truth, and led the church into the attainment of her real destiny.

59. At the same time Stephen did not break with the established worship. He was charged, indeed, with saying, " Jesus of Nazareth shall destroy this place and

shall change the customs which Moses delivered us"
(vi. 14). This was false testimony (vi. 13); but it
must have had some basis, and it may be plausibly
conjectured that he had been repeating the predictions
of Jesus concerning the destruction of impenitent Jerusalem, or had been interpreting, like Jesus, the spiritual content of the law. There is nothing, however, to
show that he declared, as Paul afterward did, that the
work of Christ had relieved the believer from obligation
to Mosaism; and, though he taught (vii. 44–50) that
tabernacle and temple were representative of a higher
sanctuary, he did not disparage the national worship
itself. He only marks the first appearance of ideas
which contained the principle of the future expansion
of Christianity. These limitations of his teaching are
a remarkable testimony to the accuracy of the report
of his address.

60. The death of Stephen was apparently an act of
violence. Some forms of law were observed in its ex-
ecution (vii. 58), but there is nothing said of a formal
decision. At any rate the decision was made quickly
and tumultuously and executed instantly. This explains its occurrence, in spite of the fact that the
Romans had taken from the Jews the right of capital
punishment (John xviii. 31). Some have inferred that
at this time there was an interruption of Roman rule,
and would date the event after the recall of Pilate
(A. D. 36). But there is no reason to think that the
strictness of Roman rule ceased when Vitellius, the
Governor of Syria, sent Pilate to Rome to answer
the complaints of the Samaritans against him. The
government of Judea was given temporarily into the
charge of a certain Marcellus (*Jos.* Antiq. xviii. 4. 2).

The martyrdom of Stephen was rather an outburst of passion which was liable to happen in spite of any law.

61. At the same time the Sanhedrim, now thoroughly aroused against the disciples, determined to suppress peremptorily the new sect. Roman rule permitted the chief court to exercise extensive civil functions, and especially to regulate and, within limits, enforce the religious law of the nation (comp. *Schürer*, HJP. II. 1. p. 184). Accordingly a general proscription of the offensive sect was issued. Men and women were imprisoned (Acts viii. 3; xxii. 4; xxvi. 10, 11). The most active persecutor was the young Saul of Tarsus, at whose feet the witnesses against Stephen at his martyrdom had laid their clothes. In consequence, the great body of disciples fled from the city. Most of them scattered through Judea and Samaria; but others, as we shall see, went much farther. The apostles, however, remained in Jerusalem. They doubtless hid until the storm was over; and their remaining indicates that Jerusalem was still regarded as the seat and head of the church. But the first period of apostolic Christianity had closed. The hope of the speedy conversion of the nation was extinguished. The consciousness of independence had been awakened in the disciples. It was evident that the faith would conquer only through conflict. These events, however, turned out to be the means by which Christianity discovered its intended destiny and attained its universal and complete message to mankind.

PART II

EARLY EXPANSION OF CHRISTIANITY

I

HISTORICAL SOURCES

62. For the history of the earliest expansion of Christianity we are again mainly dependent on Acts. The principal narrative is found in chapter viii. 4 to xiv. 28. In xxii. 1–21 and xxvi. 1–23 we have reports of Paul's addresses in which he recounted his early life and conversion. Further light on the same events is furnished by the apostle in Galatians i. 13–24, and allusions to his conversion occur in First Corinthians, ix. 1 and xv. 8. Second Corinthians (xi. 24 to xii. 9) also contains references to incidents some of which belong in this period; and in Second Timothy iii. 11 he alludes to occurrences during the journey through Phrygia and Lycaonia. In Acts, viii. 4 to xii. 25 appear to have formed the second great division of the book. It describes the transition from Jewish to Gentile Christianity. Here again Luke shows his intelligent grasp on the significance of the movement of events. We have five sections, exhibiting (1) the earliest expansion under Philip (viii. 4–40); (2) the conversion and early work of Paul, whereby the man was provided for the future diffusion of the faith (ix. 1–30); (3) the work of Peter in Syria which ended in the conversion of Cornelius and the demonstration to the church that God would accept uncircumcised believers (ix. 31 to

xi. 18); (4) the rise of Gentile Christianity in **Antioch**, whereby the new centre for the expanding religion was provided (xi. 19–30); (5) the Herodian persecution, whereby the Jewish state registered its repudiation of the gospel (xii.).

63. Extra biblical literature furnishes no information concerning Christianity during this time. Josephus, however (Antiq. xix. 4 to 8), gives an account of the life and death of Herod Agrippa I. which should be compared with Acts xii. For the history and condition of the Syrian towns the reader should consult Schürer's "History of the Jewish People in the Time of Jesus Christ" (Part II. Vol. I. ch. ii. and iii.), as well as with regard to the Nabatæans who ruled Damascus at the time of Paul's early ministry in that city (Part I. Vol. II. Append. II.). For the best information concerning the route of Paul's first missionary journey and the location of the places visited, see Ramsay's "Church in the Roman Empire" (ch. ii. and iii.) and "St. Paul the Traveller" (ch. iv. and v.).

II

THE DISPERSION

64. THE persecution which followed Stephen's **death** was the means of spreading the new faith, for " they that were scattered abroad went everywhere preaching the word " (Acts viii. 4). There were already, no doubt, disciples outside of Jerusalem (sect. 49), but the diffusion now became aggressive and widespread. It permeated especially Judea and Samaria (Acts viii. 1), but did not stop there. Both those of the disciples who settled in new homes and those who continued their wanderings regarded themselves as missionaries of the Messiah.

65. Thus Philip, one of " the seven," acting in the spirit of Stephen, repaired to the city of Samaria (Acts viii. 5, R. V.), or, as Herod the Great had called it, Sebaste, which contained a numerous pagan as well as Samaritan population. This of itself indicated liberation from Jewish prejudice (John iv. 9). Yet the Samaritans observed the law, practised circumcision, and expected the Messiah. They offered, therefore, the most natural field outside of Judea and Galilee. We may also see in Philip's conduct another effect of the example and teaching of Jesus (Luke ix. 52–56; x. 33; xvii. 11–19; John iv.; Acts i. 8). The belief of many of the Samaritans in Philip's message raised no question concerning the observance of the law, while his mission to them indicated the broadening spirit of love and the clearer comprehension of Christ's purposes which were making themselves felt. Wonder and joy were awakened in Jerusalem by the report that " Samaria had received the word of God," and from the capital the faith spread ultimately into many adjacent villages.

66. In Samaria, however, it was for the first time confronted with a form of the superstition and religious imposture of which the ancient world, especially the Orient, was full, and against which the new religion was destined often to contend. The story of Simon the Mage, whose reputation as a magician and teacher was great in Samaria, and who, astonished at Philip's miracles, professed to believe, shows that Christianity had indeed emerged from its original home and was beginning to compete with the forces which dominated the complex and corrupt pagan world. In that eclectic age religious impostors abounded, and often strangely united blatant trickery with the language of philosophy. Of this class none became more famous than Simon. Justin Martyr, himself a Samaritan, relates that he was a native of Gitton, and reports, though with some confusion of statement, that he visited Rome under Claudius and was honored as a god. One of the earliest Gnostic sects was called after him, and in later legends he figures as the arch enemy of Peter. There is no reason to doubt his historical character, nor is it improbable that he appropriated some Christian ideas to augment his influence, and thus became, as tradition states, the prototype of heresy. We learn from Acts that he was regarded by the Samaritans as an incarna-

tion of the divine power. But the new faith was not
to be defiled by such an unworthy alliance. When
Peter and John arrived and the Holy Spirit, with his
gifts and powers, came on the converts at the imposition of the apostles' hands, Simon revealed his true
character by offering money, if like power to impart
the Spirit were given to him. The offer was indig-
nantly refused ; and the incident merely illustrates the
triumph of the new faith over the subtlety of superstition, and its clear ethical consciousness amid the
temptations of the larger world into which it was
entering.

67. It is more important to observe that when the
news from Samaria reached Jerusalem, Peter and John
were sent to complete the work which Philip had begun.
This evidently implies the wish to preserve the unity
of all believers under apostolic direction. Moreover,
the Lord had indicated his will that the new converts
should be led to realize the authority of the original
apostles by withholding the outward manifestations
of the Spirit ; for only when the hands of Peter and
John were laid on them did they " receive the Holy
Spirit" (Acts viii. 15). This was not always a condition of the manifestation of the Spirit's power. Not
only did he at Pentecost come directly upon all the
disciples, but he was given to Saul of Tarsus through
the instrumentality of Ananias (Acts ix. 17), and to
Cornelius without any instrumentality at all (Acts x.
44) ; nor is it probable that in Galatia (Gal. iii. 5) and
Corinth (I. Cor. xii. 28) his gifts were dependent on
apostolic touch. At other times, however, the imposition of apostolic hands preceded the gift of the Spirit
(Acts xix. 6 ; II. Tim. i. 6) ; and in the case before us

the importance of uniting in one body Samaritan and
Jewish believers amply explains to those who believe
in the Spirit's guidance of the history the event as it is
reported. The expansion of Christianity was thus not
merely the diffusion of the faith, but also the extension
of the community which had been organized in Jerusalem under the apostles.

68. Philip's work, however, was not confined to
Samaria. Luke appends the account of the conversion
of the Ethiopian steward (Acts viii. 26–39). This took
place in southern Judea, on the road to the old and
deserted city of Gaza. The narrative is intended to
illustrate the varied progress of the faith. The steward
was apparently a proselyte, although according to the
law (Deut. xxiii. 1) he could not, if we understand the
term " eunuch " in its strict sense, have been a recognized member of the congregation of Israel. He was,
at any rate, a devout worshipper of Jehovah. He was
deeply interested also in the Scriptures, and especially
in the prophecies. He is a fine example of the way in
which the religion of Israel had touched the souls of
many in the pagan world and prepared them for a
further message from God. His conversion was to
Luke very properly representative of the widening
destiny of the gospel ; and, though we know nothing
of an Ethiopian church in the first century, the incident
was suggestive of the geographical as well as ethnic
expansion which was beginning. Luke particularly
emphasizes the fact that Philip acted under the direction of the Spirit. It was in truth the Spirit who, in
co-operation with providence, was impelling the disciples
to spread their faith. The progress was not accidental,
but divinely intended and guided. The use also of the

fifty-third chapter of Isaiah to introduce the steward to a knowledge of Jesus illustrates the means by which the unlikely story of a crucified Messiah was made credible and intelligible to these early converts. After this incident Philip seems to have settled in Cæsarea (Acts viii. 40). There, much later, Luke himself found him (xxi. 8), and may have received from the evangelist's own lips these facts which he embodied in his history.

69. But while Luke's narrative follows the movements of Philip, it seems clear that Syria was the principal region in which the faith was diffused. Into it many of the refugees must have fled. Jews resided in large numbers in the towns of both the coast and the interior, some of which were doubtless the "foreign cities" (Acts xxvi. 11, R. V.) into which even the persecution reached. Certainly Damascus had received the gospel, for thither the arch persecutor turned his steps. In most of these cities the Jewish colony had its local council, by which Jewish criminals could be delivered to the Jerusalem Sanhedrim. But in them also the refugees for the most part would be safe and could extend the influence of their faith. Here, therefore, the largest advance was made. Not long after, we find Peter visiting the disciples in Syria (Acts x. 32); and the accounts of Eneas at Lydda and of Dorcas at Joppa indicate that the faith had been well established in those regions. Finally the great Syrian metropolis of Antioch was occupied by a party of Hellenistic missionaries who had previously been to Phœnicia and even to Cyprus (Acts xi. 19). These events extended over a number of years; but they were all a part of the expansion which followed the death of Stephen, and

indicate Syria as the region mainly occupied. At the same time it is very probable that the movement reached more distant territory. It is difficult to believe that Egypt, Arabia, and Babylonia, where the Jews were in close touch with those of Judea, did not hear of the new faith. We have, however, no information on that point.

70. It should be remembered that this early expansion was at first and for some years almost wholly among the Jews. It was simply the spread of Jerusalem-Christianity ; and Peter's visit to the disciples of Syria (Acts ix. 32) shows that the latter kept in touch with the mother church and acknowledged the authority of the apostles. The diffusion was effected mainly by personal intercourse, or else by preaching in the synagogues, which were always open to visiting Hebrews. The faith itself was the same which had been preached in Jerusalem. The new believers trusted in Jesus, as the risen and glorified Messiah, for the forgiveness of sins ; received baptism in his name ; learned his spiritual interpretation of the law ; studied afresh his fulfilment of prophecy ; waited for his return in glory ; while the apostolic reports of his life and teachings were circulated from lip to lip. In most instances the disciples continued to worship in the synagogues as well as to have their own meetings. They were bound to one another, however, by the bonds of a common faith and peril ; and gradually they formed separate synagogues of their own (Jas. ii. 2 ; v. 14). But the expansion of the new faith did not as yet result in any violent rupture with the older Jewish organizations. It united at first, and in most localities for many years, faith in Jesus with loyalty to the

Mosaic ritual and law. The conversion of the Samaritans and of the Ethiopian steward did not form any real exception to this. The movement as yet was strictly a Hebrew one. It was, so far as the evidence goes, simply the extension among the Jews of the dispersion of the new faith and brotherhood which had been formed in Jerusalem.

III

THE CONVERSION OF PAUL

71. AN event soon occurred which was destined
to be of supreme importance to the growing faith.
This was the conversion of Saul of Tarsus. At
the time of Stephen's death Saul was still a young
man (Acts vii. 58). His native city, Tarsus in
Cilicia, was a place of both political and intellectual
renown. It was a free city, with large commercial
interests, and a noted educational centre. Saul's
father was of the tribe of Benjamin (Phil. iii. 5) and in
religion a Pharisee (Acts xxiii. 6). It is not known
how the family became residents of Tarsus. An old
tradition makes them to have removed thither from
Gischala of Galilee when the latter place was captured
by the Romans. Others suppose that they were settled in Tarsus by one of the Syrian kings who colo-
nized many Jews in Asia Minor. There is reason to
believe that the family connection was a large one
(comp. Acts xxiii. 16 ; Rom. xvi. 7, 11, 21). It must
have been also influential, for Saul was both a citizen
of Tarsus (Acts xxi. 39) and a free-born Roman (xxii.
28) ; while his active relations to the Sanhedrim, of
which he seems, though a young man, to have been a
member (xxvi. 10), his prominence in Jerusalem
(xxii. 5), and the description which he gives of his high

ambitions as a Jew (Phil. iii. 4–7), indicate that he
sprang from no obscure origin. Nothing is known of
the way in which his ancestor obtained the Roman
citizenship which Saul inherited. Equally uncertain is
the origin of the second name, Paul, by which he calls
himself, and by which Luke describes him after his
missionary work among the Gentiles had begun (Acts
xiii. 9). Some have supposed that he assumed it after
he became a Christian, and various explanations of its
meaning have been given. But it is more probable
that, like many other Jews (Acts i. 23; xv. 37), he had
from the beginning both names. If so, " Paulus " may
point to some connection of his ancestors with the
Roman family of the Pauli (*Conyb. and Howson*, Life
and Ep. of St. P. p. 153); or it may have been
adopted for other, and perhaps purely personal, reasons
(*Deissmann*, Bibel-Studien, I. p. 181). As a Gentile
name it was naturally employed by him in his work
among the Gentiles.

72. Although foreign born, Saul had been reared
on strictly Jewish principles (Phil. iii. 4–7). There is
little reason to suppose that he was influenced in his
boyhood by the intellectual atmosphere of Tarsus.
His earliest education more probably was in the narrower sphere of Jewish studies. Like other Jewish
boys he was taught a trade, which in his case was the
manufacture of the goat-hair tents used by travellers;
and, when yet a lad, he was sent to Jerusalem to complete his education under one of the great Rabbis (Acts
xxi. 3). His teacher was Gamaliel the elder, whose
timely address prevented on one occasion the death
of the apostles (sect. 52). At Gamaliel's feet Saul
learned the traditions of the scribes, took part in their

exegetical and casuistic discussions, and imbibed a
profound devotion to Judaism and the law.   Here also
he must have acquired that thorough knowledge of the
Old Testament which his epistles reveal.   He developed
into the intensest of Pharisees (Acts xxii. 3; xxiii. 6;
xxvi. 5; Gal. i. 14; Phil. iii. 5); and while his style
of argumentation, after he became a Christian, is
wholly devoid of the merely verbal subtleties and
trivial discussions which characterized Rabbinism, yet
all the presuppositions of his thought remained Hebrew
to the end, and prove that his mind, in its formative
period, had been saturated with Jewish belief.

73. It is true that the speeches and letters of Paul
indicate some acquaintance with Hellenic, and especially Stoic, thought.   He can hardly be said indeed to
show acquaintance with Greek literature, for his few
quotations (Acts xvii. 28; Tit. i. 12) are not sufficient
to prove this.   Nor does his style of composition show
the rhetorical training of the schools.   On the other
hand his use of some philosophical and ethical terms
indicates familiarity with pagan culture; and his passion for dialectical argument and for a systematic construction of his teaching appear rather Hellenic than
Hebrew.   Occasionally, too, he implies acquaintance
with the course which pagan history and thought had
run (Acts xvii. 27; I. Cor. i. 21; ii. 6).   This should
warn us against an unduly narrow idea of his education.   In those days of wide Greek influence, even a
pupil in the school of a Jerusalem Rabbi might learn
something of the thought of the outside world; and
Gamaliel was reputed to be fond of Greek learning.
It is more likely, however, that these foreign influences
came to Saul after he left his teacher.   It is not im-

probable that he returned, for a while, to Tarsus, since he does not appear to have been in Jerusalem at the time of Christ's crucifixion. If so, he may then have pursued other studies in his native city. Still later his eager mind, when freed from Jewish shackles and penetrating into the implications of his new faith, may be supposed to have increased its acquaintance with the world's thought which he found himself obliged to confront. But Hellenic culture never formed a constituent element of his teaching; and in his youth his whole mind was devoted to the study and observance of the Hebrew law.

74. Apart, moreover, from the religious and intellectual influences which acted upon him, Saul of Tarsus possessed a remarkable personality. He was one of those intense natures to whom truth and duty are so commanding as to be at once transmuted into life. His mental aptitudes also were singularly varied, and in every direction almost equally vigorous. He was a keen thinker. To him a principle became at once fruitful of a system, so that he followed an idea to its logical implications. Yet he had a strongly emotional temperament. He was capable of tremendous passion, and he always felt the full reality of what he enjoyed or suffered. At the same time he was a practical man of affairs, fond of public action, and born to be a leader of others. It is rare to find these qualities combined, but unquestionably they were combined in Saul. They sprang from the wonderful intensity and completeness of his nature. It would seem as if no phase of life or experience were unknown to, or at least unappreciated by, him. There also appears in his conduct a singular union of strength

and tenderness, of strenuous energy with pathetic desire
for sympathy, of heroic courage with passionate love
of friends. Most characteristic of him was the intensity of his religious disposition. To his soul, even
as a Jew, the religious view of life was the only real
one, and to it he dedicated his powers from his youth.
He could truly say late in life, " I thank God, whom I
serve from my forefathers with a pure conscience"
(II. Tim. i. 3). He was a Pharisee because Pharisaism, with all its faults, was to him the effort to em-
body perfectly in life the will of God.

75. Such was the man who first appeared upon the
scene at Stephen's martyrdom. He had, we may believe,
recently returned to Jerusalem, and had doubtless been
one of those (Acts vi. 9) who, after disputing with the
Christian in the synagogue, had prosecuted him before
the Sanhedrim. At his feet the witnesses, who cast
the first stones at the condemned man, laid their
clothes. Forthwith he became the leader of the subsequent persecution. He sought the position (Acts viii.
3) ; and when the disciples fled, he pursued them, with
authority from the high-priest, into other cities (Acts
ix. 1, 2 ; xxii. 5 ; xxvii. 11). It is probable that this
continued for a year or more. The whole intensity of
Saul's nature found a vent in this fierce religious
crusade.

76. We have some glimpses also into the motives by
which he was actuated. He himself refers to his persecution of the disciples as evidence of the sin from
which the grace of God had rescued him (e. g. Gal. i.
13 ; I. Tim. i. 13). He makes it clear that he was animated by zeal for the maintenance of Judaism, against
which, since Stephen's address, the disciples appeared

to him to be unholy renegades ; and that the more he
persecuted, the fiercer his zeal became (Gal. i. 14). As
he afterwards saw, he was ignorant of the real character of the gospel, and acted in utter unbelief of its
truth and value (I. Tim. i. 13). Yet at the time he
thought that he was doing God service (Acts xxii. 3 ;
xxvi. 9). He was a conscientious inquisitor, moved re-
lentlessly to the work by his sense of duty ; and he was
so entirely blind to any good in the new sect, that its ex-
tinction seemed to him the best tribute he could offer
to Jehovah.

77. It is thus impossible to believe that any predisposition toward Christianity existed in Saul's mind
before his conversion. His contact with Stephen had
only aroused his anger. It is wholly gratuitous to assume that in his heart he admired what he so violently
persecuted. Neither is it possible that his further acquaintance with the Christians made him feel the
wrongfulness of his conduct or doubt the truth as he
then held it. Such a supposition is directly opposed to
his own testimony (Gal. i. 13, 14). He acted in un-
doubting unbelief (I. Tim. i. 13). To him Jesus was
an impostor, whose Messianic claims were blasphe-
mous, and against whom duty compelled him to wage
relentless war (Acts xxvi. 9). It has indeed been
alleged that the words which he reports Jesus to have
used at his conversion, " It is hard for thee to kick
against the goad " (Acts xxvi. 14, R. V.), indicate that
he had been forcing himself to persecute against his
conscience and better convictions. But this interpretation agrees neither, as we have seen, with Paul's own
statements nor with the natural meaning of the meta-
phor. The " goad " rather represents the purpose of

God, external to Paul, which was really leading to a
service the very opposite of what he wished. There is
no reason to doubt that, so far as his conscious inten-
tions went, the persecutor did not question the rightful-
ness of his course nor lessen his zeal in it.

78. At the same time there is reason to believe that
the young Pharisee, with his deeply religious nature,
had not found peace in Judaism. This seems to be
implied in the reminiscence which he has given of the
disastrous effect upon an awakened conscience of the
realization of the full demands of God's law (Rom. vii.
9–11). In the following verses (13–25) he gives a
further analysis of the nature and hopelessness of this
bondage to sin in which the awakened conscience finds
itself; but that analysis is evidently presented in the
light in which the experience afterward appeared to
him as he looked back upon it, and he cannot be supposed to have realized at the time the full truth as he
came to see it. But the previous verses do describe an
experience when he was under the law, in which he was
led to perceive its deep import, and that it bore upon
the very least of his moral desires; so that before its
august and penetrating judgment he felt himself a dead
man. If we accept this key to his spiritual history,
we can hardly doubt that Saul had felt already that
the paramount necessity for him was to secure for
himself the perfect satisfaction of the law. He saw
already that peace could only come through the possession of a righteousness which would meet the claims
of a law whose universal scope he painfully perceived.
Such a man could not have been satisfied with the performance of a ritual. We may believe that he had
known profound unrest as he faced the real verdict of

the law against himself. But this only drove him, as it has many others, to greater efforts to obey, and his persecution of the Nazarenes may be partly explained as due to his intense desire to establish the law and fulfil his own part toward it. So far, however, as his conscious purposes were concerned, there was only antagonism towards Jesus and his disciples.

79. Yet this man, while on his persecuting mission, was suddenly converted. Three accounts of the event are given in the Acts; one by Luke (ix. 3–18) and two by Paul himself (xxii. 6–16; xxvi. 12–18). Each account is controlled by the immediate purpose of the narrator. Luke, with a purely historical motive, briefly relates the event itself. Paul's first account, because defending himself before the Jews, emphasizes the part which the devout Jew Ananias had in the transaction. When addressing Agrippa, on the other hand, he does not mention Ananias, and condenses the Lord's subsequent commands into one statement. Such variations are natural, and even assure us of the veracity of the reports. Other minor variations in the accounts (comp. ix. 7 with xxvi. 14 and xxii. 9) are explainable by the supposition that at first all the company fell upon the ground, but that Saul alone remained prostrate, and that while his companions heard the voice, he alone understood the words which were spoken to him.

80. We learn, then, that when near Damascus, whither he was going to arrest, by the high-priest's authority, the followers of Jesus, suddenly and at noon a bright light from heaven flashed around him and his companions. So overwhelming was its brilliance that they all fell upon the ground, and the man

of Tarsus heard, in Hebrew, the words, " Saul, Saul,
why persecutest thou me ?   It is hard for thee to kick
against the goad."   To his question, " Who art thou,
Lord ?" the reply was, " I am Jesus, the Nazarene,
whom thou persecutest."   Utterly crushed by this
revelation of the heavenly nature of the one he had
despised, Saul asked, " What shall I do, Lord ? "   The
answer was, " Arise, and go into Damascus, and it
shall be told thee what thou must do."   Meanwhile
his companions had risen and were standing in amaze-
ment.   When Saul arose, he was found to be blind,
and was led by the hand into the city.   There he continued three days in fasting and prayer in the house of
a certain Judas.   On the third day a Jewish disciple,
Ananias, who had received directions from the Lord,
went to him and in Christ's name declared the forgiveness of his sins (xxii. 16), that he had been
chosen as a messenger of Messiah, and that he might
receive with baptism the gift of the Spirit.   Thereupon
his sight was restored and he was baptized.

81.   These brief reports evidently imply more than
they actually record.   None of them affirm that Saul
saw Jesus.   But they clearly mean that he did ; for
not only did Ananias speak of Jesus as having " appeared " to him (ix. 17) in order that he should *see*
that Just One (xxii. 14), but afterwards Barnabas
affirmed " how he had *seen* the Lord in the way "
(ix. 27), and Paul himself declared that he was a
witness of what he had *seen* (xxvi. 16).   We are not
dependent, however, on the Acts.   Paul refers to the
event in his epistles.   He describes his conversion as
a work solely of divine power and favor, whereby he
was transformed into the opposite of what he had

been before (I. Cor. ix. 17; xv. 10; Gal. i. 15; Eph. iii. 7; I. Tim. i. 12, 13, 16; II. Tim. i. 11). He declares that he had seen the risen Jesus, and had thus been qualified for apostleship (I. Cor. ix. 1; xv. 8). He further relates that this objective revelation of the Christ had been accompanied by a spiritual illumination of his mind, so that he was enabled to grasp the truth about Jesus in order to proclaim it to the world (Gal. i. 16). According to his own accounts, therefore, God revealed his Son to and in him. The transaction had both its objective and subjective sides. The former, however, is represented as the basis of the latter. He describes it as a visible appearance of Jesus and a verbal declaration of his will. On the basis of this he also describes himself as subjectively enlightened and quickened by the power of God, so that he received the new truth and willingly devoted himself to it. The accounts do not represent the transaction, on its subjective side, as entirely instantaneous. It was not magical. Three days of prayer were required to complete his conversion. But the objective revelation is represented by the apostle himself as unheralded and peremptory, and he always ascribes the change wrought in him to the sovereign and gracious exercise of divine power.

82. Saul's conversion, then, must be regarded as occasioned by a supernatural revelation of Jesus to him. The transaction partook partly of the character of a spiritual vision. The figure of Jesus was not seen by Paul's companions, nor were the words understood; and we cannot say in such an event how much his physical organs were re-enforced by the awakened perceptions of the soul. Yet the light was seen and the

sound was heard by all, while the effects of the manifestation on Saul himself were physical as well as spiritual. The manifestation of Jesus was thus objectively real. That we are not dealing with a legend is proved by Paul's own testimony to it. It is equally impossible to explain it as an illusion of his mind. There was in him, as we have seen, no predisposition toward Christianity, but resolute and reasoned antagonism up to the very moment of the experience. Hence no psychological basis existed for the creation of an illusion. Yet the experience suddenly and entirely changed his belief and life ; and his whole subsequent career attests the absolute certitude which it produced in him. A fair interpretation of the whole evidence compels us to accept the explanation of the event which Paul himself has given.

83. It is sometimes said, indeed, that Paul was a mystic, and predisposed to ecstatic experiences. It is pointed out that he claims to have had frequently visions and revelations (e. g. I. Thess. iv. 15 ; Gal. ii. 2 ; II. Cor. xii. 1, 7) ; and it is suggested that the very frequency of them throws doubt on their reality. The possibility of such heavenly communications should, however, not be denied by those who accept the supernaturalness of Christianity. The only question is, whether these visions and revelations commend themselves by their intrinsic character and the rationality of the one who claims to have received them. With respect to this it should be noted that they are treated with marked reserve by Paul. Allusion is made to them only when on special occasions it was necessary for the sake of others. Further, so far as we learn anything about them, they were adapted to the specific

needs of the apostle at the time. They were not un-regulated ecstasies, but were limited to such communications as his historical situation required. And, finally, they appear in Paul's life in entire subordination to the rational attainment and presentation of truth. While he occasionally appealed to them, they did not supplant his intellectual life nor the vigor of his argumentation. To this it may be added that Luke makes Paul describe the appearance of Christ to him by a term (Acts xxvi. 19, " spectacle ") which the historian elsewhere applies to supernatural manifestations seen by persons in their ordinary state of mind (Luke i. 22 ; xxiv. 23), whereas he commonly uses another phrase for visions seen either in sleep or ecstasy (Acts ix. 10, 12 ; x. 3 ; xi. 5 ; xii. 9, etc.). Whether, therefore, we consider the apostle's own descriptions of his religious experiences, or his historian's report of the conversion, the manifestation of Jesus to Paul must still be accepted as an objective and supernatural fact.

84. But how much of Christianity did Paul possess as the immediate result of his conversion ? How are we to conceive his state of mind when he was thus transformed ? He himself describes his knowledge of the gospel as due to revelation by Jesus (Gal. i. 12, 15, 16). He represents himself as an independent witness and apostle. This implies that through the experience of conversion, as well as through subsequent revelations, he came into the possession of Christian truth. It is true that the co-operation of other agencies was not excluded. He brought to his new life a rich acquaintance with the Old Testament, which, as with the older disciples, was forthwith illumined by his new faith in Jesus. He brought also certain theological ideas, in-

cluding not only monotheism, but belief in salvation as consisting in the possession of righteousness before God, as well as the doctrines of propitiation by sacrifice, of a future judgment, a resurrection of the body, and a Messianic kingdom of glory. These ideas constituted the moulds in which his new faith would still run and to which it would naturally adjust itself. Nor are we to suppose that he sought from older Christians no information about Jesus and his teaching. Certainly he was afterwards well acquainted with the current evangelical narrative (e. g. I. Thess. v. 1 ; I. Cor. vii. 10 ; ix. 14 ; xi. 23–25 ; xv. 3, etc.; II. Cor. v. 21 ; viii. 9 ; x. 1 ; Rom. xii. 17, 20 ; xv. 3 ; Phil. ii. 7, 8 ; I. Tim. vi. 13). At the same time it is clear from his own expressions that his equipment as a teacher of Christianity was gained mainly from his wondrous experience and spiritual illumination. These were of such a marked character, and Paul himself was such an intense and independent man, that his apprehension of the faith was from the beginning controlled by the way in which he had been led to it.

85. Did he then at once realize all that afterwards he taught? Extreme views have been held on both sides of this question, and probably the truth lies between them. On the one hand his epistles reveal a mind which steadily advanced in the statement of doctrine in accordance with the needs of his readers, and apparently with the impulse of his own mind toward completeness of teaching. This makes it natural to suppose that in the earlier period, from which we have no products of his pen, a similar progress took place. On the other hand the fundamental points of his belief appear fully established in his earliest epistles, and

never changed. In Galatians (i. 16; ii. 2, 14–21) he speaks of his gospel as that which he had proclaimed from the beginning. It is probable, therefore, that immediately upon his conversion he became possessed of the essential points of his distinctive apostolic teaching, while their implications and full expression were gradually wrought out.

86. What, then, were these fundamental beliefs of the converted persecutor? His knowledge of Jesus and the glory in which he had beheld him constituted the primary fact on which his new faith rested. He now knew that the Nazarene was the Messiah. The Crucified was alive and clothed with divine power; and Paul always considered this to be proof of the resurrection to which the older apostles testified (I. Cor. xv. 3–8). He also now knew Jesus to be a superhuman and heavenly being, God's messenger and representative. This is expressed by the title " Son of God " which he at once applied to him (Acts ix. 20; Gal. i. 16). Jesus was " the Lord from heaven " (I. Cor. xv. 47). There is nothing, indeed, to show as yet how far Paul penetrated into the mystery of Christ's person; but the sight of Jesus, possessed of divine glory and power, revolutionized his religious thought and gave the fixed point about which faith and duty necessarily turned.

87. With this was joined the fact that he had been called into his new life by the pure favor of God in the very midst of his enmity against the Lord. His former life now appeared stained by the worst folly and sin. His obedience to the law had not saved him. In fact, his effort to obey it had led him into the greatest sin. His call by Christ had therefore been an act of

6

mere grace. His hope could only rest on the favor and
power of Jesus, which had been mercifully shown to
him. By this the whole of his former conception of
the way in which he was to obtain salvation was swept
away. If he had long ago realized that he had not
really kept the law, he now realized that salvation was
not to be had by him through keeping it. His salvation was of Christ by grace, and only his faith in the
Lord, who had revealed himself, could reassure him as
he now contemplated both the unbelief of the past,
with its hostility to the truth, and the sinfulness of his
heart as even the law had shown it to him. Thus the
keynotes of Paul's teaching were sounded in the experience through which he was led. Faith in Jesus as
the exalted Messiah who was able to save, and entire
dependence on God's grace in Christ, formed from the
beginning the two foci of his Christian consciousness.

88. Yet Paul's mind could not have stopped here.
Two questions imperatively demanded an answer.
How could this salvation by unmerited favor be reconciled with the claims of the law on every man? Why
had Messiah died a death of shame? We must ascer-
tain the answer which Paul gave from his own writings.
According to Galatians (ii. 14–21) he reminded Peter
that they had believed in Jesus in order that they
might be justified, that is, declared righteous before God,
since they had discovered that by the works of the law
none could be justified. Speaking of himself he adds,
" I, through the law [operating upon Christ], died to
the law [as the object of my endeavor in order to be
saved], that I might live unto God. I have been crucified with Christ." Still again (iii. 13), " Christ hath
redeemed us from the curse of the law, being made a

curse for us" (comp., too, Rom. iii. 21–26). These statements show that the death of Jesus was regarded as the satisfaction of the claims of the law upon the sinner. He had paid the penalty which the violated law demanded; had thus procured for the sinner reconciliation with God, the lawgiver; and the faith in Jesus, which Paul had found in his conversion to be the sole condition of his enjoyment of salvation, had its sufficiency explained by the completeness of the work which the suffering Messiah had accomplished in his behalf. This truth must have been realized by Paul very early. It fitted precisely into his Hebrew idea of salvation as the possession of righteousness. The only difference was that this was a righteousness provided by God, not achieved by himself. The idea appears in his earliest recorded address (Acts xiii. 39). He was doubtless helped to it also by the teaching of the Old Testament, in which he found two passages in particular, which are quoted by him at crucial points in his arguments. The one was the promise to Abraham (Gen. xii. 3; xxii. 18) that in him and in his seed should all nations be blessed (Gal. iii. 8, 16, 29), and the other was the words of Habakkuk (ii. 4), which he translates, " The just shall live by faith " (Rom. i. 17; Gal. iii. 11). In the one case he found the idea of salvation through a representative; in the other, salvation through faith. Both passages illuminated the doctrine of righteousness procured by the death of Christ for those who believe in him.

89. To Paul, moreover, laying hold of Christ as his Redeemer and Lord, faith meant trust to the point of absolute self-surrender, and the conviction that his life had been taken under the control of Christ, and was

revitalized by Christ's indwelling spirit. This was based on the thought that by the favor of God he was included in all the work of Christ and in all of its results. In the most emphatic and intimate sense he was " in Christ." The conception was primarily legal, but also vital. He could not conceive of the one aspect of this union without the other. Christ's satisfaction of the law for him involved necessarily the believer's experience of a spiritual transformation corresponding to the work of Christ. In Christ he had died to the law and to sin, and risen unto newness of life toward God. In Christ he had both obtained reconciliation with God, and experimental enjoyment of it through the bestowment upon him of Christ's quickening and transforming Spirit. Thus he had received the spiritual power by which his sinful nature, or the flesh, was controlled and would finally be destroyed. This was Christ in him as, on the other hand, Christ had stood for him. In short, as Christ had identified himself with Paul before the law, so by faith Paul identified himself with Christ in his own experience. Faith thus meant for him entire self-surrender to Christ, that both Christ's satisfaction of the law might be his, and the power of the victorious Christ might operate within him. As he wrote, " I have been crucified with Christ," so he added, " yet I live; and yet no longer I, but Christ liveth in me; and that life which I now live in the flesh, I live in faith, the faith which is in the Son of God, who loved me and gave himself up for me " (Gal. ii. 20, R. V.).

90. Thus by this mental and moral revolution Paul not only became a Christian, but was led to apprehend Christianity in a way destined to be of the greatest significance for the history of the faith.

The true relation of the believer to the law was discovered. The latter was a preparation for faith. It
was intended to disclose the sinner's need of Christ.
Therewith the death of Christ took on its full significance as the satisfaction of the law for the believer,
and the idea that the Jewish law was permanently
binding on believers received its death-blow. All this
was but the logical unfolding of the doctrine of salvation by faith in Jesus which Peter and others had
preached. It was also the logical result of that faith
in himself which Jesus had required of his disciples
(see sect. 14). But through the conversion of Paul
the truth was brought to full expression, and the man
and the doctrine were prepared which were destined
to release the new faith from Judaism and to interpret
it to the Gentile world.

91. Paul's life immediately after his conversion is
traced briefly in Acts ix. 19–30 and Galatians i. 16–
24 (comp. also II. Cor. xi. 32, 33). He soon began, on
the authority of his new commission, to preach in the
synagogues of Damascus that Jesus was the Son of
God, and to prove him to be Messiah. Filled with
the joy of personal salvation, convinced that the risen
Christ had appeared to him and made him his ambassador, illuminated in his understanding of the
Scriptures by his new faith, he bore his testimony to
the heavenly dignity of Jesus and the truth of his
Messianic claims. Such a man as he needed only
the experience through which he had passed to be at
once qualified for service. But, while he made disciples, his course roused, as was natural, the hatred of
the Jews. The latter were favored in a plot to kill
him by the fact that Damascus was then under the

control of the Nabatæans, a nation inhabiting ancient
Edom. The daughter of the reigning king, Aretas
IV., had been the first wife of Herod Antipas. In B. C.
88, the Nabatæans had conquered Damascus, and even
after the Roman conquest of Syria their hold on the
ancient city continued more or less constant. It
has been noted that from 35 to 61 A. D. there are
no Damascene coins bearing the Emperor's image.
While the precise and probably fluctuating political
relations of Damascus during the first century are
often obscure, there is no reason to question Paul's
statement that it was at this time governed by the ethnarch of Aretas (II. Cor. xi. 32). The relations of the
Nabatæans with the Jews had generally been friendly.
It is not surprising, therefore, that the ethnarch lent
his aid to the Jews and sought to prevent Paul's escape.
The latter, however, was let down in a basket from a
window in the wall and so secured his liberty.

92. In this period, however, occurred Paul's sojourn
in Arabia, to which he alludes in Galatians i. 17. It
is not mentioned in Acts, doubtless because it was of
no public importance. Paul mentions it simply to
show that after his conversion he had not sought instruction from the older apostles. The journey seems
to have taken place either during his work in Damascus related by Luke, or else after his escape from the
city. In either case he returned to Damascus from
Arabia. The length of his stay in Arabia and what
he did there are equally unknown. Some have supposed that he sought a field of work. Others, with
more probability, suppose that he sought retirement
and opportunity for reflection. Neither do we know
the place in Arabia to which he retired. But wher-

ever in the three years following his conversion we place the journey to Arabia, the principal fact is that he first made Damascus, whither he had gone as a persecutor, the scene of his confession of Jesus and of his earliest service to the cause he had so suddenly been led to espouse.

93. It was not till the third year after his conversion that Paul returned to Jerusalem (Gal. i. 18–23; Acts ix. 26–30). He tells us that he went to visit Peter, wishing, doubtless, to connect his own work with that of the original apostles. He mentions, also, that of the leaders of the Jerusalem church he saw, besides Peter, only James the Lord's brother; that his stay was limited to fifteen days; and that then, being still unknown by face to the churches of Judea, he departed to Syria and Cilicia to preach the faith which formerly he had destroyed. The account in Acts gives other particulars. We there learn that the brethren in Jerusalem were afraid of him, but that Barnabas took him to " the apostles " and related the appearance of Jesus to him and his zeal as a preacher in Damascus. It is added that in Jerusalem he preached to his old friends, the Hellenistic Jews; but that, when they sought to slay him, the brethren brought him to Cæsarea and thence sent him to Tarsus.

94. These accounts by Paul and Luke have been thought inharmonious; but they are capable of a natural adjustment when the points of view of the two writers are considered. The visit was brief, but not too brief to preclude an attempt to bear his witness before those with whom he had formerly blasphemed his master's name. His main purpose was to visit Peter, but that did not exclude his reception by other disciples in

Jerusalem. Luke states that Barnabas took him to "the apostles;" but while this expression would in the absence of other information naturally suggest the whole body of apostles or a considerable number of them, it is not incorrectly used if he was introduced to whatever representatives of that body happened to be in the city. Luke commonly restricts the term "apostle" to its narrower sense, but he applies it twice so as to include Barnabas (xiv. 4, 14). It may be, therefore, that in this instance he had in mind Peter and James, the Lord's brother, whom we know that Paul met. Or he may have intended merely to record the fact that Paul was introduced to the apostolic body without regarding it as important whether one or several representatives of it were present. In like manner, Paul's statement that he was unknown by face to the churches of Judea is not inconsistent with Luke's statement that he preached to the Hellenists, nor need the language mean that no disciples in Jerusalem except Peter and James knew him personally. Both accounts agree finally that from Jerusalem he went to Syria (Cæsarea) and Cilicia (Tarsus).

95. We infer, therefore, that the knowledge of his vocation had wakened in Paul's mind the desire for co-operation with the older leaders of the church. He makes it plain indeed in Galatians that he maintained his independent authority as an apostle of Christ, but this does not exclude the wish to work in harmony with others. The latter indeed is proved by Galatians ii. 1–10, to have been his desire throughout his ministry. Nor need we suppose that his future mission was as yet entirely clear to Paul himself. During this visit to Jerusalem must be placed the vision which he had in

the temple (Acts xxii. 17–21) in which he was directed, in spite of his wish to the contrary, to leave Jerusalem and go to the Gentiles. In coming to Jerusalem, there-fore, he seems to have wished to take part with the older apostles in their work. The full significance of his commission as stated in general terms by Ananias had not become clear; still less did he for a moment think of establishing a separate movement. The vision in the temple, however, made his commission clearer, and with the cordial recognition of his vocation by at least the leaders of the church in Jerusalem, did he seek other fields of labor.

96. Still further, there is no evidence that the ques-tion of the observance of the law by Gentile converts had yet been raised. We cannot say whether the con-version of Cornelius had occurred. If it had, the brethren in Jerusalem, not foreseeing the storm which was to arise afterwards on this subject, would the more readily assume that Paul might evangelize Gentiles without disturbing the existing status. But more probably the question had not yet been raised at all. Zeal for the extension of the faith absorbed attention, and the Jews themselves had so long engaged in prose-lyting that similar work by the Christians must have seemed not unnatural. Moreover, Paul, then as after-wards, was bent on first offering the gospel to the Jews in foreign lands and from the synagogue reaching the Gentiles. We may therefore believe that his peculiar vocation opened before him gradually. The situation, both as regards his attitude and that of the mother church, was not such as to call forth any friction; and this was true, although, as we have seen, both his reli-gious experience and the commission he had received

pointed, as subsequent events proved, to a gospel for
Gentiles independent of any relation to the Jewish law.
The expanding Christianity was, however, being pro-
vided with its future leader.

97. Paul's life for the next eight or nine years is for
us wholly in the dark. He implies (Gal. i. 23) that he
was actively engaged in preaching Jesus. The churches
of Cilicia (Acts xv. 41), with others in Syria, may have
owed their origin to his labors during this period. How
far they contained Gentiles we do not know ; yet the
fact that afterwards Barnabas brought Paul from Tarsus to Antioch, when the distinctively Gentile work in
the latter city began, seems to imply that already his
labors had been among Gentiles, and that Christ's commission of him to such work was known. But this
obscure period must have been a fruitful one in Paul's
own life. The significance and implications of his faith
must have become clearer to him. His understanding
of the mission and teaching of his Lord must have advanced. The widening work must have increasingly
attracted him. The claims of Judaism must have daily
hung more loosely upon him ; for when he next appears
in the history we find him fully committed to the freedom of Gentiles from the law. During this period he
had also many experiences in the service and fellowship
of Jesus which, though unknown to us, entered profoundly into his religious life ; for here we must place
some of the perils which he endured (II. Cor. xi. 23–27)
and the visions and revelations which he received (II.
Cor. xii. 1–9) to which he afterwards alluded. We
may, in short, believe that during this period Paul
was finally prepared, mentally and spiritually, for the
still greater service which lay before him.

IV

PROGRESS OF THE MOTHER CHURCH

98. WHILE Christianity was expanding in the regions beyond Judea, the church in Jerusalem gradually recovered from the blow of persecution. We cannot say how long the persecution lasted. The first notice of its cessation is in Acts ix. 31, but it is impossible to date that statement with precision. We may believe that the fury of the persecution lasted but a year or two, and that with the conversion of Paul it lost its chief instigator.

99. Its cessation was followed by a renewed growth of the Christian community. The disciples again appear carrying on their work in public. Peter is represented as preaching in towns of Syria (ix. 32–42) and, on his return, meeting the assembled church in Jerusalem (xi. 2). Some years later the disciples formed a sufficiently large and well-known element of the population to cause Herod Agrippa I. to seek to please the Jews by renewing persecution.

100. The hostility of the authorities and the spread of the faith had, however, the effect of separating the disciples from the synagogues and leading them to form a complete organization of their own. They were indeed still loyal to the temple and the law. The charge which had been brought against Stephen (Acts vi. 13) did not represent a change in the attitude of

the disciples as a body to the national worship. But
separation from the synagogues had in many cases
been forced upon them; and even though this may
not have been always the case, the necessity for the
further organization of their own community had become apparent. We have already noted this separation among the disciples in the dispersion (sect. 70).
We now find it in Judea. Mention is made of " the
elders " (Acts xi. 30) of Jerusalem, — a phrase which
implies that the disciples of the capital were organized
into a religious society, perhaps into several, modelled
after the synagogue. The same was true of those in
other towns of Judea (Gal. i. 20). The name " synagogue " was retained for the Christian assembly (Jas.
ii. 2), but at the same time the term *ecclesia* was also
used to denote the society itself (Jas. v. 14; *Schürer*,
HJP. II. ii. 58, note 48). The latter term was already
familiar, as a designation of the congregation of Israel,
through its use in the Septuagint (comp. Acts vii. 38).
It or its Aramaic equivalent had been used by Jesus
himself to denote the company of his disciples (Matt. xvi.
18; xviii. 17). Its meaning, too, — a body called out,
— doubtless contributed to its use by suggesting the
divine call to which believers had responded; while
the advantage of having a distinct name for the new
society was obvious. *Ecclesia* became eventually the
regular term used among the Christians, except by a
few ultra Jewish-Christian sects, and is employed by
Luke to denote the body of disciples from the beginning (Acts v. 11, etc.). Yet the new organization was
simply the transfer of Jewish forms to the new society.
As we have seen that before the persecution practical
necessity led to the erection of the eleemosynary office

of "the seven," and as thus the inherent power of the community to organize itself was exhibited, so now the time had come when complete organization was required for the independent welfare of the church.

101. Thus must be explained the origin of the Christian office of elder. No specific account of its institution is given. We simply find it existing; but there can be no question that it was copied from the office of the same name among the Jews. In each Jewish community the elders were the governing body. The time had doubtless passed when only old men filled the office, and the elders were chosen from the most influential. Originally they possessed both civil and religious authority; but oftener, in the time of which we are treating, their authority pertained chiefly to religious matters, except in those foreign cities where civil jurisdiction was granted by the government to the rulers of the Jewish colonies. The Jewish elders were thus the representatives and rulers of the congregation which assembled in the synagogue. They exercised discipline, even to excommunication, and managed in general the affairs of the synagogue. There were also other officers particularly charged with the house of meeting; such as "the ruler (or rulers) of the synagogue" who provided for the actual conduct of worship by securing readers and speakers; "the minister" (*Chazzan*), who cared for the sacred writings and performed other duties under the direction of his superiors; and the receivers of alms, who, however, were not strictly officers of the synagogue (*Schürer*, HJP. II. ii. sect. 27). But the eldership constituted the chief synagogal authority. Where more than one synagogue ex-

isted in a place, all the elders seemed to have formed one body governing the entire community. Finally, the great Sanhedrim in Jerusalem, consisting of seventy-one members, besides being the governing body of Judea, was the supreme court of the Jewish church and world.

102. When, then, we find the disciples organized under elders, the origin and character of the arrangement is evident. The eldership was not primarily a teaching office. Its functions were chiefly disciplinary and executive. As in the synagogue any one was at liberty to read or speak, so in the early churches there was freedom of utterance, and the gifts of the Spirit supplied the needs of the worshippers (comp. I. Cor. xiv. 26). The elders, however, presided. They could teach if they wished, and the superintendence of the instructions, as well as of the order, of the congregation was in their hands. Of course they possessed no priestly functions. As the synagogue was distinct from the temple, so the object of its service was instruction, not sacrifice; and those who ruled in either synagogue or church had none of the functions of those who officiated at the altar. In conformity with the synagogal origin of the office, we find Christian elders first mentioned as receiving the gifts from Antioch for distribution among the poor (Acts xi. 30); as appointed by Paul and Barnabas over the new churches in Asia Minor (xiv. 23); and as uniting with the apostles in the council at Jerusalem (xv. 6, 22, 23). It is probable that in Judea, as elsewhere (Acts xiv. 23; xx. 17), in each locality where a sufficient number of disciples existed, elders were chosen who governed the entire body of believers in that place.

Certainly in Jerusalem, where there were many disciples and doubtless many places of meeting, there was one body of elders ruling over all (xi. 30; xv. 6). Whether any other features of the synagogue were taken over, we do not know; but by the establishment of the Christian eldership, two facts are made clear; namely, that the separation from Judaism had become decided, and that the primitive conception of the church was not based on the temple, but on the synagogue, where the congregation met for instruction, praise, and prayer.

103. The rise of organized churches seems also to have modified gradually the work performed by the apostles. At first they had been the sole officials. With the appointment of "the seven," they were relieved of the care of the poor, that they might attend undividedly to teaching. With the establishment of the eldership, their work was further modified. No doubt it was they who directed the organization into churches on the same practical principles which appear in the institution of "the seven." They still continued to be the recognized authorities in matters of belief (e. g. I. Cor. ix. 1; xii. 23; II. Cor. xii. 13; Eph. ii. 20; iv. 11; Jude 17); but they now appear more and more to have directed their efforts to the superintendence and advancement of the cause at large. So Peter's activity, quite early in this period, is expressly described (Acts ix. 32). So too had Paul, as we have seen, been sent forth to Cilicia. From this time we hear no more of most of the original apostles. We cannot doubt that they went abroad, as tradition affirms (Eus. HE. III. 1), as missionaries and founders of new churches, and that to them, as well as to other

laborers, the spread of Christianity was due. Jerusa lem indeed continued for many years to be the head-quarters of the faith, and to it they may have returned like Paul himself from time to time. But the progress and organization of the Judean churches appears to have delocalized the apostolate and made it a travelling and scattered body, delivering in wider circles the gospel of the risen Lord (comp. I. Cor. ix. 5).

104. One event during this period illustrates partic-ularly how the mother church was prepared to appre-ciate the expansion of the faith that was beginning (Acts x.). Cornelius, a Roman centurion of the Italian cohort, located at Cæsarea, belonged to the numerous class of devout foreigners who had come under the influence of Judaism. He worshipped Jehovah and was constant in alms and prayers. This man was directed in a vision to send for Peter, who was so-journing in Joppa, that he might learn the will of the Lord more perfectly. The apostle was also given a significant vision. While waiting at noon on the house-top for food to be prepared, he beheld in an ecstasy a sheet let down from heaven, filled with beasts, creeping things, and fowls, and he heard a voice saying, " Rise, Peter, kill and eat." When he protested that he had never eaten unclean food, the voice replied, " What God hath cleansed, make not thou common " (Acts x. 15, R. V.). A second and a third time the vision was repeated, and while Peter pondered on its meaning the messengers from Cornelius arrived. The Spirit bade him go with them, and Peter realized that the vision and the summons were divinely connected. Probably he had never before doubted the binding force of Jewish ordinances; but he knew now that he must

not limit his mission by them. When, then, he reached the house of Cornelius and heard the cause of the summons, he did not hesitate to preach Jesus to the Gentiles who were present and to offer them salvation on condition of faith alone (x. 43). At once the Spirit fell upon the company, to the astonishment of the Jewish Christians who accompanied the apostle. That signified God's acceptance of uncircumcised believers. Peter recognized the divine will and without more delay baptized the new disciples. He even continued to live with them, in disregard of Jewish regulations, for certain days.

105. This incident was felt to be revolutionary. The news spread to Jerusalem, and while the conversion of Gentiles could not but cause joy, the conduct of Peter in living and eating with them offended the brethren. When he returned, they took him to task for it. He replied by rehearsing the facts, closing with the unanswerable question, " What was I that I could withstand God ? " (Acts xi. 1–17). He evidently felt that since God had accepted Gentile believers without circumcision, he dared not refuse to recognize them as brethren in the Lord even at the cost of the violation of ceremonial customs ; and if he reflected on the words, " What God hath cleansed, make not thou common," he could hardly have failed to perceive that he was meant to understand that the work of Jesus consisted in the cleansing from all sin ; and that on this basis the whole Mosaic ritual, its purpose having been accomplished, was no longer necessary. Whether he perceived this at the time or not, it was made clear to him that God did not intend the ritual law to be imposed on Gentiles.

106. This incident shows that the relation of Gentile believers, and ultimately of all believers, to Judaism was a subject on which, as Christianity expanded, there was certain to be difference of opinion. Hitherto it had been generally assumed that Gentile converts would observe the law; while as to the duty of Jews there was no doubt. Peter himself ventured to transgress the ordinances only after explicit direction from the Lord; and all that we know of the early Jewish believers makes it certain that nothing but belief in a revelation to that effect could have led the apostle so to act. Hence the incident was remembered in after times as a demonstration of what the will of the Lord was. Its effect on Peter can be seen in his whole subsequent career. He ever afterwards maintained the freedom of Gentiles from the law (Acts xv. 7–11; Gal. ii. 7, 8), and, though he was the apostle of the circumcision, we find him in Antioch living freely with them (Gal. ii. 12). The church in Jerusalem also recognized that at least God had granted to the Gentiles repentance unto life (Acts xi. 18), though their disapproval of Peter's conduct may not have wholly ceased, and though all may not have been ready to apply the principle involved. This is not inconsistent with the rise afterward, when the number of uncircumcised believers had increased, of a party who insisted on the necessity of circumcision. The manifest work of God silenced the voice of prejudice; and, as the incident became more significant in the light of later controversy, so at the time it indicated the larger field on which the faith was entering.

107. Thus Christianity advanced in Judea after the cessation of the first persecution. It was recruited

chiefly, as the poverty of the disciples seems to prove
(Gal. ii. 10), from the humbler classes. Not a few,
however, of the Pharisees joined them (Acts xv. 5);
for the loyalty of the disciples to the law was un-
questionable. In many respects the movement still
appeared a spiritual revival of Judaism and appealed
powerfully to the religious aspirations of the best of
the people. And this condition of affairs was hardly
interrupted by the brief revival of persecution by Herod
Agrippa I. (Acts xii.). That prince, the grandson of
Herod the Great and brother of Herodias who married
Herod Antipas, after a checkered career in Rome and
the East, had been given by his friend Gaius Caligula,
on the latter's accession to the empire in A. D. 37, the
tetrarchies of Iturea, Trachonitis, and Abilene with the
title of king; and to these were added, in A. D. 40, Galilee and Perea, which had formerly been governed by
Herod Antipas. Claudius, in A. D. 41, confirmed this
grant and added to it Judea and Samaria, which since
the death of Archelaus had been ruled by procurators.
Herod Agrippa was thus king of the Jews and governed
the same territory as his famous grandfather. His
reign lasted but three years (*Jos.* Antiq. xix. 8. 2). He
was popular with the Jews and, when in Judea, observant of their customs. It was quite in accord with
what we know of his character that to please the Jews
he instituted persecution against the new sect. This
was in A. D. 44, the year of Herod's death. James, the
son of Zebedee, was slain with the sword. Only a
divine interposition saved Peter, who, after sending
word of his escape to James, the Lord's brother, and
to the other leaders, fled from the city. No mention,
however, is made of other seizures by Herod. Peter's

language (xii. 17) has been thought to imply that the other apostles had also left the city ; and, even apart from the danger which threatened them, this may have been the case. But the trouble appears to have soon blown over. Herod died in the summer of that year in Cæsarea under strangely dramatic circumstances, which are described independently, but with agreement as to the main facts, by Josephus (Antiq. xix. 8. 2) and Luke (xii. 20–23). The only significance of the persecution was its indication of the determined rejection of Christianity by the Jewish state as well as by the Jewish church. However loyal to Judaism the disciples might be, they could not but realize that the separation between them and the existing authorities was complete.

108. It was probably a year or two before the Herodian persecution that the attention of the church in Jerusalem was called to the progress of the faith in Syrian Antioch. The events which had occurred there were, in fact, the opening of a new chapter in the history of the religion of Jesus. In narrating them we must go back to the dispersion which followed the death of Stephen.

109. Some of the refugees fled northward to Phœnicia and the island of Cyprus, which lay about fifty miles off the Phœnician coast, and came finally to the great metropolis of Syria, Antioch on the Orontes. Like the other refugees, they preached as they journeyed, but to Jews only. Some of them, Jews from Cyprus and Cyrene, and therefore perhaps less narrowed than others by Jewish prejudices, began preaching in Antioch to Gentiles.[1] This met with much success. A community of believers arose in the Syrian metropolis composed mainly of uncircumcised foreigners with whom the Jewish disciples lived on terms of equality. The incident shows that, quite independently of the

---

[1] Whether Ἕλληνας or Ἑλληνιστάς be the right reading in Acts xi. 20, there can be no doubt that the work was among the non-Jewish population.

divine preparation of Paul, and of the mother church
for work among the Gentiles, there was in some quarters a tendency in the same direction traceable to the
spirit of the faith itself. It was, in fact, the inevitable issue of the offer of salvation by faith which had
been proclaimed from the beginning, and of the widening sympathies engendered by the expansion.

110. The rise of Gentile Christianity in Antioch was,
however, specially momentous because of the character
and position of that city. The Antiochan church was
fitted to be a new centre for the diffusion of the faith.
From it the message about Jesus, separated from Jewish
complications, could best issue into the empire. The
third city of the empire, outranked in size only by
Rome and Alexandria, crowded with a mixed population and connected commercially with both East and
West, Antioch was the most important place for the
faith, advancing from Jerusalem, to occupy. From it
the new religion would be carried by report in every
direction. It lay just beyond the confines of Palestine,
and thus was not so far from the original centre as to
lose touch with the mother church. At the same time
it was the door from Palestine to the Græco-Roman
world. No place was so well suited to be a base of
operations for the progress of Christianity into the
empire. It was surely not accidental that these unknown refugees were led to begin their quiet but
portentous mission in Antioch.

111. We cannot say how soon after Stephen's death
this work began, nor how long it continued before at-
tracting the attention of the church in Jerusalem.
The report, however, evidently reached the latter shortly
before the Herodian persecution. Forthwith Barnabas

was sent to examine into it. The Jerusalem church thus assumed authority over the churches founded by the refugees. The desire for examination into the report implies likewise a sense of its novelty and of its doubtful character from the strict Jewish point of view. Yet the selection of Barnabas indicates the absence of hostility to the new movement. Being himself a Cypriote, he was naturally chosen to investigate a work which had in part originated with his fellow-countrymen. He was also a man of liberal mind and hospitable to new developments of the cause, as had been shown by his reception of the converted Paul. At the same time he was of high repute among the brethren in Jerusalem. He was thus fitted to appreciate the new movement, if it was a genuine work of the Spirit of Jesus, and to mediate, if necessary, between it and the older church. His mission illustrates, therefore, the joy of the mother church over the expansion of the faith, her willingness to recognize it if genuine, and yet no doubt the reluctance of most of the brethren in Jerusalem to go themselves directly to the Gentiles. That none of the apostles was sent may have been due to their absence; or to the feeling that, for the reasons stated, Barnabas was best qualified to appreciate the situation; or possibly because, this being the action, not of the apostles, but of the church (Acts xi. 22) one of the local officials, such as Barnabas doubtless was, was deemed the appropriate representative.

112. The choice certainly proved a wise one. Barnabas recognized the genuinely Christian character of the Gentile converts. With much largemindedness he made no attempt to exact conformity to the Jewish law. Nay, more. He departed at once to Tarsus and

brought Paul from thence to Antioch, and the two men labored together for a year in the new sphere with greater results than before (Acts xi. 25–26). All this is very significant. It seems probable that Barnabas was acquainted with Paul's commission to the Gentiles; that he sympathized with it; and that he saw in Antioch the divinely prepared opportunity for it. It is clear too that neither of them thought for a moment that Gentile believers would be bound by the Jewish laws. That demand had not yet been raised within the church. Thus the first Gentile church known to history was established in harmonious relations with the mother church; and in this new field Barnabas and Paul began the work of expansion outside of the limits of Judaism, which they were to carry on, together or separately, for many years.

113. Two other interesting facts are noted by Luke in connection with the young church at Antioch (Acts xi. 26–30). One is that here the name " Christian " was first applied to the followers of Jesus. It must have originated with the Gentiles, for obviously the Jews would not have given it to them. It implies also that they were no longer considered a Jewish sect, for the term distinguishes them from the Jews. The disciples had called themselves " believers " (Acts xi. 24; comp. I. Thess. i. 7; II. Thess. i. 10), or " brethren " (Acts i. 15; ix. 30; x. 23), or "those of the Way " (Acts ix. 2; comp. xix. 9; xxii. 4), or simply " disciples " (Acts vi. 1, 2, 7; ix. 10, 19, 26, etc.). Yet the title " Christian," while given them by others, would naturally be a welcome one, and this the more as their own consciousness of separation from Judaism advanced. There was nothing necessarily derisive in

it. It speedily became their common title among the Gentiles. The Jews indeed still called them Nazarenes (Acts xxiv. 5). Yet even Agrippa (Acts xxvi. 28) used the term "Christian," doubtless because of his acquaintance with its use elsewhere. Tacitus testifies that before Nero's persecution this was their common name in Rome (Annales xv. 44); Peter (I. Pet. iv. 16) intimates that the appellation was current in Asia Minor. The term moreover is not of Latin but of Greek origin. Denominatives of this form were frequent among the Greeks, especially among the Greek-speaking population of the East (*Lipsius*, Über den Ursprung und früheren Gebrauch des Christennamens). The title thus naturally originated in Antioch under the circumstances which Luke describes, and marks the first appearance of the faith among the Gentiles as a non-Judaic religion.

114. The other fact noted by Luke is that "prophets" from Jerusalem came to Antioch. This remark introduces us to a class of persons of whom frequent mention is made in apostolic literature (Acts xiii. 1; xv. 32; xxi. 10; I. Cor. xii. 28, 29; xiv. 29, 32, 37; Eph. ii. 20; iii. 5; iv. 11; Rev. x. 7; xi. 18; xvi. 6; xviii. 20, 24; xxii. 6, 9). The prophet was not an ordinary church official. Any one, from an apostle (I. Cor. xiii. 2; xiv. 6; Rev. i. 3) to a private member (Acts xxi. 9; I. Cor. xii. 10; Rom. xii. 6; I. Cor. xiv. 29), might possess the gift. Prophecy was the chief of those endowments which the Spirit after Pentecost bestowed upon the church as the seal of the Lord's triumph and the earnest of his people's salvation. The New Testament conception of a prophet is precisely that of the Old Testament. He

was one whom God made the organ for the communication of truth to the church, — one who spoke directly from God and whose words were the words of God. The gift might be temporary or permanent. It might operate with or without the use of rational means for the acquisition of truth by the prophet. The truth communicated might be didactic or predictive or even historical (comp. I. Cor. xi. 23). The existence therefore of prophets in the apostolic church testifies to the belief that it was an age of revelation. Besides having the historic teaching of Jesus, the disciples believed that God was continually communicating truth to them. This prophetic ministry belonged to the apostles, but, as has been said, was not confined to them, so that " on the foundation of the apostles and prophets " was the church held to be established (Eph. ii. 20). With other gifts of the Spirit, it made the worship of the disciples partake largely of the character of a Spirit-led and voluntary service. It thus checked for a time the development of official teachers in the congregation. We shall find later the value of regular, official teachers emphasized (I. Cor. x. 28; Eph. iv. 11; I. Tim. v. 17; II. Tim. ii. 2), and from the beginning the instruction of converts was never wanting (Acts ii. 42; I. Thess. v. 12; Gal. vi. 6; I. Cor. xii. 28; Rom. xii. 7). The utterances of prophecy were moreover to be tested by the teaching already given by the apostles (II. Thess. iii. 6, 14; I. Cor. xiv. 37; I. John iv. 2, 6). But the prophets were the living evidence of the continuance of the prophetic office of Messiah by whose Spirit they spake. The beliefs of the disciples, resting on this basis, were therefore to them authoritative revelations. This

belief in living prophecy, united with belief in apostolic authority, created among the Christians the conviction that a new revelation was being made to them in addition to, though including, the teaching and work of Jesus, and finally laid the ground for a belief in an inspired Christian literature, corresponding to the Old Testament, which we find expressed in the apostolic age itself (e. g. II. Thess. ii. 2; iii. 14; I. Cor. xiv. 27; II. Pet. iii. 1, 2, 16; I. John i. 3, 4; Rev. i. 3, 11; xxii. 18, 19). In the "Teaching of the Apostles" (ab. A. D. 100) we still read of prophets as itinerant preachers; and we shall not appreciate properly the consciousness of the apostolic Christians, if we omit their faith in a present revelation which was being communicated to them by inspired men.

115. Luke's reference to the prophets who came from Jerusalem to Antioch indicates the cordial relations which existed between the old and the new communities. This soon found further expression. One of the prophets, Agabus by name, doubtless in one of the public services of the church, predicted that a great famine was about to come on the whole empire (Acts xi. 28). Probably this prediction formed part of an inspired description of the woes which would fall on the world and especially on the Jews before Messiah's return (comp. Matt. xxiv. 7; Rev. vi. 5, 6). At any rate, the prediction of a famine was specific. Luke notes that this happened during the reign of Claudius. That this was so in Judea is confirmed by Josephus (Antiq. xx. 2. 5 and 5. 2) who calls it the "great famine." He locates it during the procuratorships of Fadus (A. D. 44–46) and Tiberius Alexander (A. D. 46–48?). We know also of other famines under Claudius

(*Dio Cass.* lx. 11; *Tac.* Ann. xii. 43; *Suet.* Claud. 18)
Two of these were felt at Rome, which implies that
they raged in the provinces whence the food-supply
of the capital was drawn. Eusebius (Chron. i. 79)
also refers to one in Greece. Luke's remark therefore
is quite justified; but the important fact is the action
taken by the Antiochan Christians. They expected, as
probably Agabus had declared, that the famine would
come soon; so they began at once to raise a fund for
the relief of the brethren in Judea (Acts xi. 29). This
implies that most of the Judean disciples were known
to be poor (comp. Gal. ii. 10) and also that the Antiochans recognized their special obligation to the
mother church. The two churches were thus united
in love and mutual helpfulness; and the two men to
whose labors the church at Antioch owed the most,
were chosen as the bearers of their gift. The aid was
carried to the elders of Jerusalem by Barnabas and
Paul (Acts xi. 30).

116. This mission of Barnabas and Paul has, however, occasioned difficulty because of the fact that Paul
does not mention it in the first chapter of Galatians.
It is thought by many that his argument required him
to mention every visit he had made to Jerusalem since
his conversion. Hence Luke's account in this place
has been deemed unhistorical. Others have sought to
identify this visit with that described in Gal. ii. 1–10,
when also Barnabas accompanied Paul (*Ramsay*, St.
Paul the Trav. p. 55). But to the latter view there
are insuperable objections. The visit of Galatians ii.
had for its chief object the declaration of the gospel
which Paul preached among the Gentiles and the
determination of the attitude of the mother church

toward Gentile converts.   Paul's language implies that
the recognition of uncircumcised believers was then a
burning question.   He had also private interviews with
James, Peter, and John on the subject of work among
the Gentiles.   The apostle's object is to point out that
harmony with his views and the cordial recognition of
his mission prevailed.   Only incidentally does he mention the desire of the leaders of the Jerusalem church
that he should remember the poor (Gal. ii. 10).   This
account does not correspond at all with the cordial
relations which we have found existing between the
churches of Jerusalem and Antioch when the visit
with the gifts was made, nor with the entire absence
of the question of circumcision at that time.   The request that he should remember the poor is also much
more natural if on a previous occasion he had done so,
than on the assumption that it was made without justification in his former life.   Still further, this identification supposes that the important visit recorded in Acts
xv. is not mentioned at all in the epistle, although
it had, on any reasonable view of the date of the
writing, certainly occurred.   We must conclude therefore that Paul does not mention the visit with the
gifts.   This, however, need not throw doubt on its
occurrence.   His argument in reality required him
only to mention those occasions on which he had met
the older apostles (comp. Gal. i. 16, 17).   It is worthy
of note that in Acts he is said merely to have been
sent to the elders of the Jerusalem church.   The visit
was doubtless brief, for the gifts, being probably in the
form of money, were soon turned over to the elders.
There is no sufficient reason to assume that Paul and
Barnabas remained to distribute them.   If also Acts

xi. 30 and xii. 24, when their place in Luke's narrative is observed, imply, as some believe, that the visit occurred in the very year of the Herodian persecution (A. D. 44), another reason is suggested for its brevity and for the improbability that the visitors met any of the apostles. So Paul and Barnabas hastened back to their field of labor. Luke only adds, in anticipation of his further narrative, that they took with them to Antioch the cousin (Col. iv. 10, R. V.) of Barnabas, John whose surname was Mark (Acts xii. 25).

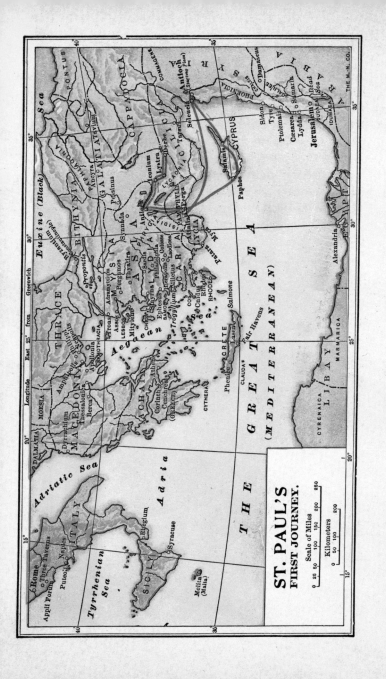

ST. PAUL'S
FIRST JOURNEY.

Scale of Miles
0 25 50   100   150   200   250

Kilometers
0   50   100   200

THE MISSIONARY JOURNEY OF PAUL AND BARNABAS

117. ANTIOCH soon became the point of departure for a greater expansion of the faith than any yet known. This originated in a revelation of the Spirit made to five prophets and teachers of that church (Acts xiii. 1, 2). Four of them, Barnabas, Simeon Niger, Lucius of Cyrene, and Paul, were Hellenistic Jews. The fifth had once been the foster-brother or comrade (*Deissmann*, Bibelstudien, p. 178) of Herod Antipas, and may have been a Jew likewise. The point to be noted is that they belonged to the circle which had already taken the deepest interest in the expansion of the faith. To them, as they worshipped, the Spirit gave the command, " Separate me Barnabas and Saul to the work whereunto I have called them ; " and forthwith the two missionaries were set apart by the laying on of hands to their new mission.

118. The work itself was undesignated, but there could be no doubt that it was to be among the Gentiles. This, of course, did not exclude work among the Jews. The synagogues were the first places in which the missionaries began to preach, and through them, indeed, they could best reach the Gentiles. But the work was not to be limited to Jews, and it was to be carried on in Gentile lands. No explicit program, however, was furnished. The messengers of Messiah were to be

guided by the Spirit and by Providence. Nor may
they at first have appreciated the magnitude of their
enterprise, but went forth in obedience to the divine
command. They were sent also by the church, acting
in the persons of the three remaining prophets and
teachers who laid their hands upon the brethren.
This did not make Barnabas and Paul apostles of
Christ in the technical sense (Gal. i. 1), but it made
them apostles of the church (Acts xiv. 4, 14). Their
mission was thus both a divine vocation and an enterprise of the Antiochan church. We may believe also
that it accorded with an already formed wish of Barnabas and Paul. It was very opportune. The men had
been prepared for the work. The work was waiting
for the men. The church had been formed which was
ready to support the missionaries, and it lay at the
gateway of the Roman world. All conspired to make
the mission the climax of the progress hitherto attained
and to open the way for further expansion.

119. The date of the journey can only be approximately assigned to the period between A. D. 44 and 50.
Nor are there any clear indications of the time consumed by it. Ramsay estimates its length at two
years and four months (Church in the Empire, pp. 61,
67, 72), but his reasoning is not demonstrative. Others
think it consumed but a single summer. We shall
perhaps be safe in locating it in 47 and 48.

120. The route first taken seems to have been determined by practical considerations. Accompanied
by John Mark as a helper (xiii. 5), the missionaries
went from Antioch to its seaport, Seleucia, and thence
sailed to Cyprus. This was doubtless because Barnabas was from that island.   Work, too, had been already

begun there (xi. 19), and the large number of Jews
provided the means by which those Gentiles who were
influenced by the synagogue might be reached. Land-
ing at Salamis, they preached in the synagogues, and
gradually traversed the whole length of the island.
No note of their success is given until they reached
Paphos, at the western extremity of Cyprus. There the
proconsul himself, Sergius Paulus, embraced the faith.
He had been influenced by Judaism and was interested
in religion; but he had fallen under the sway of a
Jewish sorcerer, Barjesus, who called himself Elymas,
or " the wise man," and had a place apparently in the
proconsul's retinue. When Elymas opposed the missionaries, Paul openly denounced the wickedness of
the renegade Jew and smote him with blindness (xiii.
8–11); and this sign secured the adhesion of the Roman
to the new teaching (xiii. 12). Luke narrates the incident because, as in the case of Simon Magus, it illustrated the triumph of the faith over those religious
impostors who were so prominent a feature of the
Roman world in the apostolic age.

121. From this time Paul — as he is thenceforth
called in Acts (xiii. 9) — appears as the leader of
the campaign (xiii. 13; xiv. 12); and it was perhaps
at his suggestion that they sailed northward to Perga
in Pamphylia. There Mark left them and returned to
Jerusalem. His conduct displeased Paul (xv. 38). We
may conjecture that Mark was unwilling to enter on
so bold and large an enterprise as that which the
apostle was undertaking in Asia Minor (see *Ramsay*,
St. Paul, etc., p. 90; *McGiffert*, Ap. Age, p. 176).
Whether the unwillingness arose from personal or
theoretical motives does not appear. It again evi-

dences the devotion of Barnabas that, in spite of his
kinsman's return, he was ready to go forward. The
stay at Perga, however, was for some unknown reason
brief; and we find the party immediately advancing
northward, probably along the Cestrus and by way of
Adaba (*Ramsay*, Ch. in Emp. p. 19), to Pisidian Antioch (xiii. 14), a city of Phrygia, lying toward the
Pisidian border, which was then the military centre
of the southern part of the province of Galatia. The
journey was a rough and perilous one. In it may perhaps be located some of the dangers mentioned in II.
Cor. xi. 26, 27. But in Pisidian Antioch the missionaries reached a place of large importance. Paul had
probably long had it in mind as the centre of the
province lying north of his own Cilicia. In it also
was a numerous colony of Jews. By visiting it, Paul
followed his well-known policy of seizing the chief
centres of population and influence.

122. The work in Pisidian Antioch began as usual
in the synagogue, and Paul's address (Acts xiii. 16–41)
aroused at once the interest of both the Jews and the
devout Gentiles who were present. It is worthy of
special notice as being the earliest recorded teaching
of the apostle. (1) In it he first reviewed briefly the
history of Israel (16–25), to show that God's purpose
culminated in the sending of a Saviour, even Jesus,
whom John the Baptist had specifically declared to be
Messiah. This part of the address is like Stephen's
in its historical point of view; but it follows quite a
different line of thought, bringing out the sovereign
power and plan of God in Hebrew history and setting
Jesus forth as the Christ of promise. Its closing
words show that the mission of the Baptist was well

known among the Jews of the dispersion (comp. also
xviii. 25 ; xix. 3), and illustrate Paul's familiarity
with the teaching of John as it is given in the gospels
(comp. verses 24, 25 with, *e. g.*, Luke iii. 15, 16 ; John
i. 20–27). (2) The address next recounted (26–37)
the death, burial, and resurrection of Jesus. Both his
death and resurrection were in precise accord with
prophecy, and demonstrated him to be the one through
whom the promises to Israel will be fulfilled. In this
section we are reminded of Peter's speeches at and
after Pentecost (comp. verse 27 with iii. 17 ; ii. 23 ; iii.
18 ; verse 28 with iii. 13 ; verses 33–35 with ii. 27; verse
37 with ii. 31) ; but the material is such as would have
been naturally common to both preachers. There are
also characteristic Pauline ideas. The ignorance of
the Jews displayed in the rejection of Jesus (comp.
I. Cor. ii. 8 ; I. Tim. i. 13), the Lord's burial (comp.
I. Cor. xv. 4), his repeated appearances to the original
disciples (I. Cor. xv. 5–7), are elsewhere emphasized
by Paul. That he does not here appeal to Christ's
appearance to himself is natural, since he was addressing strangers, and the primary point was to
appeal to the original witnesses in Jerusalem. This,
too, is in accord with his method as described by him
in I. Cor. xv. 5–7.

123. (3) The close of the address (38–41) strikes a
still more decidedly Pauline note. Like Peter (Acts ii.
38 ; v. 31 ; x. 43), but also using a form of expression
found in his own epistles (Eph. i. 7 ; Col. i. 14 ; comp.
Rom. iv. 7 and Acts xxvi. 18), he declared that through
Jesus " forgiveness of sins " was offered to them. But
he went further. As every Jew would agree, salvation
consists in the declaration by God that before him a

man is righteous. This, Paul said, is now possible. In Jesus every believer is justified, and, as he puts it with great emphasis on the word "all," is justified from all things from which he could not be justified by the law of Moses. This may be regarded as an appeal to his hearers' consciousness that the law did not secure to them real reconciliation with God, but only an apparent and unsatisfying merit (comp. Rom. x. 3 ; Phil. iii. 6, 9) ; or it may be understood as a declaration that they could not by the law, while they could by faith, be completely justified. In either case the idea is entirely Pauline (comp. *Wendt*, Apostel-geschichte). The warning also against their probable unbelief is again after Paul's manner (II. Thess. ii. 14, 16 ; Rom. ix.–xi.). While offering Jesus to the Jews, he realized fully that the nation as such, like the rulers in Jerusalem, would reject him.

124. This address then furnishes the first glimpse into the apostle's thought and method as a preacher. Luke's report is, of course, an abstract, and contains traces of his own style and vocabulary. Yet as in other cases he preserves the thought, and in great measure the diction, of the speaker. The address was certainly adapted to the mixed audience that heard it. We should not regard Paul's epistles as representative of his ordinary method of preaching. His speeches in Acts exhibit a versatility and adaptation which testify to both the authenticity of the reports and the power of the apostle. We may infer also, from allusions in the epistles, that his preaching was varied and practical as well as argumentative (*e. g.* I. Thess. i. 9, 10 ; ii. 11, 12; iii. 4 ; Gal. iii. 1 ; I. Cor. ii. 1–5). Here, the historical introduction was calculated to awaken

the confidence of his hearers in him as a loyal Hebrew. His presentation of Jesus, by emphasizing the fulfilment of prophecy and the power of God in the resurrection, was suited to make the deepest impression. His conclusion appealed to the longing of the human heart, whether Jew or Gentile, for real salvation. At the same time the thought moves entirely in the circle of Pauline teaching as we know it from the epistles. Salvation lies in justification before God. Faith alone is its condition. The death and resurrection of Christ are the means whereby salvation has been accomplished and certified. These were the leading truths which Paul taught in his epistles. We find him already teaching them in Antioch; while his intimation (verse 39) that the law cannot save shows that he stood on the ground on which he was destined soon to fight the battle of Christian liberty and defend the sufficiency of Jesus' work.

125. The favorable impression produced by the address brought a larger concourse, specially of Gentiles, to the synagogue on the next Sabbath. This, however, awakened the anger of the Jews, who feared the loss of their own influence. Hence Paul and Barnabas were led to declare that their responsibility to the Jews was at an end and that they would turn to the Gentiles. It is the first known time that this course was taken by them, but it is a typical example of their method. Unlike the gradual way in which the Palestinian disciples separated from the synagogue, in these foreign regions the separation was usually rapid. A Christian community arose in Pisidian Antioch which was mainly Gentile, and between which and the synagogue antagonism at once began. The synagogue possessed, of

course, the greater influence in the city. It was especially influential among the women (comp. *Jos.* BJ. II. 20. 2), and women occupied a prominent position in the society and even in the political and official life of the cities of Asia Minor (*Ramsay*, Ch. in Emp. p. 67). Through these agencies the civil authorities were arrayed against the missionaries, and the latter were expelled. They went to Iconium, leaving behind them a considerable body of believers.

126. Iconium was another Phrygian city, and lay about eighty miles southeast of Antioch, near the border of Lycaonia. Ramsay has made it probable that in this journey Paul and Barnabas followed one of the great Roman roads which traversed the provinces and united them for military and commercial purposes (Ch. in Emp. p. 27). The work in Iconium was like that in Antioch, and was attended with equal success. The Jews, however, again made trouble, and when the work had progressed for some time (xiv. 3), so that the city was divided between the two parties, threatened another persecution from the authorities. Thereupon the missionaries passed over into Lycaonia and visited the two cities of Lystra and Derbe. This was not, however, a mere flight for safety into an unimportant region. Lystra, which lay eighteen miles southwest from Iconium, was a Roman colony and a military centre (Ch. in Emp. p. 47); and, though the site of Derbe is still unidentified, it was probably an important place on the southeastern frontier of the province of Galatia (*ibid.* p. 54). The missionaries, therefore, still sought centres of influence and, though everywhere facing persecution, steadily pursued their plan.

127. Their stay in Lystra was made notable by Paul's

healing a lame man (Acts xiv. 8, etc.). The miracle
had the effect of persuading the populace that the
foreign, Greek-speaking visitors were none other than
the gods Zeus and Hermes; and the priest of the temple of Zeus before the city was about to offer to them
sacrifices. This was truly a new and unexpected form
of misunderstanding, and gave occasion for a new style
of address from Paul's lips (xiv. 15-18). He bravely
proclaimed, in the face of idolatry, the one living and
true God, the Creator and governor of all, the benefi-
cent author of that Nature which heathenism blindly
worshipped. Again the report is a mere abstract, but
it bears its substantial authenticity on its face. Though
there is not a word in it of the way of salvation, it is
strikingly accordant with Paul's expressions elsewhere
(comp. verse 15 with I. Cor. viii. 4; Rom. i. 20-23;
I. Thess. i. 9; verse 16 with Acts xvii. 26; Rom. i. 24;
iii. 25; verse 17 with Rom. i. 20), and reveals the
broad basis of natural religion on which his specifically
Christian teaching rested. It illustrates also his power
of adaptation to his audience.

128. It is probable that during the visit to Lystra
Timothy was converted. On Paul's next visit (xvi. 1)
he found this young disciple well reported of by the
brethren, and took him for a companion. He always
speaks of Timothy as one of his own converts (I. Tim.
i. 2, 18; II. Tim. i. 2; ii. 1), and reminds him in later
life of the perils he had undergone at this time (II.
Tim. iii. 10, 11). It is natural to infer, therefore, that
Timothy was converted during this visit. He must
have been very young. His Jewish mother, Eunice,
had married a Gentile, but had trained her son in the
Scriptures of her race (Acts xvi. 3; II. Tim. i. 5; iii. 15).

He had, however, not been circumcised. Perhaps his mixed blood made him specially sympathize with the Hebrew preacher to the Gentiles. Paul's affectionate references to Timothy's mother and grandmother (II. Tim. i. 5) suggest also that the persecuted missionary found in them receptive listeners and warm friends, and perhaps in their house a home.

129. The work in Lystra was, however, interrupted by Jews from Antioch and Iconium, who followed the missionaries and persuaded the populace against them. Where Paul had been offered worship, he was now dragged out of the city and stoned (Acts xiv. 19). Happily he was not killed, and on the next day left with Barnabas for Derbe. Nothing is said of the work in Derbe except that disciples were made. The missionaries had now reached the limit of south Galatia, and determined to return to Syrian Antioch with a report of their mission. They might have crossed the mountains southwards into Cilicia and gone by way of Tarsus to Syria, but they did not wish to leave the new converts without further instruction and organization. Hence, in spite of the danger, they resolved to return by the way they had come. It may have been that the danger had decreased, perhaps by the election of new magistrates in the cities of the province (*Ramsay*, Ch. in Emp. p. 69). But their motive was to revisit the disciples, and this they would have done in the face of danger. So from Derbe they returned to Lystra, and from Lystra to Iconium, and from Iconium to Pisidian Antioch. They not only encouraged, instructed, and warned the converts, but organized them into churches by the selection and ordination of elders (xiv. 22) in every place.

From Pisidian Antioch they returned to Perga.   There
they stopped to preach, as they had not done on the
former visit.   Thence they went to the seaport, Attalia,
and sailed to Syrian Antioch, where they related to
the church " all things that God had done with them,
and how that he had opened a door of faith unto the
Gentiles " (Acts xiv. 27, R. V.).

130. As we review this first missionary tour, we
may observe the principles on which Paul and Barnabas acted.   (a) Their plan was, in general, to move
westward into the regions next beyond those already
occupied.   It would be too much to say that Paul as
yet contemplated the winning of the empire to the
faith.   They doubtless went to Cyprus, because it was
the home of Barnabas, and then to Phrygia and
Lycaonia, because they lay just beyond Cilicia, where
Paul had lived and worked.   But their purpose pointed
westward, and thus may indicate that they sought
instinctively to carry the new religion into the civil-
ized, Roman world.   (b) Their policy was to begin
in the chief cities of each district, since these were
the centres of influence.   (c) They established in each
city an organized church, by the constitution of which
the life of the disciples would be fostered.   (d) They
always offered the gospel first to Jews, thus never
forgetting the claims of Israel ; but their churches
were mixed, in most of them Gentiles predominated,
and in them all Jew and Gentile stood on an equal foot-
ing.   In none was observance of the Mosaic law regarded as necessary.   (e) We should assume also that
everywhere they carried the story of Jesus' life, death,
and resurrection ; instructed the converts in the beliefs
and duties of the new religion ; and laid a broad

foundation for subsequent Christian life. These details are barely hinted at in our meagre reports, but Paul's conduct in his other journeys leaves no doubt as to his method.

131. Finally, it should be noted that in the universal spread of the Greek language and in the Roman government of the provinces there was an evident providential preparation for their mission. Nor had Judaism itself failed to prepare the way. Synagogues were found in all the cities, and in connection with them a large number of Gentiles who had been profoundly impressed by the religion of Jehovah and from whom most of the converts came. The existence of such devout Gentiles is amply attested both by the Acts (xiii. 16, 43, 50), secular history, and recently deciphered inscriptions. Thus the men and the means, the faith and the world, were brought together. The expansion, begun with the death of Stephen, had steadily continued, finding new fields to enter and new men to enter them. With this the church's realization of its mission had expanded likewise. In Paul finally had appeared the man who by training, experience, and revelation was prepared to maintain the principles on which the expansion could logically proceed and to carry it onward.

PART III

JUDAIC CHRISTIANITY

HISTORICAL SOURCES

132. To the phase of apostolic history included in the following part the book of Acts contributes the account of the council at Jerusalem (xv. 1–35), and that of Paul's reception by James and the elders at the close of his third missionary journey (xxi. 18–21). With the former is to be compared Galatians ii. Their harmony will be discussed in the course of the following narrative.

133. For the general character of Judaic Christianity the leading authority is the epistle of James. While Origen is the first known writer to cite this book by name, the evidence of its use goes back to the apostolic age itself. It was used by Clement of Rome (A. D. 96) and Hermas (A. D. 140 ?), and acquaintance with it is clearly disclosed in the first epistle of Peter (comp. I. Pet. i. 6, 7 and Jas. i. 2; I. Pet. i. 24 and Jas. i. 10, 11; I. Pet. i. 25 and Jas. i. 18; I. Pet. ii. 1 and Jas. i. 21; I. Pet. v. 5, 6, 8 and Jas. iv. 6, 7; I. Pet. iv. 8 and Jas. v. 20). It belongs, therefore, to the earlier part of the apostolic age, and its contents point to a date before the controversy about circumcision had begun. There is no allusion to the relation of Gentiles and Jews in the church. The difficulties and faults contemplated in it lie wholly in the sphere of Jewish life. In the communities addressed believ-

ing and unbelieving Hebrews mingle (ii. 1–13); and the
writer's teaching about justification (ii. 14–26) is not
directed against Paul's doctrine, for the two in reality
coincide (comp. Gal. v. 6, 14, 22, 23; vi. 9, 10; Rom.
vi. 12, 13), nor against a current misrepresentation of
Paul, for then he would have stated his view more
fully, but is best explained as directed against a formal,
intellectual faith which was, as Pharisaism shows,
a besetting sin of Judaism. These features comport
best with a date before the council at Jerusalem, say
A. D. 45–50. The author describes himself simply as
"James, a servant of God and of the Lord Jesus
Christ;" and this title, as well as the whole character
of the epistle, supports the view that he was the well-
known brother of the Lord.

134. So strongly Judaic is the tone of this epistle,
that a few recent critics have maintained it to be the
work of a non-Christian Jew, interpolated here and
there by a Christian hand. The conclusive reply to
this is that the work is saturated with allusions to the
teachings of Jesus (e. g. i. 2, 4, 5, 9, 12, 20; ii. 13;
iii. 1; iv. 10; v. 2, 8, 10, 12), and other Christian
ideas (e. g. i. 6, 8, 21; ii. 5, 12, 13; iv. 5; v. 8, 9),
while it contains references to the early history of
Christianity (ii. 5, 6; v. 14) and probably to baptism
(ii. 7). Moreover, an interpolator would certainly have
introduced more frequent mention of Jesus than the
two cases which alone occur (i. 1; ii. 1). Hence a larger
number of scholars date the epistle much later, and
deny that it was written by "the Lord's brother." It
is said that it lays no stress on the ceremonial law,
such as James would have done; that the worldliness
which it reproves is inconceivable at a very early date,

as is also the absence of allusions to Christ, and to his
teaching about the fatherhood of God and the kingdom
of heaven. The epistle is held, therefore, by this class
of critics to be the work of an unknown author, who
lived late in the first century. He was not addressing
Jewish Christians in particular, but expresses a legal-
istic type of Christianity which, it is said, widely prevailed outside of Pauline circles after the work of Paul
had been concluded. These criticisms in turn are not
well founded. The first forgets the Christianity of
James, which is as well attested as his attachment to
the law. It is most probable that, like Jesus, he would
lay stress on the spiritual content of the law; and if
the conflict concerning the relation of the believer to
the law had not yet risen, there was no reason for him
to exhort Jewish readers to observe its forms, even if
he had been inclined to do so. As to the worldliness
of the readers, it is sufficient to recall the examples of
Ananias and Sapphira after Pentecost, and the condition
of the young Corinthian church five years after it was
founded, to show that even in the earliest part of the
apostolic age the church was exposed to temptations
of the most carnal kind. Its alleged legalism, moreover, disappears when its teaching is carefully examined.
The argument drawn from the paucity of references to
Jesus is more plausible; but these features are equally
difficult of explanation at a later period. In either
case, the Christian element in the epistle is unquestion-
able; and its peculiarities are most naturally explained
by assigning to it an early date, and supposing that it
was addressed especially to the Jewish Christians of
Syria (*J. B. Mayor, Th. Zahn, Beyschlag*).

135. In addition to these authorities for Judaic

Christianity should be named the epistle to the Hebrews. That work, however, does not represent the opinions of Judaic Christianity as current in the churches of Palestine. While, therefore, allusions in it are valuable for our present purpose, its teaching belongs to another phase of the history.

136. Of extra-biblical authorities are to be mentioned the accounts in Josephus (Antiq. xx. 9. 1) and Eusebius (HE. II. 23) of the death of James, as well as the latter's report of the church's flight to Pella at the opening of war with Rome (HE. III. 5) and of the appointment of Symeon to succeed James (III. 11).

II

THE CHARACTER OF JUDAIC CHRISTIANITY

137. In describing the early expansion of Christianity, we have noted something of its progress among the
Jews. We have seen that the dispersion of the disciples carried the faith among the scattered Hebrew
communities, especially those in Syria; and that in
Judea, after the cessation of the first persecution, the
number of believers steadily increased. We have noted
also their gradual separation from the synagogue and
the establishment of churches modelled substantially
after the synagogal system. We have further observed
the sympathy of the mother church with the work
among the Gentiles. The latter fact is attested not
only in the Acts, but by Paul himself. He distinctly
states that while he was laboring in Cilicia the churches
of Judea heard of his activity and "glorified God in"
him (Gal. i. 24).

138. Yet it would appear that the progress of Judaic
Christianity was rather external than internal. Its
loyalty to the Mosaic system and its natural satisfaction
with the forms in which religious truth had been presented by Mosaism kept it theologically stagnant. It
is probable that most of the Jewish Christians reconciled themselves at this period to the fellowship of uncircumcised Gentiles by regarding them as the Gentile
adherents of Judaism itself were regarded; and the

o

spread of Judaism among the Gentiles was so marked
a feature of the age that the adhesion of the latter to
the new faith, without receiving circumcision, seemed
less perilous to Jewish institutions than it appeared
later. Certainly no conflict on the subject had yet
arisen. Judaic Christianity at this period may be
likened to the course of a stream which has spread out
upon a meadow, destined indeed to be carried into the
rushing torrent farther on, but as yet only slightly
moved by the current. It presents, therefore, a peculiarly interesting study.

139. After the Herodian persecution (A. D. 44) the
most conspicuous individual among the Palestinian
Christians was James "the Lord's brother" (Gal. i.
19; comp. Gal. ii. 9; Acts xii. 17; xv. 13; xxi. 18;
Matt. xiii. 55; Mark vi. 3; *Jos.* Antiq. xx. 9. 1;
Eus. HE. II. 23). He is not to be identified with the
apostle James, the son of Alphæus, for "the brethren
of the Lord" are distinguished by the evangelists from
the apostles (Matt. xii. 46; John vii. 3, 5; Acts i. 14).
Paul's language (Gal. i. 19; I. Cor. xv. 7) has indeed
been thought to imply that James was an apostle, and
the hypothesis has been advanced that after the death
of James the son of Zebedee (Acts xii. 2), the brother
of the Lord was chosen to fill his place. Others think
that in these passages Paul, contrary to his usual custom, uses the term "apostle" in a loose sense. But
his language does not compel either of these interpretations. That in Galatians i. 19 James is not necessarily to be included among the apostles is shown by
the example of other sentences similarly constructed
(*e. g.* Rom. xiv. 14; Luke iv. 26); while in I. Corinthians xv. 7 the order of words in the original would seem

to imply that James is rather distinguished from than included among them. As already observed also, it is questionable whether he was meant to be included among the apostles by Luke in Acts ix. 27 (sect. 94). Certainly, apart from these very doubtful instances, he is not called an apostle ; and, what is most significant, he does not so call himself in his epistle. It is more likely that after the apostolate had become delocalized by the progress of the organization of the Judean churches (sect. 103), James, who remained in Jerusalem, became the practical leader of the Jewish Christians , and this leadership, on account of his personal character and high spiritual gifts, rather than because of any office held by him, became so marked that he exerted an influence equal to that of the apostles themselves (Gal. ii. 9), and was remembered in after times as the head of the mother church (*Eus.* HE. II. 1).

140. At any rate the prominence and influence of James is beyond dispute. Peter, when fleeing from imprisonment, sent word of his escape to " James and the brethren " (Acts xii. 17). At the council of Jerusalem James' opinion had decisive weight (xv. 12–21). It was " certain from James," whose presence at Antioch led Peter to withdraw from fellowship with Gentiles (Gal. ii. 12). On Paul's final return to Jerusalem it was "James and the elders" who received him (Acts xxi. 18). The epistle of James witnesses to the authority and wide influence of its writer ; and the author of " Jude " introduced himself to his readers as the " brother of James " (Jude 1). To this may be added the testimony of secular history and tradition. Josephus (Antiq. xx. 9, 1) relates that after the recall of Festus

(A. D. 62 ?) the high-priest Ananus secured the stoning
of James, the brother of Jesus, and of some others, on
the ground that they had broken the law; but that the
better citizens complained of the act, so that in consequence Ananus was removed from office by Agrippa II.
The respect in which James was held by the whole city
is also attested by tradition.   Hegesippus relates (*Eus.*
HE. II. 23) that he was known as " the Just " and as
" the bulwark of the people; " that he lived the life of
a Nazarite; that he had a high reputation for piety of
a rather ascetic type.   Hegesippus' account contains
some fanciful features, and his narrative of James'
death, in which the Lord's brother is said to have been
cast by the Jews from the roof of the temple, then
stoned and finally beaten on the head, bears traces of
considerable legendary embellishment and is a less
probable account than that given by Josephus.   But
the evidence, wherever we find it, discloses a man of
large influence, impressive character, and intense piety
according to the finest Hebrew ideals, — one, therefore,
most likely to attain leadership among the Jewish
disciples.

141. In order to form a still clearer image of James
we must go back to the Nazarene home in which Jesus
was reared.   The " brethren of the Lord " were either
the children of Joseph by a former marriage, or the
children of Joseph and Mary born after Jesus.   The
latter view seems best to accord with the intimations
of the gospels.   The view advanced by Jerome and
elaborated by others that they were the cousins of
Jesus on his mother's side is beset with difficulties, of
which it is sufficient to mention the fact that it identi-
fies James with the son of Alphæus, and so makes him

one of the original apostles. There is still less foundation for the view that they were the cousins of Jesus on Joseph's side. In any event James had been the daily associate of Jesus in the Nazarene home. We infer that from early life he had been an earnest, religious character, steeped in the teaching of the Old Testament and in later Hebrew literature. The tradition of his devoted piety can hardly have been without some foundation. His knowledge of Greek, on the other hand, is explained by the bilingual character of Jewish society, especially in the region of the Sea of Galilee. Yet with all his piety James did not accept Jesus as Messiah. This does not exclude, however, sympathy with much of Jesus' teaching nor warm affection for his person. His unbelief may have been due to Jesus' rupture with many Jewish conventionalities; also to James' exalted view of the glory of Messiah, and the impression of Jesus' lowliness produced on one who had himself shared it. The fact that Jesus, after his resurrection, appeared to James (I. Cor. xv. 7) is a testimony to the latter's high character as well as to his Brother's love for him and foresight of his future usefulness.

142. We cannot wonder, then, that, when convinced of the Messiahship of his former brother but now risen Lord, James soon ranked high in the new community. It is not clear what office he occupied in the Jerusalem church. Later tradition made him its first bishop, chosen to that office by the apostles (*Eus.* HE. II. 23); and among extreme Jewish Christians of the second century he was represented as the bishop of the entire church (Clem. Homilies). But these traditions read back later ideas into the apostolic age. He was doubt-

less one of the elders of the church; and, if the eldership of Jerusalem had a permanent president, — of which there is no proof, — James presumably held that office. It is more probable, however, that his influence was personal rather than official. His relation to Jesus naturally enhanced it. He was clearly the man to lead the Jewish believers. Devoted to the ritual law, he interpreted it in the spirit of Jesus. A thorough Jew, he was not a formalist. Amid the general hostility to the church, he gave the cause reputation even with unbelievers. In the political and civil excitements of the time he kept the disciples' thoughts fixed on the true service and on the duty of patiently waiting for Messiah's return. He was thus quite as truly fitted to his situation as Paul was to the work of preaching to the Gentiles.

143. These remarks are justified by the epistle of James, which is the historic monument of early Judaic Christianity. It is addressed to " the twelve tribes of the dispersion." This phrase might have been used of Christians generally (comp. I. Pet. i. 1), but, in the absence of other indications, naturally describes Jews (comp. Acts xxvi. 7) who in their Christian wanderings realized afresh the dispersion of Israel. The phrase is thus well satisfied, if we suppose that the Jewish believers scattered throughout Syria, and perhaps not excluding Palestine, since the church as a whole was in a state of dispersion, were especially in mind; for certainly the readers were Christians (ii. 1). Yet into their synagogue an unbelieving Jew might come (ii. 2–6); and in v. 1–6 the writer utters an invective against the rich, which is plainly directed against Jewish oppressors of the poor. In

iii. 9–12 and iv. 1–10, also, while believers are included in the reproofs, they are represented as liable to sins which were peculiarly characteristic of their compatriots. The external situation of the readers thus corresponds with that mixed condition of believing and unbelieving Jews which we have found existing during the early spread of the faith among the Jews of Syria.

144. The epistle itself is an earnest homily. It begins with an exhortation to joy amid trial because of its spiritual discipline (i. 2–4). Wisdom to live aright can be surely obtained from God (5). But steadfast faith is the keynote of the true religious life (6–8). Outward circumstances are nothing in comparison with spiritual realities (9–11). God is the giver of all good; and in the joy of his spiritual quickening through the word of truth, and in the sense of deliverance from indwelling sin, which is the cause of spiritual death, his children are hopefully to trust him (12–18). Obedience also is the true worship. Hence they must seek to work out in life God's own righteousness (19–20). This can only be done by the real reception of his revealed word into the heart (21). Christian life is not one of slavery to precepts, but, looking into the perfect law of liberty, believers are to bring forth the true religious service of benevolence and holiness (22–27). The author then rebukes in turn certain faults to which his readers were liable, and which, it should be noted, were just those into which Jewish Christians were likely to fall. These are (1) the overvaluation of riches and rich men (ii. 1–13); (2) reliance on a merely formal, intellectual faith (ii. 14–26); (3) pride in knowledge and in the position

of being teachers of others (iii.); (4) absorption in civil and political strife to the injury of religious interests (iv. 1–12); (5) undue devotion to worldly business, an evil which is signally illustrated by the frequent oppression of the poor by the rich (iv. 13 to v. 8). Exhortations to patience, against swearing, to prayer and the conversion of sinners, bring the epistle to its close (v. 9–20). The work is saturated with Old Testament language and allusions, though it contains but four formal quotations (ii. 4, 23; iv. 5, 6). It also betrays familiarity with the wisdom-literature of the post-canonical period (e. g. i. 5, 19; iii. 2 with Ecclus. xli. 22; v. 11; xix. 6; xxviii. 13–26; and iv. 14; v. 6 with Wisd. of Sol. ii. 4, 12–20).

145. This conception of Christianity is what we would expect from the brother of Jesus. His ideal of life is the real working out of God's righteousness, the true performance of the divine will (i. 20; comp. Matt. vi. 33). He regards the law not as a collection of disjointed precepts, but as the revelation of a principle whereby we live in harmony with God (ii. 10). It is to be interpreted, therefore, with a view to its deep, spiritual content (i. 22; ii. 8). By the law, however, he means not only the Old Testament, but this as completed by a new revelation which the Christian has received (i. 18, 21, 22). Obedience also consists in the free service of love (i. 25). James' position, therefore, corresponds closely with that of our Lord in the sermon on the mount. In neither case was it the object to exhibit the way of salvation, but to show how a saved man should live. Hence a reason why James says so little of Christ and nothing of the stirring events of his career, which all his readers knew; though

the titles "Lord" and "Lord of glory" are enough to indicate his belief in Jesus as one sent from heaven, the exalted Messiah and the revealer of the Father. To him, we may believe, the method of salvation lay sufficiently disclosed in the temple ritual, to which he and his readers were loyal. Their faith in Jesus as their Saviour and Lord lay side by side with their use of the appointed sacrifices, without their realizing as yet the full relation of the two. What most impressed them was the fact that God had quickened them by the crowning revelation of his will. Their former Judaism had blossomed into a spiritual life of love and holiness through the teaching of Jesus and their faith in him as Messiah. Into the full joy of this rich experience James would lead them; and in so doing he reflects that side of the teaching of Jesus which would naturally impress an earnest Jew. Meanwhile he realized that the existing state of things was temporary. Not yet had the promises of glory been fulfilled. The return of Christ is therefore emphasized for the encouragement of his suffering disciples (v. 7, 8, 9) and for a warning to sinners (ii. 12; iv. 12). James thus sounds the notes of faith, spiritual service, and patient endurance which were most needful to the scattered Hebrew disciples, and his emphasis on these, in the circumstances, evinces a profound appreciation of the teaching of the Master.

146. This epistle, therefore, illuminates the early period of Judaic Christianity. The impulse to dogmatic development did not as yet exist. It needed the outbreak of controversy. There must have been much that these Jewish believers could not understand. What was to be the ultimate relation of their faith to Judaism?

What should be their attitude to national politics? In what way would their Messiah vindicate his claims? The answers to these problems must have been quite obscure. Their religion comprised faith in Jesus as Messiah, the spiritual interpretation of the divine law as he had elucidated it, the cultivation of the love and holiness which he had exhibited and commanded, the actual enjoyment of reconciliation with God through faith in Christ, the consciousness of a new life bestowed by God, the confident expectation of Christ's return in glory to make all things right. These are the main features of Christian life revealed to us by James. His epistle reflects a period of transition. It shows also that Christian life was not being fed by current Jewish thought, for there is not a trace in it of national hopes or of apocalyptic fancies, but by the Old Testament, the teaching of Jesus, and the leading of the Spirit (iv. 5). Thus, side by side with Judaism, reverencing the law and worshipping in the temple, forming its own synagogues but not breaking with the national life, Judaic Christianity strove to appropriate the message of Jesus and to await his return. It was a condition of things which could not long remain. The expansion of Christianity and the fall of Jerusalem were destined soon to disturb it; yet quite as certainly was it a condition which must have existed among the Jewish believers at this period of the history.

THE COUNCIL AT JERUSALEM

147. THE composure of the church was at last disturbed by the inevitable controversy concerning the obligation of Gentile believers to observe the Mosaic law. The controversy was inevitable, because the principle of salvation by faith alone, which had been proclaimed from the beginning and on which the expansion among the Gentiles had proceeded, was really inconsistent with the binding obligation on Gentiles of the law. In spite of the harmony which had existed, the question was certain to be raised. On its solution, in fact, the continued unity and progress of the cause depended. Three positions were possible. It might be held that all believers were freed from the law. This could be maintained only so far as it was realized that the work of Messiah had satisfied the requirements of the law and thus relieved his people from them. Or it might be held that Jews alone were bound to observe the law. This could be maintained on the ground that Mosaism was a national religion, and therefore binding on Christian Hebrews as Hebrews, though not as Christians. Or, finally, it might be held that the law was still binding upon all, and that Gentiles must accept it in order to be Christians. This view would make Christianity merely a purified Judaism, and would be really inconsistent with the doctrine of salvation by faith in Jesus,

which had been taught from the beginning. It is clear
that these opinions were certain to appear among the
Christian Jews. It is equally clear that the question at
issue would prove a burning one, for all the prejudices
and traditions of Judaism were involved in it. But the
third view meant a death-blow to the expanding faith
and to its integrity and sufficiency. The decision, therefore, was as necessary as the controversy was inevitable.

148. The controversy actually broke out in Antioch
after the return of Barnabas and Paul from their successful missionary journey. The rapid spread of Gentile
Christianity aroused the anxiety and displeasure of some
of the stricter Jewish party in Jerusalem. It seemed to
them to threaten seriously the reverence for the Mosaic
law which they held to be due from all followers of
Messiah. It even appeared possible that Christianity
might be wholly separated from Judaism and the pre-
eminence of Israel be lost. The anomalous condition
which had heretofore existed could therefore no longer
be allowed. Steps must be taken to prevent the destruction of Jewish prerogative and custom ; and since
adherents to a considerable extent had been made by
the church from the Pharisees, we can well believe that
the influence of this strict Jewish party had become
greater in the Jerusalem congregation than it had been
at an earlier period. Hence certain of them went to
Antioch, and boldly taught that unless believers were
circumcised, they could not be saved (Acts xv. 1). Later
events prove that these emissaries did not represent the
majority of the mother church, still less her leaders.
They represented only the Pharisaic party (Acts xv. 5).
There is evidence also that the visit was prompted by
a factious spirit. The disclaimer afterwards made by

" the apostles and elders " (xv. 24) seems to imply that these missionaries of Judaism had falsely declared to the Antiochans that the leaders in Jerusalem shared their views or had even sent them on their mission. Their teaching was in fact revolutionary, and they must have known it to be so. Paul, speaking of the same class of teachers, if not of these very men, calls them " false brethren privily brought in, who came in privily to spy out our liberty which we have in Christ Jesus, that they might bring us into bondage " (Gal. ii. 4, R. V.). The Judaizers might seem merely to be anxious to preserve the loyalty to the law which Jewish Christians had always professed ; but in reality they were disloyal to the principle of faith which was distinctive of the gospel, and to the fraternal liberality toward Gentile brethren which the church had long displayed. They were the means, however, of bringing this fundamental question to a definite issue.

149. In consequence of the Judaistic agitation, the church of Antioch sent a deputation, at the head of which were Paul and Barnabas, to lay the matter before the apostles and elders in Jerusalem (Acts xv. 2). This is the visit described by Paul in Galatians ii. 1–10. In both accounts the acting parties and the purpose of the visit are the same. We have already seen (sect 116) that Galatians ii. does not refer to the visit with the gifts from Antioch ; and it cannot refer to a visit later than this one, because Paul's argument absolutely requires that he should not pass this visit over in silence.[1] At the same time the two accounts of the

---

[1] The recent conjecture of J. V. Bartlet (Apost. Age, p. 57) that Galatians ii. 1–10 describes an unrecorded visit of Paul to Jerusalem *earlier* than that of Acts xi. 30, does not seem to have any tangible

visit by Luke and Paul are written from different
points of view. Luke traces historically the external
events to their issue. Paul wrote for the specific purpose of showing that his own apostolic authority and
teaching had been recognized by the mother church
and her leaders. He therefore only alludes to such
facts as were of importance for his argument. The
two accounts are thus supplementary. Their harmony
has frequently been denied, but is now generally admitted in all essential points; and a close examination
fails to show any points in which they are discordant.

150. Thus, according to Acts the visit was that of
a deputation sent by the Antiochan church. Paul, on
the other hand, relates that he went up "by revelation"
(Gal. ii. 2); yet it is easy to understand that, in so
grave a crisis, and especially when by going he seemed
to submit his preaching to the judgment of others, he
needed a revelation to make his duty clear. Again,
he mentions, while Acts does not, the presence of
Titus, and makes much of the fact that the latter was
not compelled to be circumcised. He does this because Titus, who was doubtless one of the Antiochan
delegation, was a test case for his argument, since the
reception of Titus as a Christian brother proved in
the most practical way the church's recognition of
Paul's ministry and teaching. So, too, the spirit in
which Paul and Barnabas made the visit corresponds
in both accounts. According to Acts (xv. 3) they
proclaimed, as they went, the conversion of the Gen

evidence to support it. It assumes also a doubtful interpretation of II.
Corinthians xii. 2–5. Moreover, the visit of Galatians was certainly
a public and representative one, so that its omission by Luke is
inexplicable.

tiles. In Galatians, Paul relates "I laid before them [*i. e.* the Christians in Jerusalem] the gospel which I preach among the Gentiles, but privately before them who were of repute [an additional fact], lest by any means I should be running, or had run, in vain" (Gal. ii. 2, R. V.). The last clause does not mean that he submitted his teaching to the judgment of others, being willing to retract it if they disapproved; for he immediately adds that when " false brethren" demanded the circumcision of Titus, he would not yield even for an hour. The clause in question describes rather a confident appeal to the brethren to say if it were true, as some alleged, that he was running in vain (comp. *Meyer-Sieffert*, Kommentar). In both accounts, therefore, the deputation went to Jerusalem, recognizing indeed the ecclesiastical authority of the mother church, but confident of her support and prepared to maintain their views to the end.

151. According to both accounts, also, the general sentiment of the church was disturbed in Jerusalem, as it had been in Antioch, by the Judaizers, who violently maintained that Gentile converts should be required to observe the Mosaic law (Acts xv. 3–5; Gal. ii. 3, 4). In Acts it is related that this led to the convening of a council, composed of the apostles and elders, at which the subject was discussed, addresses made by Peter, Paul, Barnabas and James, and the decision reached that Gentiles should not be required to observe the law, but only to abstain from certain acts peculiarly offensive to Jews (xv. 6–29). Paul does not mention the council; yet his declaration that Titus was not compelled to be circumcised, and that this was a refusal by the Jerusalem church to

accede to the demands of the "false brethren" (Gal. ii. 3, 4), implies that formal action of some kind was taken. He pithily states, by presenting the concrete case of Titus, the main result of the council which Luke describes. Again, in Acts (xv. 6, 22) the council is said to have been composed of "the apostles and elders," while Peter and James delivered the chief addresses. Paul speaks of having seen of the apostles only Peter and John, but the presence of these two is sufficient to justify Luke's expressions, even if no other apostles were there; while according to both sources James appears as the most influential personage (Acts xv. 13–21; Gal. ii. 7). It might seem from Acts xv. 22 that the whole church was present at the deliberation; but the language probably means merely that the decision met with its approval. It is, however, worthy of note that Paul also (Gal. ii. 2–5) represents the church as a whole as supporting his position.

152. Paul, however, adds one fact of which Acts says nothing; namely, that he had also private conferences with James, Peter, and John. He calls them by the indefinite but honorable title "those of repute" (Gal. ii. 2, 6), the "pillars" of the church (ii. 9), using terms which applied to them all, whatever their office; and while he stoutly asserts, as his argument made needful, that they added nothing to his apostolic authority or teaching, records that they gave to him and Barnabas the right hand of fellowship, and agreed that, in accordance with God's manifest will, he and Barnabas should go to the Gentiles while they labored among the Jews. His was the "gospel of the uncircumcision," while Peter's was that "of the circumcision" (ii. 7). These phrases do not describe different

gospels, but the two spheres in which the same gospel was to be carried. Paul's description of the conferences is a notable addition to Luke's narrative. Yet it was most natural that they should have been held. We can hardly conceive of their not being held between such men. The failure of Luke to mention them was obviously due to the fact that they were not part of the public history of the transaction which he was narrating. Paul mentions them only because it was afterwards charged in Galatia that the leaders of the mother church were opposed to him. In like manner the request of James, Peter, and John that he should remember the poor (Gal. ii. 10) was evidently occasioned by his previous visit with the gifts from Antioch, and by their fear lest with a division of fields of labor the needy Judeans might suffer. It is not mentioned by Luke, because it was purely a personal request.

153. Moreover, the fact that for the decision of this question a council was held throws incidental light on the organization of the church. As already stated (sect. 103), the apostles had before this time devolved the ordinary government of the churches on the local eldership. Those of the apostles who were present sat indeed in the council in virtue of their apostolic office, and are mentioned as a first and separate class in the letter which the council prepared (xv. 23); but they did not decide the matter at issue on apostolic authority, for, while doctrine was involved, the question was in form ecclesiastical. Should the Gentile converts be required to observe the law (xv. 5) as the condition of fellowship ? Men might agree on the same answer for different reasons, or

might differ in the answer though agreeing on the main point. Moreover, even in the earliest period the apostles had called out the action of the brethren in determining the organization of the church (Acts i. 16, 23; vi. 3–6); much more, now that the organization was complete, would the authority of the elders be recognized. The mode of procedure followed is therefore not inconsistent with the authority of the apostles which we have found existing from the beginning. It is to be observed also that the Jerusalem church, acting through the council, appears to have been regarded as the supreme court of the Christians in Palestine and Syria. Hence the appeal to it by the brethren in Antioch and by the Judaizers. Hence, too, the authoritative language of the letter which the council wrote (xv. 28). The most natural explanation of this is that the eldership of Jerusalem was considered, by the Judaic Christians and by the mixed churches of Syria which had originated from Jewish missions, in much the same light in which the Sanhedrim of Jerusalem was by the Jews. This was only the further carrying over into the Christian churches of the synagogal system of which the Sanhedrim was the head. We shall find hereafter that in the purely Gentile churches afterwards founded by Paul the ecclesiastical authority of the Jerusalem eldership was not recognized. Wholly independent churches, bound only by the common faith, sprang up. But for the time of which we are treating, and for the parties engaged in the discussion, the eldership of Jerusalem constituted the recognized head of the Christian synagogues.

154. The addresses made in the council are also worthy of special notice. Peter (xv. 7–11) strongly

maintained the liberty of the Gentiles, appealing to the testimony of God in the case of Cornelius. Faith, he said, was the only condition of being purified (comp. x. 15). He went so far as to speak of the law as an unbearable yoke on the Jews themselves, since they could not really keep it; and reminded the assembly that they too depended for salvation solely on the grace of Christ. This address puts Peter thoroughly on Pauline ground. The truthfulness of the report is amply confirmed by Paul's subsequent rebuke of Peter in Antioch when he faltered in the application of his acknowledged principles (Gal. ii. 15, 16), as well as by Peter's later writings. Paul and Barnabas took part in the proceedings merely by relating what God had done in attestation of the work among the Gentiles (Acts xv. 12; comp. Gal. ii. 2, 7). It was James, the Lord's brother, who made the decisive address (xv. 13–21). He was cautious, and anxious to secure harmony. Yet he admitted that the Lord's revelation to Peter practically settled the matter. He spoke, however, of the Gentile converts as an addition to Israel, such as Amos (ix. 11, 12) had predicted. He thus recognized the special privileges of the Jews. Yet to them Gentiles were to be added, and they should accept it as God's will. Hence he judged that no further burden should be laid on the Gentiles than that they should abstain from certain pollutions; namely, the food offered to idols, fornication, things strangled, and blood. These conditions of fellowship he insisted on, because they would do much to prevent offence being given to the Jews by the uncircumcised converts.

155. James' address, therefore, unlike Peter's, was conservative and prudential. Both singularly corre-

spond with the characters of the two men. They show differences of temperament and of points of view, while agreeing on the main issue. James' address and the letter drawn up at his suggestion have also some striking verbal resemblances to the language of his epistle (comp. xv. 23 with Jas. i. 1; xv. 17 with Jas. ii. 7; xv. 13 with Jas. ii. 5; xv. 14 with Jas. i. 27; xv. 19 with Jas. v. 19, 20; xv. 29 with Jas. i. 27). Both address and epistle show his thoroughly Jewish as well as Christian character; and the writer of the epistle, who makes faith the essence of true religion, urges on Jewish disciples a spiritual interpretation of the law, warns them against faults peculiar to them as Jews, and writes not a word concerning their national hopes, was quite the man to take the position which is narrated of him in the council. He cannot therefore, any more than Peter, be classed with the Judaizers.

156. The result of the deliberations was that a letter, addressed in the name of the apostles and elders to the Gentile believers in Antioch, Syria, and Cilicia, was sent by the hands of Silas and Judas Barsabbas, two of the leading men of the Jerusalem church (xv. 22–29). In it the council repudiated the Judaizers, spoke in cordial terms of Barnabas and Paul, and briefly declared that it was the mind of the Spirit and of themselves to lay nothing further on the Gentiles than the four acts of abstinence which James had suggested and which they considered necessary. This was certainly not a compromise with the Judaizers. The freedom of Gentiles from the law was fully conceded. At the same time the council protected the feelings of the Jews against what the latter regarded as abominations of the Gentiles. The decree laid down

no doctrine. It confined itself to terms of fellowship. It established a *modus vivendi*. In granting freedom from the law, the council felt that it acted in accordance with the evident will of the Spirit; but it seemed to it absolutely necessary that this freedom should in no way appear to Jewish eyes to sully the Christian name by the introduction of offensive pagan customs.

157. The requirement of these four special forms of abstinence raises, however, several difficulties. For instance, it appears strange that fornication should be classed with things ethically indifferent. Just this strangeness, however, is an assurance that the report is authentic; and the difficulty is removed when it is observed that the acts of abstinence were demanded solely in order not to offend Jews. The intrinsic quality of the acts themselves did not come into consideration. Now, fornication was regarded by the Jews, as well it might be (comp. *Lecky*, Hist. of Eur. Morals, ch. v.), as a typical pagan custom. It was often sanctified by pagan religions, and nowhere more so than in western Asia. It was too often regarded with indifference in Græco-Roman society. It therefore would naturally be mentioned by a Jew as a threatened Gentile abomination. Another difficulty is raised by the apparent identity of abstinence from things strangled and from blood. Efforts to remove this obscurity by altering the text of the Acts may be traced as far back as the second century. Perhaps the best explanation is that the second of these two prohibitions was intended to state the general principle of which eating things strangled was the commonest example, and so both to cover other instances and to state fully the principle itself.

158. But it is more important to notice the motive of the decree as a whole. It has often been maintained that it exacted of Gentile converts the same requirements made by Jews on " strangers," or, as they were afterwards called, " proselytes of the gate," who observed the so-called " precepts of Noah," but were not recognized as belonging to Israel. It is quite doubtful, however, if, at the time of the council, there was any code of requirements for such adherents of Judaism, or if there was any such class of proselytes recognized at all (*Schürer*, HJP. II. 2. 317). Outside of proselytes proper, the Gentile followers of Judaism varied greatly in the degree in which they adopted Jewish customs. Moreover, the so-called " Noachic precepts," mentioned by later writers, were seven in number (comp. *Hort*, Jud. Christianity, p. 69). It is a more plausible supposition that the acts of abstinence were suggested by the prohibitions for " the stranger," which are found in Leviticus xvii., xviii. Yet even these do not coincide precisely with those of the decree, though they may well have been at the basis of the Jewish abhorrence of the acts which the decree forbade. Any view which assumes that the Gentile converts were not recognized by the council as full members of the church is inconsistent with the whole tenor of the decree and with Paul's acceptance of its provisions. Its motive was to prevent offence to the Jews who dwelt in every city, and the simplest explanation is that these four things were prohibited because they were the Gentile customs which were most abhorrent in Jewish eyes.

159. Yet, even so, can we believe that the decree with these prohibitions was accepted by Paul, and that, as Acts xvi. 4 records, he delivered it to the churches previously founded by him and Barnabas? As already observed, he does not mention it in his Galatian epistle. Moreover, in Romans xiv. 13–23 and I. Corinthians viii. and x. 23–33, where he discusses the use of food offered to idols, he does not refer to the decision of the council, but argues the subject independently, and boldly asserts that the use of such food is in itself a matter of indifference. Fornication likewise he treats as inherently and always wrong (e. g. I. Cor. vi. 18). These facts have seemed to some to prove that he could not have accepted or even known of the decree. The inference has also been drawn that the decree was either never issued or was issued at a later time and erroneously attributed by Luke to the council. But this is to do injustice to so accurate an historian as Luke, and the apparent difficulties are capable of satisfactory explanation. For, in regard to Paul's acceptance of the decree, it should be remembered that he had gained his main point and would not be likely to refuse to do his part toward securing harmony. That would be quite contrary to all that we know of his disposition (I. Cor. ix. 19–23). It should further be noted that the churches to which he delivered the decree (Acts xvi. 4) were founded by him and Barnabas on their mission from Antioch. They were doubtless regarded as an extension of the work in Antioch, and so shared in the recognition of the authority of the mother church. Within the sphere therefore which the church then covered, the authority of the council would be admitted, and, since the freedom of Gentile converts had been acknowledged, there was nothing in Paul's character or doctrine which makes it improbable that he accepted for those whom he represented the conditions imposed.

160. The churches, however, founded by Paul after the council in his missionary work stood in a different relation to the church of Jerusalem. It is possible that the activity of the Judaizers in Antioch convinced him that it was better to have his churches independent. It is possible that the agreement with James, Peter, and John at the time of the council that he and Barnabas should go to the Gentiles, was understood to place his new churches on an independent basis. At any rate, their independence is evident. He treats them in his epistles, not only as his own spiritual offspring, but as separate societies who owned the superiority of no other church. All were indeed united in one great spiritual body in Christ, and he stimulated one by the example of others. He especially kept them mindful of their confraternity with (I. Thess. ii. 14; Eph. ii. 11–22) and their indebtedness to (Rom. xv. 26, 27) the churches of Judea; but there is not a hint that the authority of the Jerusalem eldership was recognized by them. In fact, as we shall find, this was a point on which he resisted the intrusions of the Judaizers into his territory (Gal. ii. 6; II. Cor. iii. 1). Hence it is not surprising that he does not refer to the decree, but instructs his converts independently. The Epistle to the Galatians is the one in which such a reference would be most expected, since he there describes his visit to Jerusalem at the time of the council; but since he alludes to the council only indirectly, and confines himself to the single point of the recognition by the church of his authority and teaching, it is hardly surprising that he omits also all reference to

the decree.   The Judaizers themselves had violated the
compact by denying the freedom from the law which
the council had granted, and the whole discussion had
reverted to the original question of circumcision.   It
is, however, still more important to observe that in his
instructions about food offered to idols, Paul acted precisely on the principle on which the prohibitions of the
decree were based, namely, that offence should not be
given.   The situation in Corinth was very different
from that in Antioch.   There the difficulty in the use
of food offered to idols lay in the danger of participat-
ing in heathen festivals and of wounding the conscience
of the newly converted Gentile brother.   Paul maintains the entire moral indifference of the act of eating
such food (I. Cor. viii. 4–6), but he warmly urges the
principle that abstinence for the sake of others is often
the dictate of Christian love (I. Cor. viii. 7–13 ; Rom.
xiv. 21).   He seems even to broaden intentionally the
principle of the council when he wrote, " Give no occasion of stumbling, either to Jews, or to Greeks, or to the
church of God" (I. Cor. x. 32).   It is thus clear that
on his declared principles we should expect to find him
accepting the decree for those under the authority of
the council ; while the instructions to his own separate
churches show how sincere was his harmony of spirit
with the apostles and elders at Jerusalem.

161.   Thus Judaic Christianity performed its greatest
service by acknowledging at this critical juncture the
freedom of Gentile converts from the Mosaic law.   It
was the triumph of loyalty to the manifest will of God
achieved in the face of enormous prejudice.   The
Judaizing minority had in their favor all the instincts
and traditions of their race.   It would seem that the

action of the council can only be explained by the previous occurrence of such facts indicative of the will of
God as the Acts relates. Even the teaching of Jesus,
though it plainly foretold the conversion of the Gentiles and even the rejection of the Jews (*e. g.* Matt. viii.
10, 11), and though its spirit was wholly opposed to
Jewish exclusiveness, required further revelations of
the will of God to cause it to be interpreted as reliev-
ing believers from the observance of the law. The
mother church recognized the manifest will of God,
and by following it made room, at the cost of its own
pre-eminence, for the full development of the faith.
For her decision involved the fundamental principle
that faith alone was the condition of salvation. The
law might still be obligatory on Jews, but it could not
be the means of salvation. This was fully realized by
Paul, and explains why he would not yield a moment
to the Judaizers. Yet how intense the feeling of the
Jewish Christians was, through what a conflict the
result was reached, and what variety of opinion still
existed concerning the authority of the law, appears
from an incident which occurred at Antioch not long
after the adjournment of the council.

162. For when the deputation returned to Antioch
with the commissioners and the letter of the council,
they were received with joy. Silas and Judas heartily
explained the council's action, and after a brief sojourn
returned to Jerusalem. For a while peace seemed to
be assured ; and this appeared the more probable when
Peter himself visited Antioch and freely ate with the
Gentile brethren, doubtless at their love feasts, on
terms of perfect equality (Gal. ii. 12). We must certainly place this incident here, because Paul plainly

assigns it to the period following the council and yet
mentions Barnabas as present, though the latter left
Antioch shortly before Paul's second journey (Acts xv.
39). We may well believe that Peter's generous nature
rejoiced in the conversion of the Gentiles and was
anxious to prove by acts the sincerity of the position
he had taken at the council. The disregard of Jewish
scruples had long prevailed in Antioch, and Paul and
Barnabas had not only defended the liberty of the
Gentiles, but considered themselves free to observe
the ritual law or not as they might deem best (comp.
I. Cor. ix. 20, 21). This attitude Peter also was now
willing to take.

163. The peace of the church in Antioch was, however, again disturbed. Certain men came there who
had been sent from Jerusalem by James (Gal. ii. 12).
There is no hint that they had been sent to play the
spy on the Jews in Antioch, still less that they were
Judaizers, nor that they bore any missive from James.
It is probable that they had been sent by him on an
evangelizing mission among the Jews of Syria; but
their presence led Peter and even Barnabas as well as
the other Jewish Christians to withdraw from fellowship with the Gentiles. This shows the intense feeling
on the part of the main body of the Jewish Church
against the violation by any Jew of the ceremonial law.
The council had accepted the Gentile converts as
brethren, but had never intimated that the law was
not binding on Jews; and though a minority might
feel relieved from it, the convictions of the vast majority were the other way. Possibly, too, the action of
the council made the Jewish Christians more earnest
in their own loyalty to the law; and it would seem a

fair inference that James, though fully in sympathy with Gentile freedom, supported the popular sentiment that Jews ought to be faithful to their national customs. It is not hard to understand this. The Jewish Christians were anxious not to appear to their fellow-countrymen disloyal to Moses. They themselves shared the national and traditional spirit. The new faith must be shown to be harmonious with the older revelation, and few could believe this if the sacred laws were cast aside by Jews themselves. So the sentiment was overpowering that Jewish Christians should be faithful to the Mosaic law. Peter and even Barnabas may easily have thought, in view of this state of feeling, that they would destroy their influence among their countrymen, if their free intercourse with Gentiles were known. It was at least quite in accord with Peter's impulsive character that, as he had broken the bonds of Judaism through his sympathy with the Gentiles, he should hasten to fasten them again upon himself through fear of offending his Jewish brethren.

164. But he found in Paul a remorseless logician and a fearless champion of faith. Peter's conduct had been generally condemned in Antioch (Gal. ii. 11, R. V.) and a scandal was threatened by it. If he had never consorted with Gentiles, no fault would have been found with him. But by doing so he had publicly declared that faith alone was the condition of salvation; and now by withdrawing he virtually declared that he had been wrong. He seemed to imply practically that all, Gentiles as well as Jews, ought to observe the law. For this Paul took him publicly to task. He gives a summary of his rebuke in Galatians ii. 14–21. " Why," he asked, " do you thus compel Gentiles to Judaize ? "

He reminded Peter that they both, though Jews, had sought justification through faith alone in Christ and on the ground explicitly that by the works of the law none could be justified. Could they have been wrong in this? Did Christ lead them into sin? Nay; a man who builds what he has destroyed shows himself to be the transgressor. Then Paul stated the doctrine of salvation as he knew it and as Peter must confess it. The law had made Christ's death necessary, but by that death it had been wholly satisfied. In that death Paul himself had died, so that the demands of the law had been met by him in Christ. He now lived as reconciled to God, the power of Christ working in him to do God's will, and he living by faith in the Son of God who had died for him. Hence to regard observance of law as necessary for the salvation of any believer, whether Jew or Gentile, was to imply that Christ had died in vain.

165. This address not only discloses Paul's theological position (comp. sects. 84–89), but throws light from the inside on the whole controversy about circumcision. The doctrinal principle, involved in the ecclesiastical question before the council, is now made plain. The significance of the death of Christ lay in its satisfaction of the divine law for the sinner; and just so far as this was realized, was the law seen to have fulfilled its purpose as a religious system. Its moral principles were to be now embodied in life by the believer, not in order to be saved by obedience to them, but out of love for God, to whom he had already been reconciled by Christ's obedience to and satisfaction of the law. Its ceremonial acts need not be performed at all, or only as other considerations might make advisable; for they

were but the shadow of the reality, namely, Christ. In proportion as this was realized, the death-blow was given to Judaism. Christianity could not be permanently Judaic. It could never be Judaistic. Jewish Christians might still observe their law, but only as Jews, not as Christians. The principle of faith thus wrought out its logical consequences in the history; while through the realization of the nature of Messiah's death the sufficiency of faith was rationally grounded. A crucified Messiah and salvation by faith were found to be necessarily conjoined. The outward movement of events, whereby faith had been proved to be the only condition of salvation which God required, united, with the growing perception of the meaning of the Cross, to create universal Christianity. The issue was thus the result of the working out of the fundamental truths of the gospel by the combined operation of both history and logic. Though further conflict was to follow, the result could no longer be doubtful.

166. We know nothing of the immediate effect of Paul's rebuke of his fellow-apostle. The most natural inference is that Peter acknowledged his error. It was not an error of teaching but of conduct, and he was quite the man to confess his faults. This inference is confirmed by the thoroughly Pauline character of his teaching in his epistles. Certainly there is no reason to suppose that the rebuke caused dissension between the apostles, or that it was the cause of the suspicion with which Paul was regarded for a long time by many Jewish Christians (Acts xxi. 21). Neither is it surprising that Luke does not mention the incident, as there is no reason to regard it as in itself more than a local and unimportant event. Apart from the light thrown by it on the theo-

logical position of the two apostles, its chief interest lies
in the fact that it completes our view of the condition
of Judaic Christianity at the time of the council.
The great principle of Gentile freedom was conceded,
though by the concession Judaic Christianity, as both
Paul and the Judaizers perceived, was doomed to be
only one phase of the new religion and ultimately to
perish in giving birth to a universal faith.

IV

JUDAIC CHRISTIANITY AFTER THE COUNCIL

167. BEFORE tracing the further expansion of Gentile Christianity under the leadership of Paul, it is desirable to sketch briefly the condition of Judaic Christianity in the years following the council (A. D. 50 or 51), until the destruction of Jerusalem (A. D. 70). The period was one of intense political excitement in Judea. Governmental misrule aroused repeated seditions, and a succession of rapacious procurators inflamed the anger and the patriotism of the people, until the fires of open war broke out (see *Riggs*, Hist. of the Jew. People, sects. 276–290). It is natural to suppose that such a period of violent civil agitation was not without its effect upon the disciples individually and upon the progress of the Church.

168. Amid this political ferment, however, little information can be gained of the condition of the Judaic Christians. Josephus is silent concerning them, and the only relevant statement in Acts is the language of James to Paul at the latter's last visit to Jerusalem (Acts xxi. 20–25). This, however, is quite significant. We learn that the Christians numbered thousands of the population of the city. They seem to have been recruited mainly from the humbler classes of society, for Paul's zeal in securing contributions for them from his Gentile churches implies that most of them were

poor (II. Cor. ix. 12).   Yet doubtless not a few of the
Pharisees, as at an earlier period (Acts xv. 5), united
with them.   The Sadducees were in power in the state,
and concerned chiefly with political intrigues.   The
fanatical patriots, such as the Zealots, could have had
little patience with the Christian faith.   It was naturally the more religious and peaceful class to whom the
message of Jesus continued to appeal, and who, amid
the agitations of society, felt the worth of his spiritual
teaching and waited for his return.

169. The disciples in general appear to have kept
aloof from the political strife of their fellow-countrymen.   Such would be the effect of James' influence
(Jas. iv. 1–10), and the same attitude would seem to
be implied in the tradition that at the outbreak of the
war the church fled from Jerusalem to Pella.   The
teaching of Jesus also would operate in the same direction (Matt. xxiv. 16–21).   At the same time the disciples could not have failed to feel the momentous crisis
through which the nation was passing, and thereby
devotion to the law was rather intensified than dimin-
ished.   James explicitly says of them, "they are all
zealous for the law" (Acts xxi. 20).   Perhaps this was
increased by the suspicion with which they were regarded, as well as by their own patriotism.   Their situation must have been a difficult one.   While the perils
which beset the state may have aided, as times of distress often have, the progress of the faith, the disciples
must have been sorely distraught by the contending
claims of the old patriotism and the new belief.   Most
of them showed, by intense devotion to the law, that at
least they were not faithless to the traditions of the
fathers.

170. Moreover, James' words show that the Judaic disciples were not all of one mind with respect to the Christianity which was spreading among the Gentiles. Especially had misrepresentations about Paul circulated among them (Acts xxi. 21). The misunderstanding was not shared by James and the leaders (xxi. 24). They abode by the decision of the council (xxi. 25), recognized the liberty of Gentiles, and assumed that Jews would observe the law; but many believed that Paul was teaching Jews that they ought not to follow the national customs (xxi. 21), and the prejudice against him was shared by the non-Christian Jews. The opposition of the latter to his work among the Gentiles (comp. I. Thess. ii. 14–16) increased, we may believe, their hostility to the Judaic Christians, and made the latter in turn more sensitive about the reports which were circulated of him. Hence it is not difficult to believe that, as his epistles testify, the Judaizing party did not cease after the Council to propagate their views. He was the special object of their aversion, and against him and his work they instituted a widespread campaign at home and abroad. We shall meet with them again and again in following his labors. They misrepresented him to his Gentile converts as they did to the Jerusalem church. We are here concerned with them, however, only in their relation to Judaic Christianity. The situation of the latter discloses the conditions out of which the activity of the Judaizers arose and by which it was fostered. It is plain that diverse opinions and tendencies existed among the disciples in Judea, ranging from James with his spiritual interpretation of the law and his cordial appreciation of the work among the Gentiles, through

many grades of more or less adequate comprehension
of the relation of the old to the new, down to nominally
Christian Jews who saw in Christianity only a new
method of extending Judaism; and it is plain also
that these varieties of opinion insured the ultimate
division of Judaic Christianity according as it followed the logic of the faith or the prejudice of national
tradition.

171. Apart from the narrative of the Acts, only two
events have been preserved from this period of Judaic
Christianity. One is the death of James, of which an
account has already been given (sect. 130). It occurred probably in A. D. 62, and indicates the increasing
hostility of the Jewish authorities against the Christians. When this devout son of the law, who
although a Christian was honored for piety alike by
believer and unbeliever, fell before the hatred of the
Sadducaic high-priest, it was made evident that even a
purely Jewish Christianity could not continue long to
exist within the limits of Judaism, and that the separation of the disciples from their Hebrew countrymen
was steadily advancing in spite of their zeal for the
law. The other event is the flight of the church from
Jerusalem to Pella, a town in the northern part of
Perea, shortly before or after the outbreak of the war
(*Eus.* HE. III. 5; *Epiphanius,* De pond. et mens. 15).
Eusebius states that this was in accordance with a
revelation vouchsafed to approved men before the war.
Possibly the fact was that Christ's prediction and instruction (Matt. xxiv., especially verses 16–21) was the
cause of the flight. But the latter is mainly significant because it was practically the final separation of
the church from the fortunes of Judaism. It confirms

the impression that many of the Christians held aloof
from the political agitations of the Jewish state. They
believed that the judgment of God was impending over
their nation for its rejection of the Christ. We do
not know how much of the church thus separated from
the fortunes of the nation; but the part that did acted
in accordance with the teaching and spirit of Jesus,
while the remainder, choosing Judaism rather than
Christianity, perished as a body from Christian history, as doubtless most of them perished literally amid
the ruins of their sacred city.

172. It is not surprising that, under these circumstances, Judaic Christianity remained theologically un-
progressive, and that there was even a danger of the
disciples' lapsing from the faith as the refusal of Judaism to accept their Messiah became more and more
evident. This is illustrated by the Epistle to the
Hebrews. The writer furnishes a profound exposition of Christianity from the Jewish point of view.
He gave the true consolation for the Hebrew believer
as he saw himself excluded from the revered ritual
and the latter plainly doomed to utter overthrow.
But it is also clear that the views of the author were
not current among the Christians of Judea; so that
while the epistle registers an immense advance in its
conception of the relation of Christianity to Judaism,
it does not indicate that this advance was shared by
those to whom it was addressed. On the contrary,
while confident of their faith (vi. 9, 10; x. 35–39), the
author reproves them for their immaturity and for not
realizing the truth which he set forth (ii. 1–4; iv. 1;
v. 12–14; vi. 8). The positive teaching of this epistle
can be properly appreciated only after the work of

Paul has been described. For the present we merely note its disclosures of the temptations and difficulties of its readers. It implies that a terrible crisis was impending (x. 5; xiii. 14) and that they were being tempted from the new faith through discouragement due to their surroundings (iv. 14; vi. 4-6; vii. 11; x. 23-25, 35; xiii. 13). With fainting hearts and many forebodings they clung to their unseen Messiah, while from all that their fathers had loved as the ordinance of God they were being separated. All this prevented the development of their new faith. They were in danger of a subtle drift (ii. 1, R.V.) through unbelief (iii. 12). They were still content to debate the first principles which distinguished a Jewish believer from his countrymen (v. 12 to vi. 2). Instead of being the teachers of Christianity, they had need to be taught the meaning of their own Scriptures (v. 12).

173. Thus Judaic Christianity fulfilled its real mission by transmitting to the Gentiles the faith of the apostles. It affords an example of arrested development. It was not within the sphere of Judaism that the religion of Jesus, though it sprang out of Jewish soil, could expand and mature. With the fall of Jerusalem the history of Judaic Christianity, properly speaking, closed. The church did indeed eventually return from Pella, and continued to the close of the century as a Jewish-Christian body in Jerusalem. We are informed (*Eus.* HE. III. 11) that Symeon, a cousin of Jesus, was elected its chief official. But the church of Jerusalem was now shorn of all importance. Christianity had found new centres elsewhere. Many of the Jewish Christians united with Gentile churches; others dwindled into narrow, dissenting sects. Judaic Chris-

tianity, as a separate unity and power, had run its course. The further history of the relation of Judaism to Christianity is a part of the developing and expanding faith which we shall review after we have followed the creative ministry of Paul.

PART IV

EXPANSION OF CHRISTIANITY UNDER PAUL

I

HISTORICAL SOURCES

174. THE authorities for the history of Paul's distinctive work are Acts (xv. 36 to the close) and the Pauline epistles. In the former are included the " we sections " (sect. 3), where the narrative is especially minute and full. As to the epistles of Paul, the progress of criticism during the last fifty years has certainly resulted in their vindication, exclusive of the Epistle to the Hebrews, as genuine products of the apostle. The only ones of the thirteen claiming to be Pauline about which serious question exists in the minds of any but the most extreme critics, are those to Timothy and Titus. The eccentricities of individual critics may be disregarded and the conclusion of more sober scholars safely followed. The general results obtained by B. Weiss ("A Manual of Introduction to the New Testament"), Salmon (" Introduction to the New Testament"), Th. Zahn (" Einleitung in das Neue Testament"), and Godet (" Introduction to the New Testament. I. The Epistles of Paul"), who defend all the thirteen, should be considered established. Jülicher ("Einleitung in das N. T.") and Harnack (" Die Chronologie der altchristlichen Literatur bis Eusebius," Vorrede) in like manner receive all except the Pastorals. The doubt thrown on many of these books by the Tübingen school has thus been dissipated.

175. The genuineness of the epistles to Timothy and Titus is therefore the only matter to which we need pay special attention in establishing our sources for the history and teaching of Paul. Not a few scholars refuse to receive them as Pauline, at least in their present form, and insist that they were composed wholly, or for the most part, by a later writer, who is dated variously from the close of the first to the middle of the second century, who wrote for the purpose of correcting evils in the church, and who either attributed his whole work to Paul to give it authority, or else possessed some brief notes written by the apostle, which he enlarged by extensive interpolations. This criticism is based on a variety of grounds by different writers. Some allege that the epistles are plainly directed against second-century heresies, mainly Gnostic (I. Tim. i. 4, 7, 19; iv. 1–3; vi. 4, 20; Tit. i. 10; iii. 9; II. Tim. ii. 14, 16, 18, 23; iii. 1–7, 13; iv. 3); others, that the directions about church government and officials show the stress on organization, if not the development of episcopacy, which existed in the early post-apostolic age (I. Tim. iii. 1–10, 15; v. 1–22; Tit. i. 5–9; iii. 10; II. Tim. ii. 2); others again, that the tone of address is not such as we would expect from Paul to Timothy and Titus, since on the one hand he vehemently defends his apostleship to them (I. Tim. i. 11–16; ii. 7; II. Tim. ii. 12; iv. 7), and on the other hand instructs them in the most elementary duties (I. Tim. i. 19; iv. 12; vi. 11; Tit. ii. 7; II. Tim. i. 6; ii. 1, 4, 22; iii. 14), and when dealing with error merely denounces, instead of disproving, it (I. Tim. i. 4, 7, 20; iv. 6, 7; vi. 3–5; Tit. i. 10–16; iii. 9–11; II. Tim. ii. 14, 18; iii. 1–9; iv.

3, 4). The main objections, however, brought against the epistles are based on their teaching and style, both of which are alleged to be unpauline. On the other hand, the historical references in the epistles, which are very natural and incidental and wholly unlike the work of a forger, have led recent scholars to the view that the author based his work on genuine notes of Paul (comp. I. Tim. i. 3, 20 ; Tit. i. 5 ; iii. 12, 13 ; II. Tim. i. 15–18 ; iv. 10–21). Even these critics, however, vary greatly in the determination of the Pauline portions.

176. But this criticism may be met by a greater array of opposing considerations. The negative hypothesis does violence to the explicit claims of the epistles themselves, and should not be accepted without ample proof. It also reflects severely on the perspicacity of the church of the second century which received the epistles as apostolic. It is certain that in determining the New Testament canon the church acted slowly, intelligently, and upon evidence. She is known to have rejected other works falsely claiming apostolic authorship. Her acceptance of these epistles should be presumed to have had sufficient reason, unless convincing proof to the contrary can be produced. Nor is the external evidence for the acceptance of these epistles inadequate. It is found possibly in Clement of Rome (A. D. 96) and certainly in the writings of Ignatius (about A. D. 110) and Polycarp (about A. D. 110). The letters were thus undoubtedly produced in the first century ; and the earliest post-apostolic literature shows them in circulation and used as other apostolic writings were. Their absence from Marcion's canon is no evidence against them, since he only accepted a portion of the books received as

authoritative by the church, and these epistles would, from his theological views, naturally be distasteful to him. Still further, the historical allusions contained in them, which have been already noticed, are strong testimony to their authenticity. The admission by recent negative critics of a genuine Pauline element is an acknowledgment that the historical situation evidenced by the epistles belongs to the life of Paul.

177. Moreover, the objections to their contents either disappear on examination or are insufficient to weigh against the other testimony in their favor. Thus the false teachers cannot be identified with any known heretical sect of the second century. So true is this that recent opposing critics consider the references to them to be a somewhat crude and mixed allusion to heresy in general. But they can be consistently explained, if we suppose the false teachers to have been Jews who used fanciful explanations of the Old Testament and Jewish legends to inculcate superstitious speculations and ascetic practices, combined with pretences to a higher spiritual knowledge (I. Tim. i. 4, 7; iv. 7; vi. 20; Tit. i. 10, 14; iii. 9; II. Tim. ii. 18); and the existence of similar destructive tendencies in Asia Minor appears in the Epistle to the Colossians. The errorists of these epistles even appear less Gnostic than those of Colosse, for the "myths and endless genealogies" to which allusion is made (I. Tim. i. 4; Tit. i. 14; iii. 9; II. Tim. iv. 4) were probably Jewish fables rather than speculations about the Godhead. The references therefore better suit the first century than the second. The apostle foresaw, however, that the evil would increase (I. Tim. iv. 1; II. Tim. iii. 1, 13).

178. In like manner the directions about church officials point to the apostolic age, since the bishop is still identified with the elder (I. Tim. iii. 1; v. 17; Tit. i. 5, 7), and the directions are given not in the least for the purpose of advancing the power of any office, nor to develop the machinery of church government, but to secure high character and faithful teaching in the officials already established. Neither is the author's tone of address to Timothy and Titus, nor his severe denunciation of the errorists as schismatical and opposed to established doctrine, inconsistent with Paul's position or habit. Christianity was in fact already established; and, as all his epistles show, it was his custom to emphasize the fact that an unchangeable revelation had been made in Christ, and that the Christian life was one of holiness. Writing to men to whom he had delegated for a time important fields, knowing that truth and duty had already been taught to the churches, and seeing that false and foolish teachings, often combined with failure to strive after the high moral ideal of the gospel, were being introduced, he naturally urged his helpers, and through them the churches, to be true to what they had been taught. There was no need to go over the whole argument for Christianity, but only to enforce its application. The epistles therefore fit into just the situation which the development of the churches must inevitably have created.

179. Nor can the doctrinal teaching of these epistles be shown to be unpauline. If it be said that " faith " is here used to denote the content of that which is believed (I. Tim. i. 19; ii. 9; iv. 1, 6; vi. 10, 21; Tit. i. 1, 13), and is classed as merely one of the Christian

virtues (I. Tim. vi. 11; II. Tim. ii. 22), it may be replied that these aspects of faith always formed part of Paul's representation of it (II. Thess. i. 10; ii. 12; iii. 2; Rom. x. 9; Gal. v. 22, 23), that the increase of false teaching naturally led to further stress on the former of these aspects, and that the common Pauline use of "faith" to denote the saving trust of the Christian in his Lord and the sphere in which all his spiritual activities move, appears as plainly in these epistles as elsewhere (I. Tim. i. 2, 4, 5, 14, 16; ii. 15; iii. 15; iv. 3, 10; vi. 11, 12; Tit. i. 4; ii. 2; iii. 15; II. Tim. i. 5, 13; ii. 18, 22; iii. 8, 15; iv. 7). If it be said that here stress is laid on "sound teaching" (I. Tim. i. 10; iv. 6; Tit. i. 9; ii. 1; II. Tim. i. 3; ii. 2; iv. 3), and "good works" (I. Tim. iv. 12; vi. 11, 18, 19; Tit. i. 16; ii. 12, 14; iii. 8), the reply is obvious that in other epistles Paul emphasized the duty of adherence to his teaching (I. Thess. ii. 13; iv. 1; II. Thess. ii. 15; iii. 6, 14; I. Cor. xi. 2; Col. ii. 6), and never failed to insist on the moral fruits of faith (e. g. I. Thess. iv. 1–12; Gal. v. 19 to vi. 10; I. Cor. vi. 9–11). In like manner he had ever been accustomed, as in these epistles, to hold himself before his converts for their imitation (I. Thess. ii. 1; II. Thess. iii. 7; Gal. iv. 12; Phil. iii. 17), and to make God's gracious dealing with him an illustration of his Gospel (Gal. i. 11–17; I. Cor. ix. 1, 2; xv. 8–11; II. Cor. ii. 14–17); nor does this seem inappropriate in these letters to Timothy and Titus, because the epistles were addressed to them in their official capacities and the false use of the law by the errorists suggested the re-emphasizing of the fundamental principle of grace which his own experience had illustrated. In fact,

Paul's distinctive doctrines of grace appear in these epistles. The law, though honorable (I. Tim. i. 8; comp. Rom. vii. 12), is said to be designed to bring the sinful to repentance (I. Tim. i. 9, 10; comp. Gal. iii. 19, 22) ; while we read of the sovereignty of divine grace in salvation (I. Tim. i. 14; vi. 12; Tit. ii. 11, iii. 4-7 ; II. Tim. i. 9; ii. 10, 19), of salvation itself as justification (Tit. iii. 7) obtained through redemption by the work of Christ (I. Tim. i. 15; ii. 5, 6; Tit. ii. 14 ; II. Tim. ii. 11), and witnessed by the renewal of life by the Spirit (Tit. iii. 5, 6, 9 ; II. Tim. i. 14), and of the second advent as the object of the believer's hope (I. Tim. vi. 14; Tit. ii. 13; II. Tim. iv. 8, 18). The familiar Pauline phrase " in Christ " occurs (I. Tim. i. 14; iii. 13 ; II. Tim. i. 1, 9, 13; ii. 1; iii. 12, 15), as well as other characteristic expressions and sentiments (e. g. I. Tim. i. 11, 12; ii. 7, 12 ; iv. 3, 4; vi. 1, 2, 14; Tit. ii. 9, 10; iii. 1, 2; II. Tim. ii. 8, 26). The way of salvation, in short, is the same in these epistles as in the earlier ones. The most that can be fairly said is that there is a strong emphasis on certain duties of Christian life, a tendency to use brief formulas of doctrine without elaborating them, and the employment of some new terms, — such as "godliness," " mediator" as a title of Christ, and the expression " God our Saviour," — which strike the reader as unusual. But the placing of emphasis on different aspects of truth or duty is a marked characteristic of Paul as a writer. So also is his use of new words and phrases in accordance with the changing needs of the situation and the arguments of his opponents.

180. It must be acknowledged, indeed, that the style and diction of these epistles differ considerably from

Paul's earlier letters. They contain many words not previously used by him. Many scholars miss from them his dialectical method of argumentation and the absence of his usual particles of connection. But other facts advise us that this argument cannot be pressed. The vast bulk of the language is Pauline. The comparative absence of the particles proper to argument is explained by the absence of doctrinal discussions. As already remarked, the versatility of his mind led Paul to adjust his instruction to new situations; and this caused a steady enlargement of the vocabulary of his epistles, which is in fact one of their most striking features. The argument, therefore, from style and diction should not cast doubt on these epistles. If so, the other objections are certainly inadequate. We do not hesitate, therefore, to accept them as Pauline and to use them for the construction of the history.

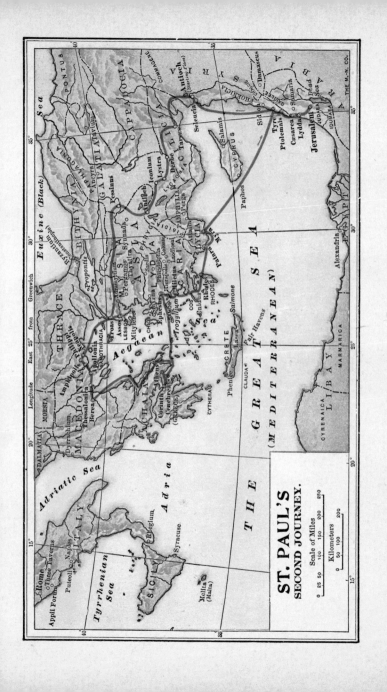

ST. PAUL'S
SECOND JOURNEY.

Scale of Miles
0 25 50   100   150   200   250

Kilometers
0   50   100   150   200

II

ENTRANCE OF CHRISTIANITY INTO EUROPE

181. RETURNING to Antioch at the period subsequent to the council and Peter's visit, our narrative must follow the expansion of Christianity among the Gentiles, for which the earlier labors of Paul and Barnabas and the decision of the council had prepared the way. The part of Acts (xv. 36 to xxviii. 31) which, with the epistles of Paul, is the source of information, describes only the missionary activity of that apostle, so that our view of the expansion must be limited to his work. Hence it is important to remember that many others were more or less closely associated with him. He was not a solitary evangelist, but rather the commanding officer of a large circle of missionaries; and the number of his co-laborers increased with the progress of the work. It is also still more important to remember that outside of this Pauline circle many other missionaries went forth, and doubtless in every direction. Paul himself alludes to Peter, Barnabas, and the brethren of the Lord as well-known evangelists (I. Cor. ix. 5, 6). The tradition (*Eus.* HE. III. 1) that the apostles scattered to various parts of the world plainly rests on a basis of fact (comp. sect. 103); and the diffusion of Christianity which existed at the close of the century can hardly be explained except by the labors of many agents. The period

was thus one of widespread evangelism. Neither was
the latter all of the same type. The Judaizing opponents of Paul actively pushed their views within
his own churches. Other Jewish missionaries carried
the message of Jesus among their countrymen in an
independent way, without opposing Paul, but doubtless
without emphasizing the phases of the gospel on which
he laid stress. We read in Acts (xviii. 26 ; xix. 1-3)
of imperfectly instructed disciples, one of whom had
heard of Jesus in Alexandria ; while in Paul's epistles
false teachers of various kinds are continually opposed.
It is clear, therefore, that quite different types of
Christianity were being disseminated.

182. Yet the expansion under Paul was the fact
of chief importance. Luke followed it, not because
he was ignorant of others, nor merely because he had
been associated with the apostle. It was through
Paul's work that Christianity was established in the
chief cities of the empire, and thus obtained the
significance which it had when Luke wrote. This
line of progress was historically the most portentous.
In Paul's Epistles, moreover, which are the index of
his teaching, the Christian system of belief was completely unfolded, so that under him Christianity
evolved its content as well as extended its area.
Later epistles from other hands prove that the Pauline
teaching was recognized by the other leaders of the
church as the correct expression of the faith. It is
true that he met with constant opposition, and that
his own churches required from him continual instruction and rebuke. But apostolic Christianity ever
presents two phases, — one the Christianity which was
taught by its founders ; the other that of the churches,

which was often quite an incomplete appropriation of the former. Paulinism was unquestionably the genuine development of the apostolic faith. Hence in following Paul, while we are not to forget other agents, we follow the expansion which was historically the most monentous and which gave its full significance to the apostolic age.

183. Paul's second missionary journey, as it is commonly called, originated from a proposal to Barnabas to revisit the churches which they had previously planted (Acts xv. 36). A sharp difference of opinion on the subject of taking Mark with them led, however, to their separation (xv. 37–39). Barnabas, with Mark, sailed to Cyprus, and thenceforth disappears from authentic history, save for the allusion to him in I. Corinthians ix. 6. The traditions about him are late and various. It may well be that he continued to perform a large part in the spread of Christianity, and to mediate, as he had done before, between Jewish and Gentile believers. Paul took for his companion Silas, who had returned to Antioch. Possessed of prophetic gifts (Acts xv. 32), a leader and probably a presbyter of the Jerusalem Church, and seemingly, like Paul, a Roman citizen (Acts xvi. 37), Silas was in complete accord with the views of the apostle and was destined to be one of his most devoted co-laborers.

184. The two men left Antioch probably in the spring of A. D. 51 (see Appendix), and the prayers of the church followed them (Acts xv. 40). Their object still appears to have been to visit the churches already founded, though this of course did not exclude further evangelization. Hence they passed first through Syria and Cilicia, and then crossed into Lycaonia (xvi. 1)

and Phrygia (xvi. 6), the scene of the former labors of Paul and Barnabas. At Lystra, Timothy, who had won the favor of the disciples there and in Iconium, and to whom the Spirit pointed as destined for important work (I. Tim. i. 18; iv. 14), was taken into the party (sect. 128). Paul caused him, as the son of a Jewess, to be circumcised in order not to give offence to the Jews (Acts xvi. 3), thus showing his entire willingness to act on the principle laid down by the council. His refusal to allow Gentiles to be circumcised was quite consistent with the observance of that rite by Jews, especially if the cause could be advanced thereby. Doubtless also at this time Timothy was formally set apart by the church as an evangelist (I. Tim. iv. 14), a ceremony in which the apostle joined (II. Tim. i. 6). Luke further notes that, as he went, Paul delivered to the churches the decree of the council. How consistently he could do this has been already discussed (sects. 159, 160).

185. The apostle had now revisited the churches previously planted, but he was not disposed to halt. Perhaps, with the replacement of Barnabas by Silas, his plans had enlarged. Perhaps, as they advanced through the older territory, the accessibility of the Gentiles impressed them anew. At any rate, it was now his purpose to enter the Roman province of Asia; but the Divine Spirit forbade it. God had chosen another field for him, and the apostle was made to realize that another mind than his own was planning for the future. The precise direction of his journey at this point is, however, much disputed. The common opinion has been that he went northeast through Phrygia, in which Pisidian Antioch lay, into the

region of Galatia (Acts xvi. 6). The latter was a large area in the centre of Asia Minor. It received its name from certain Gallic tribes who in the third century B.C., after invading Macedonia and Thrace, had crossed over into Asia on the invitation of the king of Bithynia to assist him in war. Though subdued by the Romans (189 B. C.), they had been permitted to retain self-government, and under Pompey Galatia had been made a kingdom. Under the last king, Amyntas IV., their territory was much extended to the south, so as to include part of Phrygia, Pisidia, Lycaonia, and Isauria, and after the death of Amyntas (B. C. 25), this extended territory became the Roman province of Galatia, to which (B. C. 7) further additions were made on the north (*Ramsay*, Hist. Geog. of As. M., pp. 252–254). The term " Galatia" might therefore describe the territory inhabited by the descendants of the Gauls and popularly known by this term, or the more extended Roman province to which the name was affixed by the imperial government. In the latter case it would include the region already evangelized. Hence many have maintained that Paul's Galatians were the churches which he and Barnabas founded in Phrygia and Lycaonia; while Professor Ramsay (St. Paul the Trav. chh. viii., ix., Studia Bib. et Eccles., 1896) maintains also that in Acts xvi. 6 we should translate " they passed through the Phrygio — Galatic region" and understand by that phrase the part of Phrygia which belonged to the province of Galatia. In that case Paul did not enter Galatia proper at all.

186. To whomever the epistle to the Galatians was written, it is difficult to interpret Luke's language as Professor Ramsay does, because in xviii. 23 he re-

verses the clauses and speaks of " the Galatian region
and Phrygia," thus indicating that he used the phrase
" Galatian region " as descriptive of a territory different from Phrygia (see *Zahn*, Einleit. I. 133). We must
believe, therefore, that, when Paul was forbidden to
enter Asia, he did turn into the region of Galatia
proper. Did he found churches there ? Luke does not
record it. Yet he implies it in the use of the verb
which he commonly uses elsewhere to describe an
evangelizing tour, and his failure specifically to mention it may have been due to the purpose of his narrative. His account here (xvi. 6–10) is very condensed
He was bent on describing the divine guidance which
led the apostle to Troas and so to Europe. Events
in Galatia which did not result in the occupation of
territory of special interest to one who had in mind
the evangelization of the empire, are passed over, and
the founding of churches there may have been passed
over too. It is in itself improbable that Paul lost any
opportunity of extending the work.

187. The question must, therefore, be raised here
whether the Galatians to whom Paul addressed his
epistle were inhabitants of Galatia proper or of Phrygia
and Lycaonia. Much may be said in favor of both
views. No doubt Paul could have addressed the people
of Pisidian Antioch, Iconium, Derbe, and Lystra as
Galatians, if he chose to use official Roman nomencla-
ture ; and his frequent use of the names of provinces
(Rom. xvi. 5 ; I. Cor. xvi. 15 ; II. Cor. i. 8, 16 ; ii. 12 ;
I. Tim. i. 3 ; II. Tim. i. 15), and especially his apparent
classification of his churches by provinces in the matter
of the collection for the Judean Christians (Rom. xv.
26 ; II. Cor. viii. 1 ; ix. 2 ; perh. I. Cor. xvi. 1), gives

plausibility to the view that he did so. On the other hand, we have no instance of his addressing a letter to the churches of a province under that name alone; and this is specially notable in the case of the epistle to the Ephesians, which was probably a circular letter to the churches of Asia. The Galatian epistle contains, in spite of Professor Ramsay's acute arguments to the contrary, no allusion which is not susceptible of explanation on the other view, while the description of his reception " as an angel of God" (Gal. iv. 14) hardly comports with anything we know of on the first missionary journey. If it be said that the Judaizers would most naturally operate in the nearer towns of South Galatia, where there were large Jewish colonies, it may be said, on the other hand, that Judaism had also entered Galatia proper (*Jos.* Antiq. xvi. 6. 2), and that the Judaizers would be more likely to attack Paul's own new churches which had not been so long and well established as those of Phrygia and Lycaonia. It is a serious difficulty with the " South-Galatian" view that the apostle appeals to his readers as if he alone had been their spiritual father (iv. 13–20; v. 1), whereas on the first journey Barnabas was associated with him on equal terms. The force of this fact is not lessened by the incidental allusions to Barnabas as known by the Galatians (ii. 1, 9, 13), any more than is Paul's special relation to the Corinthian church made doubtful by his reference to Barnabas and Peter in First Corinthians (ix. 6). An equally serious difficulty lies in the date which must be given to the epistle on the theory in question. It appears from iv. 13, that Paul had twice visited the Galatians. Hence on the "South-Galatian " view the epistle must have been written during his second missionary journey, since the third journey began with a third visit to Phrygia (Acts xviii. 23). Yet, if the epistle be dated before or during his visit to Corinth, we are confronted with the fact that the epistles to the Thessalonians, written from Corinth, contain no allusions to the Judaistic attacks, and no emphasis on those specific doctrines upon which these attacks ever afterwards caused him to lay stress ; while if we date it at the close of the second journey, we are confronted with the fact that in the epistle he says nothing of his intention of again visiting the Galatians, — indeed in iv. 20 writes as if he could not do so, — although Acts xviii. 19–23 makes it clear that such was his purpose, and that he at once actually did so. It thus seems quite improbable that the epistle was written during or at the close of the second journey ; and this of itself leads to the conclusion, in view of iv. 13, that the Galatians were not the Christians of Phrygia and Lycaonia.

188. We infer, therefore, that Paul not only passed through Galatia proper, but that he tarried there and evangelized. Yet the delay appears not to have been his original intention. He was afflicted on the way by a grievous, and seemingly loathsome, disease (Gal. iv. 13, 14), doubtless an attack of the mysterious "thorn [or stake] in the flesh" of which he writes elsewhere (II. Cor. xii. 7). Though suffering, he began to preach ; and his words were attended with such spiritual power that many received the gospel of the Crucified (Gal. iii. 1). No doubt this led him to linger in Galatia ; but whether he preached in its chief cities, Pessinus, Ancyra, and Tavium, or only in some of the smaller villages, is not known. Then, advancing

northward, he attempted to enter Bithynia; but again
the Spirit strangely forbade him. He was now opposite Mysia, a part of the forbidden province of Asia.
Whither did God intend him to go? Doubtful of the
future, and perhaps still suffering from sickness, the
apostle turned westward and, without preaching in
Mysia, hastened through it or along its border to Troas,
a seaport near the mouth of the Hellespont.

189. At Troas the vision of the man of Macedonia
(Acts xvi. 8–10) indicated to him at last the divine
will. Europe was his destined field of labor. We may
believe that with this vision the sense of his divine
call to evangelize the empire and to carry the gospel
steadily to the west began to break upon his mind. At
Troas also Luke joined him (Acts xvi. 10). He is said
by tradition to have been a native of Antioch, and
probably he was already acquainted with Paul. It
has been also inferred that he had been living in
Philippi, since he only accompanied the apostle on this
journey to that city (xvi. 40). But we must not read
too much between the lines. It is enough to know
that, in obedience to what they judged to be the divine
meaning of the vision, the party sailed at once for
Macedonia. Favoring winds seconded the call from
heaven (xvi. 11). On the second day they reached
Neapolis, and pushed on to Philippi, the nearest
Macedonian city. It was a place of importance and a
Roman colony. The Roman spirit is manifest in the
names of the officials, " prætors " (xvi. 20) and " lictors " (xvi. 35, 38); in the charges afterward brought
against Paul and Silas of teaching customs not lawful
for Romans (xvi. 20, 21); and in the effective use
finally made by the missionaries of their own Roman

citizenship (xvi. 37, 39). The apostle thus found him-self in the Romanized world. In a sense never before true had he entered on the conquest of the empire in the name of Jesus.

190. Only a few incidents of the work at Philippi are recorded in Acts (xvi. 12-40). Jews were not numerous, and, in the absence of a synagogue, there was only a " place of prayer " by the river to which chiefly women resorted. Thither the missionaries went on the Sabbath. The first convert was Lydia from Thyatira, a Gentile already attached to Judaism, who with her household was baptized and welcomed the missionaries to her dwelling. From this small beginning the work advanced. Even Luke's brief account implies that a deep impression was made on the population (xvi. 16, 20, 30), and that a body of dis-ciples was gathered (xvi. 40). Luke, however, was mainly interested to relate Paul's treatment by the authorities. A girl, possessed of an evil spirit of divination, bore testimony to Paul and Silas as servants of the Most High God (xvi. 16, 18), as the demoniacs of Galilee had done to Jesus. But, like his Master, Paul would not receive aid from such a source, and in the name of Jesus expelled the demon. Hence the girl's owners accused Paul and Silas before the magis-trates and the populace of being troublesome Jews, and of teaching customs unlawful for Romans. The charge was devised so as to appeal both to the popular dislike of the Jews and to the colonial pride of the Philippians. It was temporarily successful ; for the populace became excited, and the magistrates hastily had the accused beaten and thrown into prison. During the night an earthquake opened the prison doors and shook off the

prisoner's chains; but Paul and Silas made no effort to escape. Their conduct, with the impression produced by the earthquake and the knowledge that they were religious teachers, was the means of awakening the conscience of the jailer and led to his conversion; so that the hour of peril became one of spiritual triumph. Moreover, in the morning the magistrates, having doubtless realized the hastiness of their previous action, sent word by the lictors to let the prisoners go. But Paul revealed the fact that they were Romans, and demanded an apology for the illegal treatment to which they had been subjected. Hence the magistrates themselves went to release them, and respectfully requested them to leave the city.

191. While Luke's narrative exhibits the new atmosphere into which the gospel was being carried, much more was accomplished at Philippi than he records. The church in that city steadily grew in numbers and power. The zeal, consecration, and liberality amid poverty of the churches of Macedonia, of which that of Philippi was a leader, are attested gratefully by the apostle in II. Corinthians (viii.), while his epistle to the Philippians testifies to their affectionate relations to himself (i. 7, 25; ii. 9; iv. 1) and their steadfastness in the faith (i. 5, 27; ii. 12). Twice after his departure they sent him financial aid (Phil. iv. 14), as later they again did to him at Rome (iv. 10). They were organized into a church, with bishops, or presbyters, and deacons, after the model of those in Syria (Phil. i. 1). Luke remained among them and was doubtless one of their leaders; while in the epistle to the Philippians we read of Epaphroditus (ii. 25) and Clement (iv. 3), with other workers, men and women

(iv. 2, 3), active and honored in the cause. The Philippian church, dim though the outline of its history is, presents a beautiful picture of successful and uninterrupted progress. The opposition of paganism, of which Paul had had a foretaste, did not cease (Phil. i. 28–30); but it only evoked the zeal of the disciples. The apostle left Philippi with the seal of success plainly placed on the entrance of the gospel into Europe.

192. In company with Silas and Timothy he next went westward, about a hundred miles, to Thessalonica (Acts xvii. 1). The object seems to have been to occupy the most influential centres. Such a centre was Thessalonica. Situated on the Thermaic gulf, which empties into the Ægean Sea, it commanded the whole region lying to the north. Soon Paul could write to the Thessalonians: "From you sounded out the word of the Lord not only in Macedonia and Achaia, but also in every place your faith to Godward is spread abroad" (I. Thess. i. 8). It was in fact the metropolis of Macedonia. It was a free city, having municipal self-government, as the peculiar titles of its magistrates, "politarchs" (xvii. 6), indicate. In it Paul's work was again very successful. For three Sabbaths he preached in the synagogue (xvii. 2), for there was a large colony of Jews in the city. He proved to them from Scripture that Jesus is the Christ, and that his death and resurrection were necessary (xvii. 3). The result was the formation of a church composed of a few Jews and many devout Gentiles, with some women of high social standing (xvii. 4).

193. More information is given by Paul himself in his letters to the Thessalonians. The predomi-

nantly Gentile character of the church is there confirmed
(I. Thess. i. 9).   He refers also to the spiritual power
which had attended his ministry (I. Thess. i. 3, 5) and
the many practical as well as doctrinal instructions
which he had given them (I. Thess. ii. 3-8, 11, 12; iv.
1-7, 11; II. Thess. ii. 5, 15).   He set them an example
of industry and sobriety by supporting himself among
them by manual toil (I. Thess. ii. 9, 10; iv. 11; II.
Thess. iii. 8).   It is evident that he remained longer
than the three weeks mentioned by Luke.   They were
but the commencement of his mission.   It is also evident that, while in the synagogue he argued from the
Old Testament, he also fully instructed the disciples
in the duties as well as the doctrines of Christian life.
The epistles show that his instructions took a wide
range, but that he especially dwelt on the gospel as a
call to repentance and holiness (I. Thess. ii. 12; iv. 7;
v. 23) as well as to salvation, and on the return of
Messiah to judgment and to his kingdom (I. Thess. i.
10; ii. 19; iv. 15; II. Thess. ii. 5).   It should not be
imagined that Paul's ordinary instructions consisted
solely in those doctrinal discussions which form the
core of his theological system.   He dealt with the
needs of men as he found them.   He was as precise
and definite in his practical teaching as he was logical
and elaborate in his doctrinal.   His ministry was also
attended with mighty operations of the Spirit; so that
the new religion appeared both as an intellectual system of truth and as a revelation of supernatural power.
He proclaimed himself to be an ambassador from God,
clothed with authority to direct the belief and lives of
the disciples (I. Thess. ii. 6, 13; iii. 2, 15; v. 27;
II. Thess. iii. 6, 9, 14).   It is not difficult to imagine

the spiritual freshness and the directly supernatural character of the faith as he proclaimed it. At the same time the converts were but children, and required constantly additional encouragement and instruction, a fact which none realized more clearly than Paul himself (I. Thess. iii. 1–6).

194. The anger of the Jews in Thessalonica led finally to the apostle's departure from that city. The charge made by them against the Christians of disloyalty to Cæsar, on the ground that they preached another king (Acts xvii. 7), strikingly agrees with the prominence in the apostle's preaching of the doctrine of the Lord's second advent. It was of course a charge manipulated for a purpose, and came with bad grace from the Jews. His accusers, however, did not succeed in arresting the apostle (xvii. 6); yet the brethren, apprehending further danger (comp. I. Thess. ii. 14), sent him and Silas by night to Berea, an inland town on the eastern slope of the Olympus range. Timothy appears also to have accompanied them. There Paul was well received even by the Jews. They were impressed by his expositions of Scripture, and many converts, both Jew and Gentile, were made (Acts xvii. 11, 12). The Thessalonian Jews, however, followed him to Berea and roused popular feeling against him. Hence the brethren again sent him away, this time to the coast and so by sea to Athens (xvii. 13, 14). Silas and Timothy remained behind, and Paul sent back word for them to join him at Athens (xvii. 15). We infer from I. Thessalonians iii. 1, 2, that Timothy did so, but was again sent back to Thessalonica on account of the apostle's anxiety about that church. Acts itself indicates that the order for Silas and Timothy to join

Paul at Athens was not fully carried out, for it relates that they rejoined him at Corinth (xviii. 5). Silas may have found it necessary to remain at Berea, and may have joined Timothy on the way to Corinth. The apostle, however, seems to have waited some days at Athens before Timothy arrived.

195. Though alone in Athens, and in a sense a fugitive, he could not be idle. His soul burned as he observed the popular idolatry of the famous city, and he discussed with those he met, both in synagogue and agora; but he seems to have had little success. Perhaps, as often, a philosophic atmosphere was peculiarly inhospitable to the gospel. He found, however, a group of philosophers, Epicureans and Stoics, who became superficially interested in the travelling teacher, though they regarded him rather with amused contempt than with serious desire to learn what he had to say (Acts xvii. 18). They gave him a chance to expound his doctrines. It has been the common opinion that his famous address before them was delivered on that part of Mars' Hill, called the Areopagus, where the celebrated Athenian court bearing the same name was accustomed to hold its sessions. If so, however, we must not imagine a formal sitting of the court, but a group of listeners using this retired place as a convenient auditorium. Others (*Curtius*, Stadtgesch. von Athene, p. 262; *Ramsay*, St. Paul the Trav. p. 243) think that by Areopagus Luke meant the court itself, and that the address was delivered near the agora. In this case it has been supposed that there was either a trial on the charge of introducing new divinities or an informal assemblage of the court to decide whether the stranger should be allowed to teach or not. The

notion of a formal trial is certainly to be rejected, since the Areopagus did not have jurisdiction in such cases (see J. J. Manatt, Andover Rev., Nov. 1892), and Luke's narrative seems to imply a gathering too occasional even for an informal meeting of the court. There is thus no sufficient reason to abandon the usual conception of the scene.

196. Wherever the address was delivered, the apostle strove for the only recorded time to present Christianity so as to appeal to philosophers. He cleverly took for his starting-point an inscription which he had chanced to see on an altar, " TO AN UNKNOWN GOD " (xvii. 23, R. V.). With all their reverence for deities, there was then one whom the Athenians knew not. This deity he would proclaim to them. Then he set forth God as the Creator and Lord of the universe, and drew the inference that paganism with its temples and material offerings was unworthy of his majesty (xvii. 24, 25). Next he set forth God's government of the world, bringing out the unity of the race, its universal subjection to God, and his purpose that men should seek and find him (26, 27). God, being ever near us and the universal Father, desires not the coarse and absurd worship of idols, as though he were like them, but man's spiritual fellowship with himself (28, 29). The times of ignorance, which he permitted, are now past. A revelation has been made. God's command is that men repent. The time of judgment is approaching; and Jesus, whom he raised from the dead in token of the authority conferred on him, is to be the universal judge.

197. Such was the substance of the address, according to Luke's meagre but evidently faithful outline.

There was much in what was said about the absurdity of idolatry, and the spirituality of God, with which the auditors, especially the Stoics, must have agreed. So far the argument was fitted to win them, and the quotation from the Stoics Aratus and Kleanthes (xvii. 28) were in the same line of appeal. On the other hand, Paul's pure theism, his doctrine of the unity of the race and of the religious aim of the world-wide purpose of God, still more his doctrine of the resurrection, were equally offensive. The mention of the resurrection evoked actual derision. There is also a notable absence from the address of the doctrine of redemption, and the appeal was to the reason rather than to the conscience. Of course on other occasions in Athens the apostle may have spoken quite differently; but this address, like the one at Lystra (Acts xiv. 15-17), moved outside of his usual themes as we elsewhere know them. Yet it was of the highest value, because it presented aspects of truth which were to be of fundamental importance in the coming conflict between Christianity and paganism. It illustrates also the breadth of Paul's thought, and his acquaintance with current culture; and every element of it may be found expressed elsewhere in his writings. While, moreover, apparently designed to appeal to his philosophic audience, it was in no sense a compromise with error, for it emphasized ideas which he must have known would offend. The result, however, was disappointing: one Areopagite was converted, also a woman and a few others (34), and Paul finally moved on to Corinth resolved to know nothing but Jesus Christ and him crucified (I. Cor. ii. 1, 2).

III

PAUL IN CORINTH

198. PAUL'S ministry at Corinth, which lasted eighteen months (Acts xviii. 11), was one of the most momentous in his whole career. New Corinth, rebuilt by
Julius Cæsar on the ruins of the old city, was a place of
large commercial importance, a *colonia*, and the residence of the procurator of Achaia. Its population included representatives of all races and classes. It was
a pleasure-loving city and Corinthian morals were a by-
word. To leave Athens for Corinth was to exchange
an intellectual for a sensuous atmosphere. Yet in
Corinth the apostle attained a success which he had
not found in Athens. At first he still cherished the
wish to return to Thessalonica, but though anxious
and waiting for Silas and Timothy to rejoin him, he
could not be idle (I Thess. iii. 4–7). On his arrival he
obtained lodging and work with the Pontic Jew Aquila,
(Acts xviii. 2, 3) who with his wife Priscilla afterwards became his co-laborers in the nobler work of
the gospel (Acts xviii. 18, 26; Rom. xvi. 3; I. Cor. xvi.
19; II. Tim. iv. 9). They had moved recently to
Corinth from Rome because of the edict of Claudius ex-
pelling Jews from the capital (Acts xviii. 2). This
edict is mentioned by Suetonius (Claud. 25), who relates that it was caused by the tumults of the Jews
"*impulsore Chresto.*" The date of it has been assigned

by different scholars to the years A. D. 49, 50, and 52;
but even if the earliest of these dates, which is the
least probable, be accepted, it does not follow that
Paul reached Corinth in that year, for some margin
must be allowed for the journey of Aquila to Corinth
and, in spite of the words "lately come," for the period
between his arrival and Paul's. The language of Suetonius has also led many to suppose that " Chrestus "
was equivalent to " Christus," and that the Jewish
tumults in the capital were between Christian and non-
Christian Jews. But Suetonius makes " Chrestus " the
instigator of the tumults; and from what we elsewhere
learn of the beginnings of Christianity in Rome, there
is little reason to think that it had at this time attained
sufficient strength to cause open conflicts in the Jewish
colony (Acts xxviii. 21, 22). At any rate Luke does
not intimate that Aquila and Priscilla were Christians
when Paul met them. Doubtless they were led to the
faith by their lodger. From their home, the apostle
went forth to preach to the Corinthians. He visited the
synagogue every Sabbath. During the week he supported himself by his trade. Silas and Timothy had
not yet come; and in spite of many discouragements
and of conscious weakness (I. Cor. ii. 3), the solitary
ambassador of the Cross disputed with the Jews and
their Gentile adherents and told the story of Jesus
(I. Cor. ii. 2).

199. At last Silas and Timothy joined him, with a
good report on the whole from Thessalonica (I. Thess.
iii. 6); and forthwith his energy became more intense
(Acts xviii. 5). This led finally to an open rupture
with the Jews, so that he established himself with his
disciples in the house of a devout Gentile, Titus Justus,

next door to the synagogue. The contiguity of the
two societies was of course fruitful in disputes. The
apostle's company, however, grew rapidly. Even
the ruler of the synagogue, Crispus, believed (xviii. 8;
I. Cor. i. 14); but most of the converts were from the
lower classes of the populace, and most of them were
Gentiles (I. Cor. i. 26). The work continued for many
months and not only spread through Corinth, but
churches were formed in adjacent towns (II. Thess. i.
4; II. Cor. i. 1: Rom. xvi. 1). It was, however, an
agonizing ministry for the apostle, and was performed
with an intensity of spiritual ardor scarcely equalled
in his career. There is reason to believe that he
passed through a period of severe mental struggle,
out of which he came with the resolve to preach more
simply and plainly than ever. We read of a vision
vouchsafed for his encouragement (Acts xviii. 9, 10).
In I. Corinthians he speaks in strong terms of his
fears and weakness while first laboring among them
(I. Cor. ii. 3). The vow which he took (Acts xviii. 13)
may have been connected with the same experience.
He felt, no doubt, a temptation to make his message
more ornate in style and philosophical in substance;
but was enabled to remain true to the proclamation of
a crucified Redeemer (I. Cor. ii. 1–5), in spite of its
offensiveness to Jew and Greek (I. Cor. i. 23), and to
rely on the Spirit's demonstration of the truth to the
consciences of men.

200. Thus the great church which Paul founded in
Corinth was begotten with much travail (I. Cor. iv. 15;
II. Cor. vi. 13), and he ever looked on it as peculiarly
his own. Its subsequent condition caused him great
anxiety. Around his relation to it some of the most

perplexing problems of his life cluster, and out of it grew some of his most important teaching. Many of his converts were with difficulty separated from their pagan usages. They were but babes in Christ (I. Cor. iii. 1, 2). Diverse elements also existed in the church, to unite and mould which required all the authority and patience of the apostle. Nevertheless the progress was rapid. This led finally to an attempt of the Jews to arrest it by force (Acts xviii. 12-17; I. Thess. ii. 15, 16). On the arrival of Gallio, the brother of the philosopher Seneca, as procurator of Achaia, they accused Paul of persuading men to worship God contrary to the law; but Gallio with justice refused to take cognizance of the case, declaring that the religious quarrels of the Jews were no concern of his. His action illustrates the attitude of the Roman government at this time to Christianity. It was regarded as a Jewish sect and therefore protected; and under the shield of Judaism itself, which was a *religio licita*, it made its early progress throughout the empire. The pagan populace, moreover, seeing the Jews repulsed by the procurator, let loose their enmity against them and beat Sosthenes, the ruler of the synagogue, before the very judgment-seat itself. Thus the effort of the Jews to arrest Paul resulted in their complete discomfiture.

201. The apostle's sojourn in Corinth was also made notable for all time by the composition of his first two extant epistles, those to the Thessalonians. Few now doubt that both were written from Corinth. In them he associates with himself Silas and Timothy (I. Thess. i. 1; II. Thess. i. 1), the latter of whom had recently come from Thessalonica with a report of the condition of the church (I. Thess. iii. 6). The condition of the

Thessalonians, as reflected in the epistles, was clearly
that of a newly formed community. They required
the most elementary moral instruction (I. Thess. iv.
1–8); were disturbed by the death of some of their
members (I. Thess. iv. 9–12); and were bitterly opposed by the Jews (I. Thess. ii. 13–16). The apostle
refers also to his sojourn among them as if it were
recent (I. Thess. ii. 1–12), and in the first epistle there
is an absence of allusion to doctrinal controversy which
further implies an early date. If I. Thessalonians was
thus written from Corinth shortly after Timothy's
arrival, the second epistle was evidently penned from
the same place some months later. The situation of
the readers is the same, though certain difficulties had
become more acute. The second advent is, as in the
first epistle, the leading doctrinal topic; but its discussion has advanced to a new stage. In fact the first
epistle is referred to (ii. 15) and its language is echoed
in numerous phrases (comp. II. Thess. i. 2, 3, 4, 5, 8,
11; ii. 13; iii. 6, 12, 7–10; ii. 1; with I. Thess. i. 1,
2, 3, 12; iv. 5; i. 3, 4; v. 9; iv. 11, 12; ii. 1–13;
iv. 17 respectively).

202. By these two letters, therefore, we are introduced to Pauline literature. It is noteworthy that
the apostle writes as an authority whom the Thessalonian Christians were bound to obey (I. Thess. iv. 2;
ii. Thess. ii. 15; iii. 6, 14); that his epistles were
public documents to be read in the assembly of the
church (I. Thess. v. 27); and that he assumed that
the same authority would be attached to them as to
his oral teaching or to a revelation of the Spirit, or to
the word of God (II. Thess. ii. 2). The authoritative
character of apostolic literature thus appears from its

beginning to have been acknowledged by writer and readers. At the same time these productions are real letters, as of a pastor to his people. They were written in the conventional epistolary form of the day. In them we still feel the beating heart of the writer, and they deal with the specific needs of his first readers. This combination of the personal and occasional with the authoritative and universal is one of their peculiar characteristics.

203. The First Epistle to the Thessalonians was written partly out of joy over their steadfastness, and partly because of several perils which threatened them. Of the latter there were three in particular, the existence of which gives a suggestive picture of this early Christian community. There was a disposition on the part of some to neglect their daily work and to fail to exercise moral restraint (I. Thess. ii. 9, 10; iv. 1-8, 11, 12). There had developed, moreover, dismay at death, for they feared that the dead saints would lose their part in the coming kingdom (iv. 13-18). There were also indications of friction between the regular officers and teachers of the church and those who professed to have inspired spiritual gifts (v. 12, 13). These difficulties were chiefly those of a young community just emerging from paganism. They arose also out of the excitement caused by the new spiritual experiences through which the disciples had passed, and out of their vivid, and often crude, expectation of the Lord's return. But there does not appear to have been any difficulty as to the way of salvation, a sure sign that the Judaistic controversy had not arisen among them. Indeed the absence of any warning about such errors proves that the controversy had not

yet entered at all into the apostle's field of work (sect. 186).

204. This epistle, written under such circumstances, is a warm, pastoral exhortation. It urges to industry and purity of life, and tells of his anxieties about them. Only one important doctrinal passage occurs, that, namely, in which he assured them, on the authority of a special revelation which he had received, that dead believers will not fail of participation in the glory of the returning Lord (iv. 13–18). It provides, however, a graphic picture of the moral perils to which these early Christians were exposed; and, on the other hand, of the large view which the apostle took of the new life to which they had been called.

205. The Second Epistle to the Thessalonians was occasioned by further reports of more specific trouble which had arisen concerning the Lord's advent. Some erroneously believed that "the day of the Lord" (*i. e.* the time of final judgment; comp. Acts ii. 20; I. Cor. i. 8; iii. 13; v. 5; II. Cor. i. 14; I. Thess. v. 2) had already come, and that, therefore, the return of Christ might be expected at any moment (ii. 2, R. V.). By this they were further tempted to idleness and disorder (iii. 6–12), as well as to doubt whether their persecutions were reconcilable with God's just judgment (i. 4, 5). The agitation was apparently increased by alleged revelations of the Spirit and interpretations of Scripture, and also by the report of a letter from Paul containing such teaching (ii. 2). This made the situation acute, and the apostle hastened to correct the error.

206. He began by acknowledging the gratitude which he should still feel for their faith and love amid persecution, and pointedly reminded them that

their endurance was itself a proof of God's just judgment, since it showed that he had accepted them, and would surely vindicate them in that day when Christ will return and pass final sentence upon all mankind (i.). But he begged them not to be disturbed by the idea that the day of the Lord was present (ii. 1, 2). He reminded (comp. ii. 5) them that before that day there would be an apostasy (doubtless within the church) culminating in the appearance of " the man of lawlessness " (or Antichrist) who would impiously claim the homage due to God alone (ii. 3, 4). For the present, as they knew, the development of this apostasy was being checked (perhaps, by the Spirit) ; but " the restrainer," would be taken away, and then would the lawless One be revealed in Satanic power, only, however, to be destroyed by the returning Christ (ii. 6–12). Grateful was he, in view of this fierce conflict, that they had been chosen to salvation (ii. 13, 14). Let them, therefore, stand fast in his teaching (ii. 15–17). He added a request for their prayers (iii. 1–3), an assurance of his confidence in them (iii. 4, 5), and a repeated command, sharper than before, to imitate him in a sober and industrious life and to separate themselves from all who would not obey his word (iii. 6–16). In view of the fact that a letter, falsely ascribed to him, was said to be in circulation, he called attention to his signature which was appended by his own hand to every epistle ; and closed with his blessing (iii. 17, 18).

207. These two epistles furnish a partial, but clear glimpse into the condition of Thessalonian Christianity. It is not an ideal picture. It is, however, one which might be expected in a church emerging out of paganism. These early believers needed instruction about

the most elementary duties and doctrines. It required
the firm hand of the apostle to prevent fanaticism and
childish error. Yet at the same time the genuine fruits
of the Spirit were manifest among them, and the central
truths of Christianity were firmly held and loyally con-
fessed. The doctrine chiefly explained is that of the
second advent and the judgment. In I. Thessalonians
the advent is presented as the time of reward to believers
(i. 10; ii. 12, 19; iii. 13; iv. 15–18; v. 4, 9, 10). In
II. Thessalonians it is presented as the time of judgment to the ungodly (i. 7, 9; ii. 8). The apostle taught
a personal, physical, public return of Christ to gather
his people into the everlasting kingdom, and to execute
judgment upon all the wicked. He looked forward to
it eagerly, speaking as if he might live to see it (I.
Thess. iv. 17) though not saying that he would. He
also taught that certain events must happen first, and
that the period before the advent, whether long or
short, would be one of conflict within, as well as
without, the church. His teaching about the coming
" apostasy " and " the man of lawlessness " was evidently based on the language of Jesus (comp. Matt.
xxiv., especially verses 4, 5, 6, 10, 11, 12, 23, 24). We
may also see in his words the influence of the Book
of Daniel (comp. Dan. vii. 23–25; xi. 36). The term
" man of lawlessness " seems, however, to be of his own
coining; but the expectation of apostasy within the
church and its final embodiment in some mighty Antichrist is found in the New Testament (e. g. Matt. xiii.
25; Luke viii. 13; xviii. 8; I. Tim. i. 6–10; iv. 1–3;
vi. 3–5; II. Tim. i. 15; iii. 1–8; I. John ii. 18–27; II.
Peter iii. 3; Rev. ii. iii. xiii. xvii. xviii.). Having this
expectation, Paul did not look for a peaceful develop-

ment of the faith. The early Christians were trained by him for conflict with foes without and within; nor is it strange that they were deeply concerned in these questions which were made so practical by their persecutions. The situation illustrates the stir of thought and hope, the possibilities of error of every kind, together with the power of prevailing faith, with which Christianity arose among the Gentiles.

208. After eighteen months in Corinth, Paul turned his face again to the east. Aquila and Priscilla sailed with him as far as Ephesus (Acts xviii. 18, 19), whence he, after promising to return (xviii. 20, 21), took ship again to Cæsarea. Apparently he visited Jerusalem (xviii. 21, R.V.) and then returned to Syrian Antioch. He had probably been absent about two years and a half. But the apostle now realized that he had been called to a larger mission than he had imagined when he and Silas had set forth from the Syrian city, and he only waited a few months before entering upon another campaign.

PAUL IN EPHESUS

209. It was probably in the spring of A. D. **54 that** Paul left Antioch on what is usually called his third missionary journey. He had already promised to visit Ephesus, and the Asian metropolis was now his object. The former prohibition of the Spirit (Acts xvi. 6) had evidently been removed. He first visited in order the churches of the Galatian region and Phrygia (xviii. 23). The order of words, contrasted with the similar phrase in Acts xvi. 6, indicates that he first went to Galatia proper. It is possible that this was due to information received in Antioch that the Judaistic party was carrying on, despite the decision of the council, the propagation of their views, and were threatening especially the Gentile churches which he had founded ; for Galatians i. 9 seems to state that when last in Galatia he had warned his converts against such perversions of the gospel. Doubtless, also, the success of his work in Europe had increased the alarm and enmity of the Judaizers. It was clear that under him Christianity would become independent of Judaism and of the mother church. Hence these over-zealous and, as Paul plainly called them (Gal. iv. 17 ; v. 10), unscrupulous sectarians determined to undo his work, to wean his converts away from him, and to perpetuate the Mosaic law among the Gentiles. It does not ap-

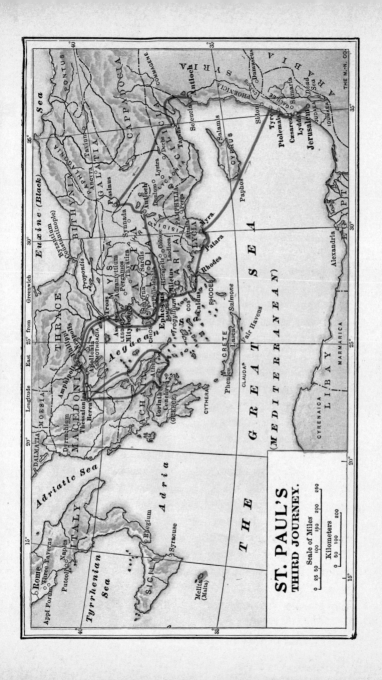

ST. PAUL'S
THIRD JOURNEY.

Scale of Miles
0 25 50   100 150 200 250

Kilometers
0   50 100   200

THE M.-N. CO.

pear that as yet they had actually entered Galatia; but it was soon proved that Paul was right in fearing that they might. That his special anxiety was already about the Galatians seems also to follow from the fact that Luke does not report him to have visited Lycaonia. He passed through Phrygia, simply because it lay on the way from Galatia to Ephesus.

210. Before he reached Ephesus, there occurred the interesting fact of the arrival of Apollos, the eloquent Alexandrian Jew, who preached Jesus though knowing only the baptism of John, and who, after having received further instruction from Aquila and Priscilla, passed on to Corinth and continued the apostle's work in that city (Acts xviii. 24-28; 1. Cor. i. 12; iii. 4-6). The incident illustrates the influence of John the Baptist even outside of Palestine, and the spread of faith in Jesus as the Messiah among some who had never come in contact with the apostles. If Apollos had learned of Jesus in Alexandria, he provides the first known evidence of the extension of the gospel into Egypt, a land where the beginnings of Christianity are quite obscure, yet where it was certainly flourishing early in the second century. The twelve disciples also, whom Paul met shortly after reaching Ephesus (Acts xix. 1-7), present a similar instance of what we may call non-apostolic Christianity. As Judaism had prepared the way for Christianity among the Gentiles, so in some measure had the mission of John and the reports about Jesus prepared the way among the Jews of the dispersion. It was not of an unknown personage that the apostles spake when they testified in the synagogues that Jesus was the Christ. Here and there actual believers in him were waiting for the full report.

211. When Paul at last reached the Asian capital, which he had long desired to occupy, he entered on an extended and vigorous campaign. The importance of Ephesus as a centre of the faith is attested not only by his long residence, but afterwards by the mission of Timothy to it, and still later by the residence in it of the apostle John. Already Aquila and Priscilla were there, and perhaps still earlier the message of Pentecost had been brought (comp. Acts ii. 9). But with Paul's settlement in the city the real history of Ephesian Christianity began. For three months he taught in the Jewish synagogue (Acts xix. 8) ; then, since the Jews disbelieved, he organized his disciples into a church, and daily taught for two years in the school of Tyrannus, doubtless a Greek lecture-hall (xix. 9, 10). Besides this, he visited from house to house among his disciples (xx. 20). If we assume that he arrived in the autumn of A. D. 54, the two years and three months would reach to the beginning of 57. At that time he proposed to leave for Macedonia, and sent Timothy and Erastus ahead of him (Acts xix. 21; comp. I. Cor. iv. 17 ; xvi. 10) ; but he himself tarried longer (Acts xix. 22) because of the great work in hand (I. Cor. xvi. 8), and other events occurred, pertaining to the church at Corinth, which detained him till the summer or early autumn of A. D. 57. His whole stay in Ephesus, therefore, amounted to three years (Acts xx. 31).

212. His Ephesian ministry was marked (a) by special thoroughness of teaching (Acts xx. 18–21, 26, 27, 31), due probably to his experience of errors among his earlier converts and to the now known plans of the Judaistic party ; (b) by extraordinary miraculous attestations (Acts xix. 11, 12; comp. II. Cor. xii. 12),

which seem to have been intended specially to offset
and overcome the power of magic and sorcery in Ephesus
(Acts xix. 13–19); (c) by varied and widespread success, for not only were representatives of the most
diverse classes, from the common people (xix. 26, 27)
to the wealthy men who had filled the position of
Asiarch (xix. 31 ; comp. *Lightfoot*, Ignatius and Polycarp, Vol. II. p. 987; *Hicks*, Expositor, 1890, p. 401),
won by him personally, but throughout the entire
province his influence extended (Acts xix. 10), while
his co-laborers carried his message to and founded
churches in neighboring cities (comp. not only Acts
xix. 22; xx. 4; Col. iv. 7, but also I. Cor. xvi. 19;
Col. i. 7; ii. 1; iv. 13)); (d) by fierce opposition
(comp. I. Cor. iv. 9–13; xv. 32; xvi. 9; II. Cor. iv.
7–10; vi. 4, 5), of which the exciting demonstration
caused by Demetrius, whose trade in the shrines of
the temple of Artemis (*Ramsay*, St. Paul the Trav.
p. 277, etc.) was endangered by the progress of Paul's
work (Acts xix. 23–41), was only one, and probably not the most serious, illustration (comp. I. Cor.
xv. 32; xvi. 9); and (e) finally by constant attention
to the difficulties existing in distant churches, the care
of which pressed upon him daily (II. Cor. xi. 28).
The details of Paul's life in Ephesus would furnish a
story of physical, intellectual, and spiritual activity
marvellous for its intensity and versatility. The incidents recorded in Acts are, however, less important
for our purpose than the light cast on apostolic history
during Paul's Ephesian ministry by the epistles to the
Galatians and the Corinthians.

213. The Epistle to the Galatians was written probably soon after Paul's arrival in Ephesus. It may be

assigned to the spring of A. D. 55. This is on the
hypothesis, for which reasons have been given (sect.
186), that it was addressed to churches in Galatia
proper, founded on the second missionary journey. It
cannot indeed be proved that the epistle was written
soon after his arrival in Ephesus, for the phrase (Gal. i.
6), " I marvel that ye are *so quickly* removing from him
that called you," may refer to hasty action rather than
to shortness of time since he had been with them, and
on any interpretation the phrase is quite vague. Still
the impression made by his passing allusions to his
second visit to Galatia (i. 9 ; iv. 13) is that it had been
recent; he implies elsewhere (II. Cor. xi. 28) that while
in Ephesus he had been pressed by anxiety about many
churches ; and the reason usually assigned for dating
the epistle later — namely, the close connection of its
thought with the Epistle to the Romans — is insufficient, since Galatians presents the doctrine of salvation
in a much less complete form than is done in Romans,
and therefore probably preceded the latter by some
time. Hence the probability that this epistle was
written early in the Ephesian ministry.

214. It was occasioned by a report from Galatia
which fired the apostle's indignation and filled him
with grievous apprehensions. The Judaizing missionaries had invaded his churches and had actually
succeeded in perverting their immature faith. They
had assailed the apostle, too, as well as his teaching.
They declared that he was no apostle, but at best a
mere scholar of the true apostles; that he vacillated in
his teaching to please men, now opposing circumcision
and now teaching it; that the Galatians should look for
instruction to the leaders of the mother church, and

that these were not in sympathy with Paul. Then, too, they taught the continued obligation of the Mosaic law as a condition of salvation for all Christians. Their mission thus struck at the very heart of the gospel as well as at the authority of Paul. That they came from Judea is rendered practically certain by the appearance of such teachers at the time of the council (Acts xv. 1), and by the appeal which these in Galatia evidently made to the names of the authorities in Jerusalem. That they misrepresented the church in Jerusalem and her leaders is proved by Paul himself (ii. 1–10). He charges them with acting from selfish motives (iv. 17) and stigmatizes their party as false brethren (ii. 4). Their mission was thus a revival of the old conflict which the council had sought to settle. They were themselves faithless to the decision of the mother church. In the name of Christ they preached Judaism. They had not yet indeed induced the Galatians to be circumcised, but they had caused a dangerous reaction. Like Jewish proselyters generally, they had begun by recommending some of the easier and more attractive features of the ritual. The Galatians were now observing " days and months and seasons and years " (iv. 10). This involved the recognition of the law as binding, and the demand for circumcision would follow, if it had not been made. Paul saw that the gospel of faith was imperilled. We can see that the whole question of a universal and non-Judaic religion was at stake. Hence this epistle, written in the white-heat of inspired indignation, became the *magna charta* of Christian universalism and liberty.

215. He first proceeds, after a brief introduction, to the vindication of his independent apostolic authority

(i. 11 to II. 21). He had received his gospel by immediate revelation from Christ (i. 11–12). Formerly he
too had been a "Judaizer" (i. 13, 14), but God had
sovereignly called him and revealed his Son in him, that
he might preach him among the Gentiles (i. 15, 16).
In the fulfilment of this commission he had not been
dependent for anything on the older apostles, and for
years had only on one brief occasion seen Peter and
James (i. 17–24). When he and Barnabas went up to
Jerusalem at the time of the council, he had declared
boldly the gospel which he preached (ii. 1, 2), and the
mother church had approved his teaching against the
Judaizers (ii. 3–5), while the leaders had given him
the right hand of fellowship (ii. 6–10). He added
the account of his discussion with Peter at Antioch
(sects. 163–165) to illustrate further his independence,
and perhaps also to prevent any misuse of Peter's conduct which the Judaizers might make (ii. 11–21).

216. Turning next to the doctrine at stake (iii., iv.),
he exclaimed at the folly of the Galatians in forgetting
the crucified Saviour who had been portrayed to them,
in whose crucifixion their whole salvation was assured
(iii. 1). Had not their experience been conditioned
upon faith alone? (iii. 2–5). And was not this, according to Scripture, the original Abrahamic way of salvation? (iii. 6). Abraham's children, therefore, to whom
the promise was made, are not those who keep the law,
but those who believe (iii. 7–9). The law, since it
requires perfect obedience as the condition of salvation,
brings only a curse upon those under it, and hence cannot be the instrument for the fulfilment of the promised
blessing (iii. 10). It was the work of Christ, as the law
itself foretold, to redeem us from it, and for this very

purpose he accepted its curse by dying in our place that we through him might receive the promise and the Spirit (iii. 11–14). To make this truth, which was the heart of the whole controversy, more clear, the apostle further pointed out that since God solemnly ratified his covenant of salvation by faith with Abraham and his seed, the law, which came later, could not disannul the original arrangement (iii. 15–18), but was intended as a temporary discipline to make sinful men realize that sin is transgression of God's commandment (iii. 19, 20). It was, therefore, a tutor to bring men to Christ (iii. 21–24); so that by believing in him who alone has fulfilled the law for us, and who is, with his people, the true seed of Abraham, we may inherit the promise in him (iii. 25–29).

217. The apostle then added three more reasons for their fidelity to his gospel (iv.). The first was an appeal, based on the analogy of Græco-Roman customs, not to go back to a state of infancy when the time for their entrance on the inheritance had come (iv. 1–11). The second was an appeal to their former affection for himself (iv. 12–20). The third was an illustration of the freedom of the true son of Abraham, drawn from the narrative in Genesis of the relation to Abraham of the sons of Sarah and Hagar (iv. 21 to v. 1). The rest of the epistle is a masterly application of the principles of the preceding chapters. Its substance is: (1) maintain your liberty (v. 2–12), yet (2) do not abuse it, but walk by the Spirit and bring forth his fruits (v. 13–25); (3) use your liberty for the spiritual good of others (v. 26 to vi. 5), and (4) remember your responsibility in its exercise (vi. 6–10). The letter ends with a postscript (vi. 11–18), in the apostle's own handwriting, in

which he summarizes the contents of the letter and dismisses all further attacks upon him as useless, since, as he said, "I bear in my body the brands [slave-marks] of Jesus."

218. It is impossible to overestimate the value of this epistle. The relation of its historical statements to the narrative of Acts has been already discussed (sects. 91–94, 116, 149–152). Its chief importance lies in its exhibition of the theological grounds on which rested the emancipation of Christianity from Judaism and its establishment as a universal religion. Chapter ii. 11–21 shows that the doctrine of the epistle was not a new one, but was the recognized basis on which Gentile Christianity stood. The centre of that doctrine was the death of Christ, the significance of which it was especially Paul's privilege to make clear. Knowing that the divine law requires of every man righteousness through perfect obedience, that no man can obtain such righteousness through his own works, and that the penalty of sin is death; considering the perfect life of Jesus, and assured at Damascus of his Messiahship, — Paul was led to realize that the death of Messiah was the divinely provided satisfaction of the law for his people. At once its mysteriousness and offensiveness was removed. It became God's crown-ing act of grace. It explained why faith, whereby the work of Christ was appropriated, had been made from the beginning the only condition of salvation. With this, of course, the obligation to observe the law in order to salvation passed away. Evidently, too, since the Scriptures had ever promised salvation through Christ and by faith, the law had never been intended to be the way of salvation at all. The Jews

had misunderstood its object. It had only been intended to prepare for Christ by awakening the sense of guilt. Its great moral principles, indeed, would ever remain as a guide to the interpretation of God's character and will; but its ceremonial ordinances had no further function. To regard them as necessary was in fact to fall away from the gospel. To bind them on the believer was to imply that Christ had died in vain. Thus Christianity was at once delegalized and denationalized. The blessing of Abraham, through the work of Christ in dying for sinners, had come to the Gentiles, and faith alone was the condition of salvation for all alike. Of this transition the Epistle to the Galatians is the abiding monument. We may believe that it had its intended effect on the Galatians themselves. The apostle anticipated that it would (v. 10), and later allusions to the " churches of Galatia " (I. Cor. xvi. 1; I. Pet. i. 1, and perhaps II. Tim. iv. 10), even if those addressed in the epistle may not be exclusively intended, seem to imply that the threatened defection was averted.

219. If the earlier part of Paul's residence in Ephesus was made anxious by the Galatian churches the latter part was disturbed by affairs in Corinth. The First Epistle to the Corinthians was written probably in the spring of A. D. 57. Chapter xvi. 8, and possibly v. 7, 8, imply that the spring was approaching, and xvi. 5 apparently refers to Paul's purpose to pass through Macedonia to Achaia mentioned in Acts xix. 21, 22, which was toward the close of his sojourn in Ephesus, and therefore in A. D. 57. He had, however, previously written a letter (v. 9), which has not been preserved, in which he gave instructions concerning

the attitude of the disciples to those about them who
led impure lives. This was a practical matter in Corinth, where the Christians were surrounded by a society
in which the principles of morality were constantly
violated. His direction "not to keep company with
fornicators" required subsequent explanation (v. 9–11);
but it illustrates the sort of difficulties by which the
Corinthians were confronted. We learn further that
Timothy had been sent to Corinth (iv. 17 ; xvi. 10).
If this was the mission mentioned in Acts xix. 21, he
was to go by way of Macedonia, and the hesitating
language of I. Cor. xvi. 10, — "*If* Timothy come," —
implies that Corinth was not the sole object of his
journey, and that he possibly might not reach it.
Hence we may suppose that he was sent early in 57 to
Macedonia, ahead of the apostle, with directions to go
on to Corinth, if he deemed it best to do so. Paul
expected him to reach Corinth, and directed the
church to follow his instructions (iv. 17). After
Timothy had gone, messengers arrived from Corinth
with alarming reports (i. 11). There was worse trouble
than association with impure pagans. Factions had
arisen in the church which threatened discord, if not
division. Then, too, we learn that a delegation from
Corinth had visited the apostle (xvi. 17). It seems to
have brought a letter inquiring how the church should
act in view of certain perplexing social difficulties
(vii. 1). Besides all this, other perils, practical and
doctrinal, were reported. There were abuses in public
worship, extravagant pride in the more emotional and
less useful gifts of the Spirit, errors about the resurrection, and, worst of all, actual immorality in the church.
The nascent Christianity of Corinth was evidently in a

critical condition, and to meet the emergency this epis-tle was written. It was doubtless carried to Corinth by the returning delegation.

220. In it he takes up in order the subjects on which the Corinthians needed instruction; and the epistle is not only a masterly example of the apostle's firmness and tact, but an instructive description of the actual situation of these early Christians. He first reproved them for the factious spirit of which he had heard (i. 10 to iv. 21). Paul himself, Apollos, Peter, and even Christ had become party names. Actual division of the church had not resulted, but it easily might; and the situation implied a total misunderstanding of the relation of their teachers to Christ. The Peter-faction naturally implies the presence of a Jewish Christian element, though not necessarily of Judaizers. It does not imply that Peter had been at Corinth. Acquaint-ance with the part he had played in the founding of the church is sufficient to explain the partisanship of those who called themselves after him. The Christ-faction is more of an enigma. Many, on the ground of II. Corinthians x. 7 and xi. 22, suppose that it was the party of the Judaizers; but a more careful examination of II. Corinthians fails to show that an allusion is there intended to any of these factions. Perhaps the best explanation of the Christ-faction is that some were disposed to reject all apostolic authority and, in opposi-tion to the other factions, to profess allegiance to Christ alone.

221. The apostle, however, merely mentions these two, and deals at length with the Paul and Apollos factions. Apollos had probably preached more elo-quently and philosophically than Paul; and, though

faithful to the gospel (iii. 8), had aroused the speculative spirit of the Greeks as well as admiration for himself. There was danger of their forgetting the simple message of the Cross. We thus for the first time see Christianity facing Hellenism and tempted by the pride of philosophical achievement. This gives peculiar interest to the apostle's treatment. He reminded them that the Cross was and ever would be foolishness to the Greek, as it was an offence to the Jew; and that it assumed the total failure of human wisdom to solve the problem of man's salvation (i. 18–31). Hence he had preached to them Christ crucified, without rhetorical ornament, relying only on the demonstration of the Spirit (ii. 1–5). This, indeed, was not because the gospel is itself foolishness. On the contrary, it is the profoundest wisdom; but a wisdom divinely revealed to chosen men (ii. 6–16). He and Apollos were, therefore, co-laborers under God. He had laid the only possible foundation, and Apollos had builded on it; but the work was God's (iii.). Let not their ministers be made the heads of factions (iv. 1–5). Neither let any despise him and his scriptural teaching (iv. 6); for, though persecuted and hated, he was an apostle of God (iv. 7–13). He was also their spiritual father, whose warnings they should heed, lest he be forced to chastise them (iv. 14–21).

222. This important passage shows that to Paul the gospel was as distinct from Hellenism as it was from Judaism. It was a direct revelation of salvation by grace through a Redeemer. Yet both Judaism and philosophy had negatively prepared for it: the former, by producing through the law the sense of guilt and of **the need of righteousness;** the latter, by demonstrat-

ing the inability of man to solve the problem of salvation for himself. Christianity, moreover, provided the blessings which Judaism and philosophy had respectively sought, namely, righteousness before God and the knowledge of God. It was, according to Paul, the goal of both, though both rejected it. It is thus evident that he realized the relation of his message to its entire environment. He was neither dependent on the influences about him nor blind to their existence and significance. To the Jew he offered in the gospel righteousness, and to the Greek the true wisdom. He did the latter, however, not like Philo, by interpreting revelation in the interest of philosophy, but by stoutly maintaining the failure of philosophy to solve the problem of salvation, and by presenting revelation in and by Christ as the gate of knowledge.

223. The rest of this epistle is mainly occupied with the practical difficulties in which the Corinthians were vitally concerned. With great indignation the apostle rebuked them for failure to discipline a man who had been actually guilty of an incestuous marriage (v.). There was, in fact, too little regard for church discipline among them (vi. 1–8) ; and sins of impurity in particular should never be regarded with indifference (vi. 9–20). He then discussed two subjects about which they had asked instruction (vii. 1 to xi. 1). The first was marriage and divorce (vii.). In this it is most important to note that he commands fidelity to marital obligations (3–5) ; forbids, on the ground of Christ's command, any seeking after divorce (10, 11) ; directs that a marriage already formed between a believer and an unbeliever should not be broken, but admits that, if the unbeliever break it by desertion, the believer is released from the bond

(12–16). While frankly avowing his preference for the unmarried state " by reason of the present distress " (26), he upholds the sanctity of marriage and its place in Christian life. The other question concerned eating food which had been offered to idols (viii. 1 to xi. 1). It was a difficult question; for the food bought in the markets was consecrated to idols, and in any social gathering the guests were liable to be called on to eat or drink in honor of a god. The apostle's directions are bold and tactful. He lays down the principle that, since the idol is nothing, the food was as good as any, and might be eaten freely; but, if the use of it at certain times and places would be understood to be a recognition of the idol, it should then be avoided, out of love to brethren who might be made to stumble and from a desire to honor Christ (viii.). This, he says, was the principle on which in all things he had acted (ix.). They should be careful also not to be, like Israel of old, led away by their pagan surroundings; and, with specific reference to the matter in hand, they should remember that they belonged to Christ alone, that all lawful things are not always expedient, and that they should seek the good of others. Hence, ordinarily they might eat without question ; but if, in a mixed assembly, the food was eaten in honor of an idol, they should abstain, that none might be made to stumble (x. 15 to xi. 1).

224. He next corrected abuses which existed in public worship (xi. 2 to xiv. 40). These reveal most instructively the immaturity of Christian life among the Corinthians and their tendency to sensuous excitement. Women sometimes were inspired to prophesy in public. Paul directs that they should do so with

covered heads (xi. 2–16). Ordinarily no woman should
teach in public (xiv. 34; I. Tim. ii. 12); but if the
Spirit made an exception, modesty and feminine subjection must not be laid aside. Again, the love feasts,
closing with the Lord's Supper, had become occasions
for actual revelry. Paul insists that they must be
observed reverently, as a religious act, in obedience
to the purpose of Christ in the institution of the Supper
(xi. 17–34). Then, at great length, he deals with the
exercise of "spiritual gifts" (xii. to xiv.). These
existed in abundance. The Spirit of Jesus had wrought
mightily among them. But grave abuses had arisen.
Spiritual pride was being manifested. Emotional and
showy gifts were valued more highly than instructive
and helpful ones. We should remember that an age
of miracles is not necessarily an ethically ideal age,
but that the same temptations operate in it as at other
times. Paul's instructions show his clear insight into
the relation between the miraculous and the ethical.
He first acknowledges the necessity of the operation of
the Spirit for Christian life. He then enlarges upon
the variety of the Spirit's operations which secures the
full development and real unity of the body of Christ.
Of all the gifts of the Spirit he gives the pre-eminence
to love, thus placing the ethical work of the Spirit far
above his miraculous effects. In regard to the latter,
moreover, those gifts should be valued most which,
like prophecy, edify the church. The gift of "tongues"
in particular should be exercised with restraint. It
was the emotional utterance, in unintelligible sounds,
of the soaring thoughts of the soul; the outcries of
a mind rapt in praise or prayer (comp. sects. 33, 34).
It was adapted to private devotion, and should not be

indulged in public unless one having the gift of "interpretation" were present. It is evident that the ordinary worship of these early Christians did not follow a prescribed order, but that the Spirit moved different persons to take part according to his gifts. But Paul points out that the purpose of the Spirit should be kept rigidly in view; for his manifestations did not carry the assembly away, but were subject to the control of the recipients. Didactic and moral results were the Spirit's object. Edification of the church should therefore be the guiding motive in their public exercises. There can be no better proof than these instructions that, although early Christian life with its supernatural features was liable to the excesses by which belief in miraculous powers is always tempted, the apostle himself accurately distinguished the ethical and didactic from its miraculous accompaniments, and thus brought out those elements of Christian life which were to be permanent and universal.

225. Finally, the one doctrinal subject by which some in Corinth were disturbed is taken up, namely, the resurrection (xv.). Doubts on this point probably arose from philosophical influences. They do not appear to have been widespread (xv. 12); so their refutation is reserved for the end of the letter. Yet they touched a fundamental truth, and were likely to arise again as Christianity made its way in the face of Hellenism. So Paul reminds his readers that the resurrection of Christ was a fundamental fact of the gospel, rehearses the apostolic evidence for it (1–11), and argues that, as without Christ's resurrection their whole faith was vain, so did it involve the future resurrection of believers (12–19). The latter will take

place at the second advent, and will be part of Christ's completed victory over death (20–28). He begs them to remember the fundamental character of this belief (29–34); and, in reply to the speculative inquiry, " how are the dead raised," illustrates its possibility by the way in which God gives a new body to the seed cast into the soil; explains that objections based on our knowledge of the present natural body do not hold good of the future spiritual body; affirms the identity of the two, yet the vast differences between them, since, though both are material, the one is the organ of the present natural life and the other will be the perfect organ of the glorified spirit; and closes with a magnificent exposition of the resurrection as the completion of redemption (35–58). It is to be observed that this teaching is a further and consistent explication of the subject of the second advent previously taught to the Thessalonians.

226. The epistle closes with directions about certain gifts from his Gentile churches which he was collecting for the brethren in Judea and with items of personal news (xvi.). These gifts were a matter about which he was much concerned. They were his practical answer to the charges of disloyalty to his nation and of hostility to the mother church. Hence he directs the Corinthians to prepare their contribution.

227. The despatch of this long and careful epistle did not end the apostle's anxiety about the church at Corinth. In fact the closing months of his stay in Ephesus were full of distress on their account. The facts can only be gleaned from II. Corinthians, written after he had left Ephesus. From this it appears that he made a brief visit to Corinth in much distress, to

which he afterwards looked back with deep sorrow (II. Cor. ii. 1; xii. 14; xiii. 1, 2). This must have been after sending our I. Corinthians, since it contains no reference to the visit. It is a probable supposition that he had heard, perhaps through Timothy, that the church refused to exercise discipline upon the incestuous person, and that therefore he himself hastened to Corinth, and with much sorrow, and apparently in the face of opposition (II. Cor. xii. 21), pronounced the sentence. It would seem that he then returned to Ephesus, but only to be further distressed by the report that his discipline had not secured the peace of the church. In fact, the condition of affairs grew worse. Judaistic emissaries, bitterly hostile to Paul, had gone to Corinth (II. Cor. iii. 1; xi.; xiii.); and there was one member of the church who openly defied his authority (II. Cor. ii. 5, 10; vii. 11, 12). It is most probable that this offender was the same incestuous person, and that he had rebelled, after Paul's judgment upon him, against the apostle himself. We infer also that the Judaistic emissaries had supported his rebellion. Thus there was now a distinct antipauline party in Corinth. It is easy to imagine the apostle's distress. We judge it to be this to which he refers (II. Cor. i. 8–14) as so intense that he almost despaired of life. This language will not appear too strong if we remember that his character was assailed (II. Cor. i. 17; x 2, 10), that his converts were being turned against him (II. Cor. vii. 2, 7), and that his work might be undone (xi. 3, 13, 14). Under these circumstances he sent his trusted friend Titus, with an unnamed brother, to Corinth with sharp directions to act at once in the further discipline of the offender

and in securing the peace and loyalty of the church
(II. Cor. ii. 13; vii. 6, 7, 13–15; xi. 18). It is also
probable that Titus carried a brief, stern letter from
the apostle, written with many tears, commanding
obedience to his behests. The existence of this second
lost letter is to be inferred from II. Corinthians ii. 3, 4,
9; vii. 8, which can hardly refer to our I. Corinthians.
In this letter Paul explained that he did not go himself
to Corinth, because he did not wish to visit them again
in grief. He seems also to have stated that it had
been his purpose to go directly to them and thence to
Macedonia (II. Cor. i. 16), instead of the opposite as
originally intended (I. Cor. xvi. 5), but that he could
not bear to see them under the circumstances. So
Titus departed on this difficult mission. He was to
meet Paul, with his report, at Troas; for the apostle
intended soon to leave Ephesus. But when, in the
early fall of A. D. 57, Paul reached Troas, Titus was
not there, and the apostle's distress was intensified
(II. Cor. ii. 12, 13). It is a very pathetic picture of
the great missionary which these facts furnish. His
Ephesian ministry, successful though it was, closed
under this heavy cloud. The cloud, however, was
destined soon to lift and his bitter experience to be a
cause of thanksgiving, because of the spiritual good
which finally came to him and to all out of the trial
(II. Cor. i. 1–7; ii. 14–17; vii. 9–16).

FROM EPHESUS TO ROME

228. Not having found Titus at Troas, Paul passed over to Macedonia, doubtless to Philippi (Acts xx. 1; II. Cor. ii. 13). Yet his distress of mind did not cease. As he himself puts it, " Without were fightings, within were fears " (II. Cor. vii. 5). At last comfort was restored by the arrival of Titus and the report which he brought. The Corinthians had obeyed their apostle and disciplined the offender; and the man himself was now filled with sorrow for his sin (II. Cor. ii. 5–11). The majority, too, had with deep repentance vindicated themselves from apparent complicity in his sin and assured the apostle of their loyalty (II. Cor. vii. 9–12). Thus the main cause of Paul's distress was removed. Yet there was still a disaffected minority, and the work of the Judaizers had not ceased.

229. In these circumstances our II. Corinthians was written in the early autumn of A. D. 57. It, too, was intrusted to Titus, who was sent back to Corinth with two others, one of whom had been appointed by the Macedonian churches to be their representative in bearing their gifts to Jerusalem (II. Cor. viii. 18–22). The main duty of Titus was now to complete the gifts of the Corinthians which Paul proposed, after visiting Corinth, to carry to Judea. He took the opportunity in this letter of pouring out the feelings of his lately

distraught but now comforted mind to his dear disciples. It was written with unusual emotion. It reflects the agony through which he had been passing. It is an unequalled revelation of the personality of the apostle. In it he relates his religious experience, describes his actions and his motives, justifies his authority, pours out his love, reviews his life, rebukes and pleads, chastises his traducers and cheers his friends; and all with a rush of language and sudden transitions of thought which betray the highly wrought condition of his mind. No other of his letters is so autobiographical. In none are we permitted to approach so near to the personal life of the apostle.

230. The epistle is divided into three well-marked sections. The first (i. to vii.) deals with the distress through which he had been passing on their account, and then gives a glowing, yet pathetic, description of the character of his ministry. It is an outpouring of his soul, a laying bare of his very heart to his beloved children, in which it is easy to see his sensitiveness to the attacks which had been made upon him and his joy in the restored fidelity of his converts. The second section (viii., ix.) urges to liberality in their gifts for the Judean saints, and directs them to receive Titus and other brethren who were about to visit them in this interest. The third section (x. to xiii.) is an indignant defence of his apostleship, evidently directed against the Judaizers, to whom a passing allusion had already been made (iii.) and to a minority in Corinth who sided with them. It is written in the apostle's most vehement style, and contains not a few references to events in his history otherwise unknown (xi. 23 to xiii. 2).

231. After Titus, with the other brethren, had re-

turned to Corinth, Paul appears to have further visited, during the autumn of A. D. 57, the churches of Macedonia (Acts xx. 2). He went as far as the boundary of Illyricum (Rom. xv. 19). Finally he reached Corinth, where he abode three months (Acts xx. 3). No incidents of this winter in Corinth have been preserved. We may believe, however, that he finally adjusted the remaining difficulties in that church, and we know that he received its contributions for the Judean saints (Rom. xv. 25-28). With him was a considerable company of friends (Acts xx. 4; Rom. xvi. 21-23). Some of them were to accompany him to Jerusalem as representatives of the contributing churches, for he was unwilling to have the money in his sole charge (II. Cor. viii. 20).

232. It was, however, during this winter at Corinth that Paul wrote the Epistle to the Romans, and this important letter throws additional light on the entire situation. We suddenly find from it that Christianity was being preached vigorously in the world's capital. Its beginnings there are shrouded in obscurity. It is possible that some of the " sojourners from Rome " (Acts ii. 10, R. V.) carried it back after Pentecost. It is possible that some of those who fled from Jerusalem after the death of Stephen travelled as far as Italy (Acts viii. 4). We have already alluded to the interpretation put by some on the decree of Claudius as implying that Christianity had caused contentions in the Jewish colony by the Tiber (see sect. 197). But this epistle throws the first clear light upon the subject. From it we learn that the progress of the new religion in Rome was already widely known among the churches (i. 8, 13; xvi. 19). It must then have existed for several

years. The Roman Christians, moreover, possessed the gifts of the Spirit and some organization (xii. 7, 8). Yet the epistle is not addressed to " the church at Rome," but " to all who are in Rome, beloved of God," a phraseology which suggests that their organization was not compact or unified. This inference is, perhaps, confirmed by the allusion to several groups of believers in the capital (xvi. 3–5, 14, 15; yet comp. I. Cor. xvi. 19). The impression given, however, is that of a large but imperfectly organized community. They are addressed as Gentiles (i. 6, 13; xi. 13, 30; xv. 8–13, 15, 16), and as trained in Pauline teaching (ii. 16; vi. 17; xiv. 1–14); yet evidently they included also not a few Jews (ii. 17 to iii. 20; xiv. 1; xv. 10, xvi. 3, 7, 11). The closing salutations are especially instructive (comp. *Lightfoot*, Philippians, p. 171), and show that Paul had many friends in Rome. Some of them had worked with him elsewhere (xvi. 3, 5–7, 13). They had evidently gone to the capital from Pauline churches. We are not to suppose, indeed, that his friends were the only missionaries on the ground; but the epistle shows that his mission to Europe had already embraced indirectly the metropolis of the world. So far as our information goes, these friends of Paul were the founders of Roman Christianity. With this accords the contemptuous and evasive allusion to the Christians by the elders of the Jewish colony, when Paul afterwards addressed them (Acts xxviii, 22).

233. It is not surprising, therefore, that Paul wrote to the Christians of Rome. But his doing so when and as he did is highly significant. He had long wished to preach in Rome (Acts xix. 21; II. Cor. xi. 16; Rom. i. 9, 10, 13; xv. 23, 24, 28), and to go from thence to

Spain (Rom. xv. 28), but had been prevented. Now he
was about to return to Jerusalem, and knew not what
might befall him (Rom. xv. 30, 31; Acts xx. 22, 23).
He naturally wished to send a message to his friends
in the capital, and to explain that in returning eastward
he was not relinquishing his purpose to visit them.
But why did he write so elaborate a letter? It is not,
except incidentally (*e.g.* i. 5; xv. 17–21), a defence of
himself and his apostleship. Neither is it, except again
incidentally (*e. g.* ii. 17, etc.), or from the very nature
of the argument, a polemic against either Jews or
Judaizers, or followers of his own school who had fallen
into error. Still less is its motive the conciliation of
different parties. Its purpose is chiefly didactic. It
is an elaborate presentation of the way of salvation,
argued with superb dialectical completeness. Why,
then, did he send this statement to Rome? The probable answer is very instructive. He evidently realized
the future importance of the church at Rome. He had
long believed that Christianity would become the religion of the empire; and he knew that, as his plan of
evangelizing the great cities must culminate in the
evangelization of the capital, so the Christianity of the
capital would be likely to determine that of the world.
In this he reveals the statesman as well as the missionary. He knew further that his gospel would continue to be attacked and that his Judaizing antagonists
were following westward in his tracks. Already they
had invaded Corinth. The controversy with them
also had brought to full expression the true gospel;
and Paul's own mind, which ever sought completeness
of truth, impelled him to a formal statement of it
The Epistle to the Romans therefore illuminates the

whole situation, and illustrates the broad intelligence with which Paul laid the foundations of Christianity in the empire.

234. Hence in this epistle the conception of Christianity as a scheme of salvation is elaborately wrought out. The apostle characteristically presents it as the revelation of a righteousness provided by God for the believer (i. 16, 17). He proves at length the universal want of such a righteousness, by the Jew as well as by the Gentile (i. 18 to iii. 20). He then describes the righteousness revealed in the gospel as provided by Christ's redeeming death, through which God has made it possible for him, the righteous one, to declare the believer free from guilt (iii. 21-26). This way of salvation is then shown to have been that whereby Abraham, the father of Israel, was saved (iii. 27 to iv. 24); to be implied in the Christian's experience of salvation by the mere grace of God (v. 1-11); and to proceed on the same principle of moral government on which God had dealt with the race in the person of its first representative, Adam (v. 12-21). The objections to this doctrine which would be inevitably raised are next acutely discussed (vi., vii.), and the scheme is shown to make provision for the sanctification of the believer as well as for his justification, and for the glorification of both his body and his soul (viii.).

235. Yet the apostle was not content to present a mere scheme of doctrine. He fully realized the difficulty offered by the fact that Israel denied and rejected what he declared to be the teaching of her own Scriptures. It was necessary for personal, historical, and dogmatic reasons that he should reconcile this fact with his argument. He did this in chapters

ix. to xi. He maintained that God's purpose had always referred to a sovereignly chosen portion of the Hebrew nation, which election He had the right to make (ix.) ; that the rejection of Israel as a nation and salvation by faith has been explicitly announced by the prophets (x.) ; yet that the rejection was not final, but that eventually the Hebrews would obtain the fulfilment of all the promises (xi.). Thus the scheme of salvation, revealed in Christianity, was adjusted to the historical situation.

236. This epistle, then, is the monument of Pauline teaching concerning the way of salvation. All its doctrinal presuppositions are Hebrew. Its conception of God as the sovereign, holy, and omnipotent governor of the universe; of righteousness as his attribute and his requirement; of salvation through an imputed righteousness based on redemption ; and of the relation of the race to Adam, are of Hebrew origin. The absence of Hellenic influence is sufficiently proved by its teaching the participation of the body in the benefits of redemption. The only indication of non-Hebraic ideas may be found in the doctrine of adoption (viii. 15 ; Gal. iv. 5), which may have been suggested by Roman customs. The teaching of this epistle is therefore the direct unfolding of the ideas with which Paul began his Christian life. Yet it is not the product of a doctrinaire. It keeps close to life. It does not forget that truth is in order to holiness. To it, imputed righteousness is the basis for personal growth in sanctification. Legal union with Christ involves a vital union and the devotion of the heart and will to God. If the Epistle to the Galatians is the *magna charta* of universal Christianity, the Epistle to the

Romans is its constitution. Here the missionary and theologian gives his completest interpretation of the work of Jesus for the salvation of all who will believe.

237. From Corinth Paul and his companions set forth for Jerusalem in the spring of A. D. 58. It was at first his plan to go directly by sea to Syria, but a plot of the Jews led to a change of route (Acts xx. 3). At Philippi Luke joined the party (xx. 4–6), and he describes the journey with great minuteness (xx. 7 to xxi. 16). It followed the coast of Asia, thence crossed to Tyre, thence to Ptolemais, and so to Cæsarea. Paul was anxious to reach Jerusalem by Pentecost (xx. 16), doubtless because that was the feast at which freewill offerings were made by the Jews. Hence he did not visit Ephesus, but met the elders of that church at Miletus, where he took an affectionate farewell of them (xx. 17–38). At Tyre the disciples besought him not to endanger his life at Jerusalem, for the Spirit warned them of the peril he was facing (xxi. 4); but he resolutely went forward. Again at Cæsarea, where they lodged in the house of Philip, the prophet Agabus predicted that bonds awaited him ; but, when he resisted all efforts to dissuade him, some of the disciples accompanied him to Jerusalem and took him to the house of Mnason, a Cypriote, with whom he could lodge in safety (xxi. 9–16). Thus, fully aware of the dangers which confronted him, the apostle bore to the mother church the gifts of the Gentile Christians.

238. He was received cordially by James and the elders ; but they were anxious about his reception by the church, because of the reports that in his foreign work he had taught Jews to forsake Moses. They

proposed that he show publicly his respect for the law by joining in the rites of purification about to be undergone by four brethren who had taken a vow, and by defraying their expenses. To this he consented ; but the act of conciliation resulted in the very trouble it was intended to prevent. Certain Jews from Asia saw him in the temple, and circulated a false story that he had brought Gentiles into the sacred place. A fierce riot followed, which would have resulted in Paul's death had not the captain of the Roman guard in the adjacent castle of Antonia intervened. He supposed Paul to be an Egyptian Jew who had previously made a sedition and escaped (*Jos.*, Antiq. xx. 8. 6). Discovering his mistake, he allowed the apostle to address the people from the castle steps. They listened to him till he uttered the word " Gentiles," when the riot broke out afresh, and Lycias, the captain, hurried him into the castle. He was only prevented from examining his prisoner by scourging through the latter's revealing his Roman citizenship (Acts xxi. 17 to xxii. 29).

239. On the next day Lycias took him before the Sanhedrim, that the Jewish court might adjudicate his case (xxii. 30). It was a perilous position for the apostle, and we can hardly blame him for resorting to a strategy. He declared himself a Pharisee and that he was accused for teaching the resurrection (xxiii. 1–6). This was certainly only a half-truth. Probably in less excited times it would not have helped him. But in this case it served his purpose, for the council divided and broke up in confusion (xxiii. 7–10). We should remember too, in further explanation of the result, that many of the Pharisees were not unfriendly to the Christians. The course of events was thus to

Paul's advantage ; and that night he was further encouraged by a vision in which the Lord assured him
that he should see Rome (xxiii. 11).

240. The discovery of a plot of certain Jews to slay
the prisoner, led Lycias at once to transfer him to
Felix, the procurator, at Cæsarea (xxiii. 12–30). The
apostle was now safe from violence in the hands of the
Roman authorities (xxiii. 31–35) ; but his first trial
before the procurator was unsatisfactory. To the
accusation of the Jews that he was guilty of sedition
and of defiling the temple (xxiv. 1–9), he replied with
a demand for witnesses to prove the charge (10–21).
Felix, who knew something of the Christians (22), put
his decision off, and for two years the apostle remained
a prisoner in Cæsarea. The procurator, in fact, was hop-
ing for a bribe (26) ; so he delayed the case until his
recall to Rome left it for the disposition of his successor (27).

241. It would be interesting to know how the
apostle was occupied during his Cæsarean imprisonment. His friends were allowed to see him, and Felix,
with his wife Drusilla, listened occasionally to his message (xxiv. 23–25). In fact the apostle seems to have
been treated with marked consideration. He was evidently regarded as a person of importance. Professor
Ramsay, in view of Paul's whole conduct at this period,
in view also of Felix's hope of a bribe and the expense
involved in the subsequent appeal to Cæsar, as well as
in view of the fact that Paul lived in Rome in his own
hired house, draws the inference that in some way the
apostle had come into the possession of considerable
property (St. Paul the Trav. p. 310). This is not inconsistent with his earlier support of himself bv manual

labor (I. Thess. ii. 9; Acts xviii. 3; xx. 34), nor with his acceptance, both at former and later times, of gifts from friends (Phil. iv. 15, 18). The treatment he received, however, may have been due to the high standing of his family (sect. 66). But these two years could hardly have been spent in idleness, though the confinement must have been an irksome restraint on the tireless energy of the prisoner. We cannot, indeed, accept the view that any of his extant epistles were written in Cæsarea (sect. 250). Yet he may have kept in communication with his churches, and he may have prepared himself by reflection and study for the work of the future, to which he still eagerly looked forward. None can tell how much the world owes to the enforced solitudes of its great leaders. It may be that his Cæsarean confinement gave opportunity to the apostle of working out the ideas concerning the person of Christ and the eternal and world-wide purpose of God which his later epistles contain.

242. The new procurator, Porcius Festus, was at once besought by the Jews to order Paul to Jerusalem for trial (Acts xxv. 1-3). Festus, however, bade them send their representatives to Cæsarea (4, 5), and when they came they were unable to substantiate their charges (6-8). Nevertheless Festus asked Paul if he was willing to go to Jerusalem. Thereupon the apostle, realizing the hopelessness of justice in Palestine, made a formal appeal as a Roman citizen to Cæsar (9-12). He was accordingly remanded to prison till there should be an opportunity of sending him to Italy.

243. Shortly after this, Agrippa II. and his sister Bernice came to congratulate Festus on his entrance

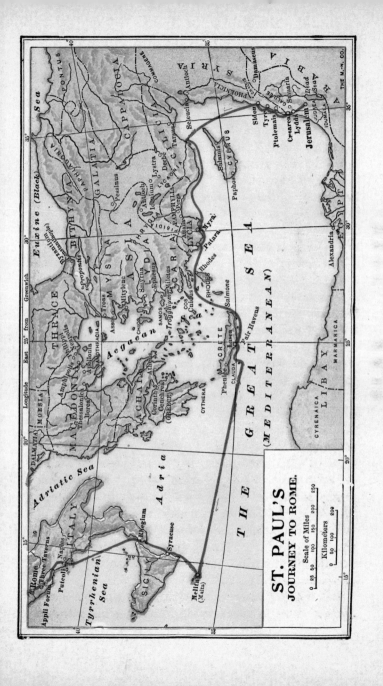

ST. PAUL'S
JOURNEY TO ROME.

Scale of Miles

0 25 50   100   150   200   250

Kilometers

0   50   100   200

THE M₋N. CO.

into office (xxv. 13). Partly out of compliment to Agrippa, as the titular king of the Jews, and partly to learn what account of Paul he should forward to Rome, Festus proposed that together they should hear the prisoner's defence (14–22). Hence on the next day the apostle delivered before this distinguished audience his most famous apology (xxv. 23 to xxvi. 32). He declared his loyalty to Israel's historic hope; related the story of his conversion and mission to the Gentiles; and finally appealed to Agrippa to hear Him of whom the prophets had spoken. When the assembly broke up, Agrippa expressed the opinion that the prisoner might be released, if he had not appealed to Cæsar. Such an appeal, when once made, had to be carried out. But evidently Festus had no charges of impor- tance to send to the emperor, and Paul's ultimate lib- eration, after reaching Italy, became practically assured.

244. In the early autumn (A. D. 60) the apostle was sent to Rome with other prisoners, under the escort of Julius, a centurion of the Augustan cohort (comp. *Schürer*, HJP. I. ii. p. 53; *Ramsay*, St. Paul the Trav. p. 314, etc.). Luke and Aristarchus of Thessalonica accompanied him. Professor Ramsay (St. Paul the Trav. p. 316) proposes the interesting conjecture that they secured passage as his slaves. Be that as it may. Luke has narrated the journey (Acts xxvii. 1 to xxviii. 16) with a minuteness and picturesqueness which could only have come from an eye-witness (see *James Smith*, Voyage and Shipwreck of St. Paul; *Ramsay*, St. Paul the Trav.). It is sufficient to say that the party sailed from Cæsarea to Myra in Lycia. There they boarded an Alexandrine merchantman, perhaps a corn ship, bound for Italy. The voyage ended, after a fearful

storm, in utter shipwreck on the island of Melita
(Malta), which lies about sixty miles south of Sicily.
During the voyage Paul was kindly treated, and even
exerted marked influence on both the centurion and the
crew. At Melita, too, he won by act and word the regard of the islanders. In the spring (A.D. 61) the
party was placed on another Alexandrian ship, which
had wintered at the island, and finally landed at Pu-
teoli, a seaport of southwestern Italy. There Paul
found Christian brethren, a fact which reveals the
spread of the faith throughout Italy even at this early
period. A delay of seven days made it possible for
news of his arrival to reach Rome; so that at "the
market of Appius" (forty-three miles from the capital), and again at "the Three Taverns" (ten miles
farther on), delegations from the Roman Christians
met him.

245. On arriving at the capital the prisoner was
granted the privilege of lodging by himself with the
soldier who guarded him (Acts xxviii. 16). Afterwards he was allowed to hire a dwelling, in which,
though still in chains (Eph. vi. 20 ; Phil. i. 13), he
lived during the following two years in which his trial
was pending (Acts xxviii. 30, 31). A tradition, preserved in the authorized version of the English Bible
(Acts xxviii. 16), states that the centurion delivered
the prisoners to the captain of the guard. This has
been generally supposed to refer to the prefect of the
pretorian guard, who may have been the celebrated
Burrus (*Lightfoot*, Philippians, p. 7). The revised version, however, with the best manuscripts, omits this
statement. Yet the tradition may be itself correct.
Professor Ramsay (St. Paul the Trav. p. 348) believes

that Paul was turned over to the chief of a corps called *legiones frumentarii,* whose task was mainly the superintendence of the grain supply, but who also performed police duty. To this corps Julius is supposed to have belonged. But it is not at all clear that such a corps existed so early (comp. *Hastings,* Dict. of Bible, art. Prætorium), and the best interpretation of Philippians i. 13 is that Paul was under the charge of the pretorians. Thus the apostle found himself at last in the great city on which his thoughts had long been fixed, " an ambassador in bonds."

VI

PAUL IN ROME

246. The mildness of his imprisonment enabled Paul to pursue in Rome his work as an apostle; and the two years of his life in the capital were, in fact, a period of constant and far-reaching activity.

He first summoned the chiefs of the Jewish colony to explain to them how he came to be there on an appeal to Cæsar against his own nation (Acts xxviii. 17-20). They replied that they had received no letters about him, though they added that the sect of Christians was everywhere spoken against. It is not surprising that the Jews of Jerusalem had sent no advices to those in Rome, since Paul's appeal had only been made the previous summer, and also because the favorable attitude to him of the Roman officials probably made his enemies despair of securing his conviction. The way in which the Jews referred to the Christians is surprising. They certainly knew more than their language implied. Their words, indeed, are hardly consistent with the view that a Jewish Christian church had been long formed in Rome, and that conflict between it and the synagogue had led Claudius to expel the Jews (sect. 198). They accord better with the view that the Roman church was from the beginning mainly Gentile (sect. 231). At the same time the language was evasive. They were unwilling to say all that they knew.

Nevertheless, they and others accepted Paul's invitation to hear his message (xxviii. 23). He wished, as on other occasions, to offer the gospel first to the chosen race. But the result was again disappointing. Most of them disbelieved; and forthwith the apostle bent his efforts upon preaching to all, Gentile or Jew, who could be brought to his dwelling or under his influence.

247. For the remaining facts of the Roman ministry of the apostle, we are dependent on the few items furnished by his epistles. Acts relates only his continued and unhindered activity during two years (xxviii. 30, 31). The purpose of that book was attained when it had described the rise of Gentile Christianity and brought its leader to the capital of the world. We must therefore turn to the epistles. From them we learn of the zeal and success of the " ambassador in bonds " (Col. iv. 3, 4; Eph. vi. 19, 20; Philem. 10). His success increased with time. He succeeded in winning to the faith many of his military guards (Phil. i. 12–14, R.V.). His influence also permeated the large imperial household itself (Phil. iv. 22), even as the retinue of other noble households had previously been reached (Rom. xvi. 10, 11). Onesimus, the runaway slave, illustrates another class of people of which doubtless he reached not a few. Yet there is reason to believe that the faith penetrated at this period in Rome not only among the lower classes, but also here and there into the upper strata of society, while still larger numbers of the middle class were affected by it (comp. *Jas. Orr*, Neglected Factors in the Study of the Early Progress of Christianity, ch. ii.); and Paul certainly had his share in this diffusion. He was surrounded also by many friends and co-workers. Luke and Aris-

tarchus had accompanied him, and the latter seems to
have shared his imprisonment (Col. iv. 10). Others,
like Timothy, followed him; while others came on
errands from different churches. We read of Epaphroditus going with aid and comfort from Philippi (Phil.
iv. 18), and of Epaphras from Colosse, who also seems
to have for a while shared the apostle's imprisonment
that he might report and consult about the work abroad
(comp. Col. i. 7, 8; iv. 7, 9–14; Philem. 1, 10, 24;
Eph. vi. 21; Phil. i. 1; ii. 19). The apostle was confident too of his release (Philem. 22; Phil. i. 25; ii.
24), so that he did not lessen his energy. At the same
time there were opponents even in the Christian community. These appear especially in the latter part of
his residence (Phil. i. 15–18). They were doubtless
Jewish-Christian teachers, who had moved westward as
he had done. So decided was his own success, that he
was able to speak of them with unusual equanimity and
even to rejoice in what good they did. His house in
Rome was thus the centre of a vigorous and far-reaching propagandism.

248. In this way was fulfilled the apostle's long
cherished desire of preaching at Rome. It is interesting to remember the condition of the great city at the
time, its luxury and idleness, its military splendor, its
love of pleasure, Nero's increasing tyranny and de-
bauchery. Amid the vast population the Christians
were a feeble company. Yet they were becoming
known and hated even by the Roman populace (*Tacitus*, Ann. xv. 44). Strange tales were being circulated
about them; and that popular hostility to them as
"enemies of the human race" was already rising, which
the Emperor used afterwards as an excuse for his per-

secution. As yet, however, no notes of danger were heard. While the world gazed in wonder at the splendid horrors of Nero's rule, the obscure prisoner, waiting at his bar, with equally obscure co-laborers, was spreading quietly through the capital and even into the imperial guards and household the peaceful and pure religion of a divine Redeemer.

249. The epistles written by Paul from Rome are documents of high value for the history of Christianity not merely in the capital but throughout the empire, and the study of them again best reveals the history. They fall into two groups. One, comprising those to the Colossians, to Philemon, and to the Ephesians, was sent by Tychicus, who was accompanied by Onesimus (Col. iv. 7; Philem. 10, 12; Eph. vi. 21, 22). The other, comprising the epistle to the Philippians, was sent by Epaphroditus (Phil. ii. 25), who had come to the apostle with a gift from the Philippian church. The first group is to be dated probably in A. D. 61 or 62, and Philippians in A. D. 62 or 63.

250. The Epistle to the Colossians introduces us suddenly to a new phase of apostolic history. No mention has been hitherto made of this Phrygian city on the Lycus. The epistle implies (ii. 1) that Paul himself had not been there, but that the otherwise unknown Epaphras had been the minister and apparently the founder of the church (i. 6, 7; iv. 12, 13; Philem. 23). Probably the gospel had been carried to Colosse during Paul's residence in Ephesus (Acts xix. 10, 26). Philemon also, a Colossian, had been one of Paul's converts (Philem. 19), and he too may have heard the apostle in Ephesus and carried the faith to his home. It was, at any rate, a Pauline church. Epaphras had

recently come to Rome and reported its condition; and there were some features of the situation which so seriously threatened its welfare that the apostle despatched this epistle.

251. The danger at Colosse arose from the appearance of a new and insidious form of false teaching. It was an eclectic movement, combining Jewish rites with a mystic theosophy, and threatened to undermine the believer's confidence in the all-sufficiency of Christ. It was not the old Judaistic error against which Galatians had been written; for the apostle does not meet it by the same arguments. In fact the unity of Jew and Gentile in Christ is spoken of as acknowledged (i. 6, 12, 21–29; ii. 7, 11, 19). Yet the influence of Judaism is plain from the warnings against Jewish observances (ii. 11, 14, 16, 20–22). On the other hand, the error included a mystical, speculative element. It claimed to be philosophical (ii. 8), and in particular included a worshipping of supernatural beings besides Christ, while into the mysteries of the celestial hierarchy the initiated alone could peer (ii. 18). There was also an ascetic tendency (ii. 18, 23), perhaps because considered conducive to spiritual illumination and because the errorists were touched by the widely prevalent notion that matter is inherently evil. In this teaching lay evidently the germs of an entire subversion of the original gospel. It is difficult to account in detail for the origin of each element of the error and for the special form of their combination. But the movement as a whole was clearly a phase of the religious syncretism then prevalent in the East and into which Jews of the dispersion, like the Essenes in Palestine, sometimes fell. At Colosse the same type

in its purpose. The perfection of his work as a Saviour of men was seen to rest on the fulness of his divine dignity. His life and work on earth appeared as the climax not only of Hebrew history but of the whole cosmic process of the self-revelation of God. In the light of this vast vision of revealed deity and of its relation to the entire universe, faith in Christ appeared more than ever the condition of salvation, and Christianity itself the only true religion.

254. Onesimus, who accompanied Tychicus to Colosse, carried also the epistle to Philemon. This beautiful little letter illustrates the personal relations of the apostle with his friends and the fine ethical spirit which animated him. Onesimus had once been a slave of Philemon, who was now a leading member of the Colossian church; and, after robbing his master, had run away. He had drifted to Rome and had there been converted by the apostle. The latter acquired the warmest affection for the converted slave. He would like to have kept him by his side; but he felt it to be only right for Onesimus to return to Philemon and make amends for his fault. The letter was written to ask Philemon to receive and forgive the runaway. It is couched in the most delicate language. It is an appeal to Philemon's Christian principles rather than a command such as the apostle might have issued. Paul even offered to repay any money that Onesimus might owe. The whole letter is suffused with the most delicate suggestions of love and duty on the part of all concerned. It is therefore of far more importance than the incident which occasioned it. It reveals the social ethics of apostolic Christianity. The new religion, though teaching the equality in

Christ of servants and masters, did not free the former from their obligations to the latter. Neither did it undertake the reconstruction of the social order. It left that to the gradual operation of the principles involved in the relation of all believers in Christ to God. It rather directed every one to discharge existing relations in the spirit of Christ (comp. I. Cor. vii. 17–24). The slave should serve his master with fidelity. The master should treat his slave as a Christian brother (comp. Col. ii. 22 to iv. 1 ; Eph. vi. 5–9; I. Pet. ii. 13–25). The new community was thus a spiritual fraternity. It controlled, without destroying, the existing relations of life. It infused into society the sense of spiritual oneness, the passion of mutual love, and a keen regard for the rights of others. This was the seed out of which alone in time social reconstruction and civil progress could emerge in stable and harmonious forms.

255. Tychicus carried a third letter which is of pre-eminent importance to the student both of Pauline teaching and of apostolic Christianity. This was the so-called Epistle to the Ephesians. It was really addressed, however, not to the Ephesians alone. Had it been, it would almost certainly have contained salutations to Paul's many friends in the Asian metropolis. Indeed certain expressions (i. 15 ; iii. 2, 4) seem to imply that some of its readers were not personally acquainted with him at all. Though clearly addressed to a specific circle of readers, the epistle has also the character of a general discussion. Moreover, in the two best manuscripts of the New Testament the words "in Ephesus" (i. 1) are not found. Origen did not have them in his text, and Basil, in the fourth century,

states that in his day also they were not in the ancient
copies. It is known too that Marcion, in the second
century, called this the Epistle to the Laodiceans. On
the other hand, it was generally known in the church,
as far back as the second century, as " to the Ephesians." These facts are best explained by the supposition that it was a circular letter addressed to the
churches of Asia. It is no doubt the one referred to
in Colossians iv. 16 as " the epistle *from* Laodicea,"
one copy having been left there; and from Laodicea
Marcion may have derived his. Yet, as Ephesus was
the metropolis of Asia and a church of large importance in early Christian history, and as it was included
in the churches addressed, the letter became commonly
known as the Epistle to the Ephesians. It was the
mission of Tychicus to distribute copies of this circular to the churches of the province.

256. This epistle is closely related in language and
thought to Colossians. Frequent echoes occur of
phrases used in the companion document (comp. *e. g.*
Eph. i. 1 and Col. i. 1; Eph. i. 3, 20; ii. 6; iii. 10; vi.
12 and Col. i. 5; Eph. i. 6 and Col. i. 14; Eph. i. 7 and
Col. i. 14; Eph. i. 10 and Col. i. 20; Eph. i. 11 and Col.
i. 12; Eph. i. 19, 20 and Col. ii. 12, 21; Eph. i. 21 and
Col. i. 16; Eph. i. 22 and Col. i. 18; Eph. i. 23 and
Col. ii. 9, etc.). Evidently the two were written under
the influence of the same impressions. Yet Ephesians
is by no means a mere repetition of Colossians. Even
when the phraseology is nearly the same, it is modified; and the themes of the two are not identical. In
Ephesians the thought is widened so as to include the
whole doctrine of the origin, salvation, and destiny of
the Christian community. In Colossians emphasis is

on the person of Christ and the sufficiency of his work; in Ephesians it is on the church, the body of Christ. In Colossians Christ is the "fulness" of God; in Ephesians the church is the "fulness" of Christ. In Ephesians the apostle's thought goes beyond the divine dignity and all-sufficiency of Christ to the eternal purpose of God in Christ, of which the church, the whole body of the redeemed, is the result. Hence this epistle is the climax of Paul's teaching about salvation. True, it does not treat of eschatology; but in other respects it sums up his teaching. It lays down the fundamental principle of his system of thought, namely, God's sovereign purpose of grace, to illustrate which in the redemption of his elect he has ordered the course of history and revealed his will and power in his Son.

257. In this epistle, then, Paul's teaching about the essence of Christianity is presented in the most complete form. The way of salvation taught in Galatians and Romans is assumed, but the whole plan of God embodied in the mission of Jesus is unfolded. The experience of salvation in Christ is traced back to its origin, and carried forward to its goal. It is the manifestation in time of the eternal purpose of God with man. Stress also is laid on the creation, by means of the election and redemption of individuals, of a new and spiritually organized community. The result is the presentation of a complete theodicy. Christianity appears as the goal, not only of human history, but of the eternal divine thought. We are given a world-view of its significance. It is not merely a system of belief, but the divine creation of a renewed humanity, to which the title "the church" emphatically belongs, and which, as it originated in the purpose of God and

has been effectuated by the work of Christ, is organized by the divine, indwelling Spirit.

258. It is clear that, while the apostle was moved to write by the needs of his Asian churches, yet the epistle embodied his mature thought and makes a distinct progress in the delivery of his doctrine. It is the culmination of his teaching at the culmination of his life work. We may conjecture that three factors in particular entered into the historical formation of his thought. One was the success of his missionary work throughout the empire, by which a new spiritual community of all races had been actually formed. Secondly, his Judaistic controversy had made perfectly clear that such a community was the goal of history and of God's purpose. Thirdly, his own reflection, ever reaching after ultimate truth, could not rest until these historic facts were contemplated as parts of the ordered unfolding of the divine scheme concerning the universe as a whole. The result was this sublime production. Here the church appears as the universal company of the redeemed and spiritually united people of God. It is not identified with an external organization. It is a spiritual community, and knit together by spiritual bonds. In this great temple "each several building" (ii. 21, R.V.) has its place, and the unity of the whole is "the unity of the Spirit" (iv. 3). Yet the spiritual reality is conceived of as manifested in all the activities of the church and in all the relations of life. This was the new Israel, the new temple, the new humanity, which Paul describes as the goal of God's purpose with mankind, and as realized alone through Christ in the Christian community.

259. The Epistle to the Philippians, written later

than the three which Tychicus and Onesimus bore to
Asia, is a warm greeting from the imprisoned apostle,
partly to thank his beloved Philippians for a gift which
they had sent him by Epaphroditus (ii. 25; iv. 14–18),
but abounding in personal news, in the frank confi-
dences of a friend, and in such instructions as suggested themselves to his mind. It was not elicited by
any special crisis at Philippi, nor by the wish to set
forth any special truth. It is a typical specimen of a
pastoral letter to a devoted congregation. It is of
chief interest for the information it contains, and for
its tender expressions of lofty Christian experience.

260. It throws, in the first place, some light on the
condition of the Philippian church. Thus we find it
organized under "overseers (bishops) and deacons"
(i. 1). They were specially mentioned in the saluta-
tion, probably because they were the official agents
through whom the gift had been sent to the apostle;
but the language advises us that these were the two
classes of regular officers in the churches. The title
"overseer" was replacing "elder," although the latter
was still used and the two denoted the same office
(Tit. i. 5, 7; I. Tim. iii. 12; iv. 17; Acts xx. 17, 28).
The term "overseer" seems to have arisen among the
Gentile churches, and it may be that its adoption was
occasioned by its employment to denote the presiding
offices of civic or social societies (*Hatch*, Organization
of the Christ. Chh. sects. ii., iii.; *Lightfoot*, The Christian Ministry). It would thus be the Hellenic equivalent for the Hebraic "elder." On the other hand, the
use of the term in the Greek Old Testament (comp.
II. Kings xi. 18; II. Chron. xxxiv. 12, 17; Neh. xi. 9, 14,
22; Is. lx. 17) may have prepared the Christians to

employ it much in the same way in which *ecclesia* was substituted for *synagogue* (sect. 100). Whatever its origin, the office of "overseer" was the same as that of "elder," but the term described the office from the practical point of view of its duties. Apart, however, from these officers, there were many in the church, both men and women (iv. 2, 3), who were active in the cause.

261. As to the apostle himself, this epistle illustrates, as already observed (sect. 247), his successful zeal, his trials and his courage, and his strong expectation of release. In point of doctrine it does not add essentially to what we have already learned of Paul's teaching. The great passage on the self-humiliation of the divine Son (ii. 5–11) makes perfectly clear his belief in the eternal and essential divinity of Christ, and beautifully describes the ethical spirit illustrated by the incarnation; but it does not advance save in detail beyond earlier utterances (Gal. iv. 4; II. Cor. viii. 9; Rom. i. 3, 4; viii. 3; ix. 5; Col. i. 15–17; ii. 9). The same may be said of chapter iii. It should be noted, however, that here reappears the expectation of a physical transformation of believers at Christ's advent (iii. 21), which shows that the absence from Colossians and Ephesians of his earlier eschatology was not due to any change of views. With the few items of information furnished by this epistle, our knowledge of Paul's first Roman imprisonment ends. The little that we do learn suggests, of course, that much more must have been done by way of influence on the capital and abroad. We leave him still awaiting his trial, but none the less leavening the world by his teaching. It is easy to understand why the Roman church of the next age looked back to Paul as one of its founders.

VII

THE LAST YEARS OF PAUL

262. HAD Paul's life ended with the Roman im
prisonment recorded in Acts, he would still have performed the work which has made his name historic.
Not only had he personally established Christianity
in most of the chief centres of the empire, but from
them the faith had rapidly spread into the contiguous
regions. There is evidence, shortly after, that it had
permeated the whole of Asia Minor (I. Pet. i. 1), had
entered Illyricum, or, as it was later called, Dalmatia
(II. Tim. iv. 11), and had possibly found its way into
Gaul (II. Tim. iv. 11, R.V., marg.). Converts had been
made in various ranks of society. The majority were
probably of the middle class; and it should be remembered that even the slaves, to whom frequent
reference is made (Eph. vi. 5; Col. iii. 22; I. Pet. ii.
18), often included intelligent and educated men.
Even in Corinth, where most of the early disciples
were from the lower orders (I. Cor. i. 26; vii. 11), we
read of Crispus, the ruler of the synagogue (Acts
xviii. 8), and Erastus, the treasurer of the city (Rom.
xvi. 23, R.V.); while in Ephesus some of the wealthy
"Asiarchs" (see sect. 197) were the apostle's friends.
Gentile and Jew, masters and slaves, educated and
ignorant, rich and poor, had been united in a few
years into a new confraternity. Moreover, the apostle

had by his epistles put in permanent form his whole
system of instruction. He had fully interpreted to
the Gentiles Jesus, the Messiah. Through his ministry, whatever others may have done, Christianity
had unfolded its message to the world and attained
complete consciousness of its independent mission.

263. There is reason, however, to believe that Paul's
life did not end with his appeal to Cæsar, awaiting
the issue of which Luke's narrative closes. That the
apostle was martyred at Rome under Nero is the
constant testimony of tradition from the earliest times,
and may be accepted without doubt. The year of his
death is more open to question. Tradition, first mentioned by Eusebius (*Chronicon*), placed it in A. D. 67
or 68. (See Appendix.) Even if this be too late, a
period of time certainly elapsed between the close of
the two years mentioned in Acts (xxviii. 31) and his
martyrdom; for it is utterly incredible that he died
before the outbreak of Nero's persecution in the
summer of A. D. 64. Did he then continue a prisoner,
or was he released on his appeal to Cæsar and allowed
to resume his work? The reasons for the latter supposition, quite apart from the question of the genuineness of the Pastoral Epistles, are very strong.

264. In the first place, he confidently expected to
be released (Phil. i. 25; ii. 24), and his expectation
must have been based on his knowledge of the situation. In the second place, his previous treatment
by Roman officials makes his release probable. He
was regarded as a Jew who had a controversy with
his fellow-religionists; and as Judaism was a legalized
religion, its internal dissensions were no affair of the
state. Not until the outbreak of the Neronian perse-

cution were Christians punished by the Romans for
being such; and although the Jews accused Paul
of offences of which the officials could take cognizance
(Acts xviii. 13; xxiv. 5), yet in every case when he
made his defence and the real nature of the dispute
appeared, he was either discharged or acknowledged
to be guiltless. It is altogether probable, therefore,
that when his case came before Cæsar, he was acquitted. In the third place, tradition asserts his
release. Clement of Rome (A. D. 96) wrote of him that
" he taught the whole world righteousness and reached
the furthest bound of the west; " which in one writing
from Rome can hardly mean less than that the apostle
had visited Spain, and this implies his release. In
like manner the Muratori Fragment (A. D. 170–200)
mentions the journey to Spain as if it were generally
believed, and the same tradition appears in early
apocryphal " Acts " (comp. *Zahn*, Einleit. I. sect. 36,
note 7; *Steinmetz*, Die 2te Gefangenschaft d. Paul.
p. 90). Finally Eusebius (HE. II. 22) gives it as the
current report that the apostle was released, resumed
his ministry, and was again arrested and suffered
martyrdom at Rome. It is true that the witnesses to
the tradition are not many, but there is no opposing
tradition. It is true also that no trustworthy historical remains exist of Paul's work in Spain. There is,
however, some evidence that Christianity existed in
Spain as early as the reign of Nero (*Steinmetz, ibid.* p.
86). The absence of historical remains of Paul's visit is
no disproof of the visit itself, nor is the tradition sufficiently explained as arising out of the apostle's known
wish to visit Spain (Rom. xv. 24). Taking the evidence
as a whole, when combined with the probabilities of the

founding new churches, as in Crete, and in revisiting the older ones. With him others co-operated, some of them men formerly associated with him, and others, like Artemas and Zenas (Tit. iii. 12, 13), of whom we have not heard before. Meanwhile, in all probability, the Neronian persecution had broken out in Rome, and it could not but have made the apostle more anxious to complete his work. In I. Timothy and Titus, however, there is no allusion to it. We only learn from them of the restless activity of the apostle, and his intense desire that his churches should be true to the faith and should honor by their lives the Christian name.

267. The First Epistle to Timothy and that to Titus illustrate the growing need which the apostle felt of care in the regulation of the organized life of his churches. His purpose was not in the least to advance organization. He does not direct any addition to existing offices nor exalt one above another. The only factor, not hitherto mentioned, is the list of widows supported by the church, and this too was evidently an established custom. His aim was rather to prevent abuses in the selection of officials and of subjects of aid. His language shows his sense of the importance of the church as an organized society (I. Tim. iii. 14–16) and the need of maintaining a holy and commendable life. This was only the practical application of the idea of the church universal which he had given in the epistle to the Ephesians.

268. Yet these epistles do disclose something of the organization of the churches. Timothy and Titus had clearly been left in charge temporarily, not as permanent officers, but as apostolic delegates. The perma-

nent officials consisted of overseers, or elders, — the two terms being convertible, — and deacons (see sect. 260). The former were rulers, the latter ministers to the poor. On the elders had devolved more and more the work of teaching (I. Tim. iii. 2; v. 17; Tit. i. 9; II. Tim. ii. 2). That this was not confined to them appears from the very injunctions against false teachers. Neither did all the elders devote themselves to teaching (I. Tim. v. 17), but those that did were to have double honor. In short, we notice that while the freedom of public teaching had not ceased, the burden of regular instruction was devolving more on the overseers of the church; and it was plainly the view of the apostle that this was a needed safeguard of the truth. This indeed was but a further application both of the original duty of the elder and of what Paul had already taught in Ephesians iv. 11–16. Yet a new emphasis is evident. Out of the eldership the idea of an established teaching, as well as ruling, body had begun to emerge.

269. The epistles further show the perils to which the churches were exposed from false teaching and unholy living. This is a strange but instructive fact. The apostle predicted that it would become more and more the case. His view of the future was not that of an idealist. Error and sin were manifesting themselves within the body. The congregations contained many elements. Some were attracted who did not fully apprehend the gospel. Half-converted Jews brought in religious fables and fanciful speculations about Scripture and the spirit-world. Religious excitement sometimes engendered fanaticism. Philosophic theories were substituted for the apostolic faith. Christianity

had to defend its purity and its lofty moral ideal
as well as prove its right to exist at all. Hence the
apostle's stress on holy character. Christianity, he
repeats, must be kept honorable. Zeal for righteousness and all the kindred virtues is urged no less than
fidelity to truth. Perhaps he was partly influenced
by the growing hatred of the church by paganism, and
by the vile misrepresentations of the new sect which
were beginning to be circulated. There were also real
perils within the churches themselves. These epistles
testify to the strenuousness with which the apostle of
faith wrought out, as the fruit of faith, a holy life, and
insisted upon it to his converts. He knew that only a
holy life could successfully meet the world's attack
upon the faith itself.

270. Second Timothy discloses an entire change in
Paul's situation. He is again a prisoner at Rome (i. 8,
12, 17; ii. 9; iv. 6), charged with being a malefactor
(ii. 9, R. V.). He has had one trial at which, though
deserted even by his friends, the Lord delivered him,
as he puts it, "out of the mouth of the lion" (iv. 16,
17); but he fully expects death (iv. 6). He is sorely
troubled also by the defection and absence of some of
his friends (iv. 10) and by the positive enmity of others
who bore the Christian name and who hailed from
Asia (i. 15). Alexander, the coppersmith, had done
him much evil (iv. 11); many suppose that he had
testified before the tribunal against Paul. Yet other
friends, some of them new to the history (iv. 21), were
with him. These scanty allusions evidently imply that
he had been again arrested — where or why we know
not — and had been again sent to Rome. He was now
charged with crime by the Roman authorities them-

selves. It may be that he was charged with complicity in the burning of Rome (*C. and H.*, Life and Ep. of St. Paul, ii. 472). It may be that the charge was "hostility to established customs and weakening imperial authority" (*Ramsay*, St. Paul the Trav., p. 361). There were evidently several charges, for, though at first not condemned, he was still held a prisoner. He does not say that he was charged with being a Christian. Yet that was evidently the animus of the charge. The Roman authorities were also adverse to him. He had no hope of final acquittal. Clearly their attitude had much changed since Philippians was written. This makes it probable that the Neronian persecution had meanwhile occurred. However inadequate the proof of guilt might be, the Christian apostle was certain that he would be condemned.

271. Under these circumstances his second letter to Timothy was written. He wished Timothy to come to him (iv. 9, 21). While calling him to his side, he takes the opportunity of pouring out his heart to his beloved friend in exhortation and encouragement. There is certainly no reason to suppose, as some have done, that we have here two letters combined, — one urging Timothy to come to Paul; the other directing him how to carry on his work; for the charge to Timothy in this letter is not, like those in I. Timothy, to carry on a specific work in a specific place, but is a general exhortation for Timothy's subsequent life, and Paul's impending death made him feel that he must not lose an opportunity of giving his farewell testament to his "son." Hence he exhorts Timothy to be true to him and to his teaching amid increasing perils (i.), to be faithful to duty, giving heed to his own life and faith,

diligently upholding truth and resisting temptation (ii.). He warns him that error will increase, and encourages him to resist it by recalling how he himself had suffered in the service, and by pointing him to the Scriptures as the sure rule of faith and life (iii.). With a repeated charge to fidelity (iv. 1–5), he tells of his own expectation of death and joy in it, of his desire to see Timothy again (iv. 6–9), and closes with items of news and greetings (iv. 10–22). With this letter our knowledge of Paul's life ends. Tradition affirms that he was beheaded on the Ostian Way.

PART V

PROGRESS OF CHRISTIANITY TO THE CLOSE OF THE APOSTOLIC AGE

HISTORICAL SOURCES

272. THE anonymous Epistle to the Hebrews is valuable both for its incidental references to the condition of Judaic Christianity (sect. 172) and for its own teaching. In the latter aspect it is a source for the period now before us. Its authorship has ever been a subject of dispute; for even in ancient times, while the eastern churches received it as Pauline, there was dissent in the west, and Tertullian states that it was ascribed to Barnabas. There is, however, no book more certainly written in the apostolic age, since it was used freely by Clement of Rome (A.D. 96). Its internal features make strongly against the tradition that it was written by Paul. Its anonymity is unlike Paul. The writer appeals to the confirmation of the Lord's message which he and his readers had received from those who had heard him (ii. 3; iv. 2). He had apparently been associated with his readers in the earlier days of their Christian life (ii. 4; x. 32; xiii. 7, R.V.). His smooth style and his greater fondness for the Septuagint point also to another hand than the apostle's. The "Alexandrianism" of the epistle has indeed been exaggerated. Its interpretations of scripture assume, like Paul's and unlike Philo's, the historical reality of the inspired narrative, and his conceptions show no dependence on the philosopher (comp. *G. Milligan,*

The Theol. of the Ep. to the Heb., ch. ix.). Yet there remain a number of phrases and observations which indicate the writer's familiarity with Alexandrian terminology. Most decisive, however, is the difference of the form of theological conception from Paul's. Both entirely harmonize. But the Pauline expression of salvation "in Christ" is replaced by that of the believer as "sanctified" by the work of his priestly representative (ii. 11; x. 10, 14, 29; xiii. 12). Salvation is not described as "justification," but as the "perfecting" of man's relation to God (vi. 1; vii. 11, 19; ix. 9; x. 1, 14, 40). The law is presented from the ritual, not from the moral, point of view. Salvation by works is not rejected because of man's inability to keep the law (Rom. vii. 9–24), but because material offerings cannot remove guilt (ix. 9, 10). To Paul, man is carnal (Rom. vii. 14); to this writer, the law is (ix. 10; x. 4; xiii. 9). Paul's versatility was great; but his theological conceptions did not thus change their moulds. At the same time this epistle notably coincides with Paul's both in substantial doctrine (comp. i. 2–4 and Col. i. 15, 16, Eph. i. 20; ii. 10 and Rom. xi. 36; vii. 25 and Rom. viii. 34; vii. 27 and Rom. vi. 9, 10; ii. 9 and Phil. ii. 8, 9; ii. 3 and I. Cor. xv. 27; ii. 4 and I. Cor. xii. 11; ix. 27, 28 and Tit. ii. 13) and in a peculiar form of quotation (x. 30 and Rom. xii. 19). Hence it probably emanated from one of his friends. It is impossible to affirm positively who wrote it; but of all the guesses that have been made, the most plausible is that which attributes it to Barnabas.

273. The epistle was certainly addressed to Hebrews (see especially i. 1; iii. 1–6; xii. 18–24; xiii. 13). They were a definite community (v. 12; vi. 10; x. 32–

34; xiii. 7, R. V.) which had long existed (v. 12), had suffered imprisonment and loss of goods (x. 32–34), but
had not as a community endured bloody persecution
(xii. 4). A great crisis was impending which threatened painful separation from their former associations
(x. 25; xii. 27; xiii. 13, 14). These allusions point to
Christians of Palestine. To no other was the reproach
so applicable that " by reason of time ye ought to be
teachers " (v. 12). It cannot be ascertained, however,
whether it was sent to the church of Jerusalem, or to
some neighboring community, or to a portion of the
Jerusalem church which had on the approach of the
war left the city. It is to be dated shortly before
the fall of Jerusalem, since the temple service was still
in operation (viii. 4, 5; x. 25; xiii. 10–14). We may
assign it to 67 or 68 A. D. Its place of composition is
unknown. The phrase " they of Italy salute you " (xiii.
24) may indicate that the writer was in Italy or merely
that certain Italians were with him.

274. The First Epistle of Peter was addressed to the
Christians in the provinces of Asia Minor. Its allusions
to persecution (i. 7; iii. 15; iv. 12, 16) point clearly
to the period following the outbreak of Nero's cruelty
(A. D. 64). The apostle was in " Babylon " (v. 13).
This term has often been regarded as a pseudonym for
Rome, and the supposition would seem to be supported
by the allusions to persecution; yet the simple epistolary character of the document makes the literal sense
more probable. The letter was known to and freely
used by the earliest post-apostolic writers, nor is there
reason to doubt its claim to be the work of the apostle.

275. The genuineness of the Second Epistle of Peter
has been more doubted than that of any New Testa-

ment book, but substantial reasons may be given for accepting its explicit claims. Traces of its use in the second century, though few, are not wanting and have been re-enforced by the lately recovered apocryphal Apocalypse of Peter, dating from about A. D. 150, which draws largely from it. It explicitly claims to be by Peter, and we should be slow to believe that the churches, which rejected other works pretending to be his, were imposed on by so daring a forgery. The writer alludes to his previous epistle (iii. 1) and shows the same fondness for reminiscences of his life with Jesus (i. 14, 16–18) which is found in First Peter (i. 3, 8, 21 ; ii. 21, 23 ; v. 1, 5). In it, as in the other, stress is laid on prophecy (i. 19–21 ; iii. 2, 13) and the mind is fixed on the glory to come (i. 4, 11, 19 ; iii. 4, 10, 12–14). It is true that he emphasizes more than in the first epistle (iv. 5, 17) the advent as the time of punishment (ii. 1, 3, 9, 13 ; iii. 7), but this was because he was rebuking false teachers and evil men. The doctrinal point of view of both epistles is the same (comp. *e. g.* II. Pet. i. 3 and I. Pet. i. 3, 4 ; II. Pet. i. 4 ; iii. 9 and I. Pet. i. 9, 13 ; II. Pet. i. 10 and I. Pet. i. 2 ; v. 10 ; II. Pet. ii. 1 and I. Pet. i. 18) ; and while some new phrases occur in the second epistle, they belonged to the common Christian vocabulary. In both epistles there is the same stress on practical faith and godliness, the same absence of doctrinal discussion, the same use of Old Testament illustrations (II. Pet. ii. and I. Pet. ii. 6, 20). In both epistles also is to be noted the disposition to use the writings of Christian contemporaries. First Peter contains many echoes of the epistles of James and Paul, while in Second Peter there is not only a specific reference to Paul's epistles (iii. 15, 16), but an extensive use of the Epistle of Jude (comp. ii. 1 and Jude 4; ii. 4 and Jude 6; ii. 10 and Jude 8; ii. 11 and Jude 9; ii. 12 and Jude 10; ii. 13 and Jude 12). A certain roughness of style, when compared with First Peter, is to be acknowledged, but is quite an insufficient ground on which to deny a common authorship. The epistle was probably written from Rome shortly before the apostle's death. It was addressed to part at least of the same circle of churches to whom the first epistle had been sent.

276. The Epistle of Jude seems to have been written about A. D. 65–67. The author calls himself "a servant of Jesus Christ and brother of James" (1). He was therefore not an apostle, but one of the brethren of Jesus, and, like James (Jas. i. 1), felt himself worthy to be called only a servant of his Messiah-brother. His language implies that James was better known than himself, and probably that he wrote after James' death. It might seem also to indicate that he addressed Jewish Christians; but First Corinthians (ix. 5) shows that the brethren of the Lord were, like Peter, evangelists well known to the Gentile churches, and since Peter in his later years addressed Gentiles, Jude may have done the same. It is, moreover, difficult to suppose that the persons whom Jude denounced had appeared in Jewish-Christian churches (4–8). Their errors look rather like the abuse of Pauline teaching (comp. Rom. vi. 1–11). We may conjecture that the readers lived in some part of Asia Minor. The same facts point also to a date contemporaneous with the Pastoral Epistles. The false Christians of Jude cannot indeed be identified with the false teachers of First Timothy and Titus. They agree more nearly with those de-

scribed in Second Timothy (iii. 1–9). Jude and the Pastorals, however, belong to the same general situation.

277. During the seventh decade appeared also the synoptic gospels. The first, from the earliest times attributed to Matthew, was written from the point of view of a Jewish Christian emancipated from Judaism. As early as about A. D. 140 (Papias) we find the statement that Matthew wrote originally in Hebrew. If so, the relation of our Greek gospel to the original is a difficult problem about which the last word has not yet been written. Many modern scholars believe that the original consisted only or mainly of a collection of Christ's discourses, and that our gospel was called Matthew's because it embodies these discourses with historical matter derived from another source. But from what we know of the apostolic preaching, it is improbable that an early gospel did not contain the acts as well as the words of Jesus, and especially that it did not contain a history of the passion. This theory, moreover, rests upon an interpretation of the word "logia," used by Papias to describe Matthew's work, in the sense of " discourses," whereas the term is employed in the New Testament, by Philo and by the early fathers, in the sense of " oracles," or divine communications, and is constantly applied to inspired books, either in whole or in their parts. We are not warranted, therefore, in departing from the belief, which the same line of tradition affirmed, that our first gospel was the work of Matthew. Possibly he issued both a Hebrew and a Greek edition. The efforts of recent scholars to recover the original Hebrew by retranslation either of this gospel alone, or of it in

combination with Mark and Luke, cannot be regarded as successful.

278. Our second gospel was universally considered in the second century to have been written by Mark at Rome and to have embodied largely the preaching of Peter, whose "interpreter" Mark was said to have become. Its connection with Peter is somewhat confirmed by the fact that it lays stress on the miraculous events of Jesus' life as Peter always did (Acts ii. 22; x. 38; I. Pet. i. 3; II. Pet. i. 16, 17), and contains a number of vivid details which indicate the recollection of an observant eye-witness (e. g. iii. 5; v. 39, 40; viii. 12, 34). It was plainly written for Gentiles (comp. i. 9; v. 41; vii. 3, 4; xii. 42; xiv. 13; xv. 42), and is a graphic, pictorial narrative descriptive especially of the power of Jesus, the Son of God. There is no reason to doubt that we possess it in its original form, save that the last twelve verses are wanting. The original conclusion seems to have been lost, and was replaced, not later than the beginning of the second century, by our present text, compiled from the other gospels and other sources.

279. Our third gospel was written by the author of Acts (Acts i. 1, 2), who has already been identified as Luke (sect. 3). This gospel shows more of the spirit and method of an historian than do the other synoptics. He expressly states the care with which he collected his material (i. 1–4), deriving it doubtless both from earlier documents and personal communication with the original actors in the primitive history. He seems to have contemplated from the start the composition of both his works and to have aimed at a systematic presentation of the rise and establish-

ment of Gentile Christianity. His gospel should probably be assigned also to the years A. D. 60–70. At any rate his report of Christ's prediction of the fall of Jerusalem is not, as some maintain, sufficient ground for dating the book after that event; since his language (xxi. 20) is only an interpretation of Christ's words (comp. Matt. xxiv. 15; Mark xiii. 14) designed to make their meaning clear to Gentile readers, and that the Christians, on the basis of Christ's teaching, expected the destruction of the city is proved by Mark's report as well as by much other evidence. It is not improbable that Luke gathered his materials while Paul was in prison at Cæsarea, and that he wrote his gospel in Rome. The influence upon him of Paul appears from the stress he lays on the universal mission of Christ (e. g. ii. 32; iv. 16–30; xiii. 28–30; xiv. 16–24; xix. 10; xxiv. 47), and from the connection between certain passages in his narrative and Paul's statements (comp. Luke x. 7 and I. Tim. v. 18; Luke x. 8 and I. Cor. x. 27; Luke xxii. 19–21 and I. Cor. xi. 23–25; Luke xxiv. 34 and I. Cor. xv. 5).

280. At some time subsequent to the composition of the third gospel Luke issued the Acts, a discussion of which has already been given (sects. 3–6). Its exact date is still a matter of dispute. Its closing words cannot be held to prove that it was written, as many have thought, immediately after the two years of Paul's first Roman imprisonment. It can only be dated roughly in the period following Paul's release up to the probable term of Luke's life, say, A. D. 63–75. Its high value as a source for apostolic history has been repeatedly shown in our narrative.

281. Finally, we have from the closing years of the

first century the Johannean literature. It is true that the apostle's authorship of all or some of the five books which go by his name has been hotly debated. But that they existed and were used like other apostolic books at the beginning of the second century is certain (comp. *e. g. Resch*, Aussercanon. Paralleltexte zu d. Evang. 4tes Heft. 1896). That the author of the fourth gospel wrote also the epistles is indisputable from the identity of vocabulary and style. Examination also confirms the traditional belief that he was the writer of "Revelation" (comp. *Harnack*, Chronologie, p. 675). It is true that the latter book has many grammatical constructions peculiar to it; but these were due to its apocalyptic style and the influence on it of the language of older prophecies. The gospel and "Revelation" are both in thoroughly Hebraistic style, have a large body of peculiar words and phrases in common, while their leading doctrinal ideas are identical and some of them unique among the books of the New Testament (*e. g.* comp. John i. 1 and Rev. xix. 13; John i. 28; xix. 36 and Rev. v. 6; xiii. 8; John iii. 29 and Rev. xxi. 2, 9; John xix. 34 and Rev. i. 7; John viii. 44 and Rev. ii. 9; John vii. 37 and Rev. xxii. 17). Still less is there ground for supposing that any other John than the apostle was the author. Besides being evidently a Jew, and showing himself intimately familiar with the geography and customs of Palestine during Christ's time, he closes his gospel with the explicit statement that he was the disciple whom Jesus loved (xxi. 20, 24), and none will doubt that by that phrase we are to understand the son of Zebedee. It is to be noted that the statement is not only that "this is the disciple which testifieth

of these things," as if the author obtained his information from John ; but it is added that he " wrote these
things." We learn also from the first epistle that he
was an eye-witness of Jesus' life (i. 1), and wrote in
the name of the apostolic body (i. 3–5). The gospel
and first epistle are to be dated A. D. 80–90.

282. With regard to the " Revelation" it may be
further remarked that its style and vocabulary proves
it to be the work of one hand throughout. The opinion
has recently found favor that the author incorporated
into his book earlier apocalypses. Such a procedure
is not in itself inconceivable ; but the arguments advanced for it assume interpretations of some passages
and views of the relation of thought between visions
and parts of visions which are not demonstrable, and
which, in view of the literary unity of the book, go
beyond the limits of safe criticism. On the other
hand, critical opinion appears to be steadily returning
to the traditional view that the Revelation was composed in the latter part of the reign of Domitian,
between A. D. 90 and 96. We are not concerned with
the value of the Johannean writings for the life of
Christ. They throw, however, much light on the external situation of the churches of Asia during the
last quarter of the first century, and still more on
the currents of thought which were then felt among
the Christians.

II

THE LAST YEARS OF THE APOSTLE PETER

283. It remains to sketch briefly the progress of Christianity outside of and subsequent to its expansion under Paul. His influence indeed extended and may be traced in the literary remains of his contemporaries and immediate followers. Information concerning his fellow-workers is, moreover, scanty and sporadic; but enough exists to afford glimpses into the course which the new religion took, its successes and its perils, its progress and its unity, until its creative period drew to a close. We naturally inquire first concerning the work of Paul's chief fellow-apostle, Simon Peter.

284. The life of Peter after the council at Jerusalem is wrapped in obscurity. The tradition, first mentioned by Eusebius (HE. II. 14–17), that he went to Rome during the reign of Claudius (A. D. 41–54), and died under Nero in the same year with Paul; still more, that, as reported by Jerome (De vir. illustr. 1), he was the head of the Roman church for twenty-five years,— is inconsistent, save as regards the time of his death, with the data furnished by the New Testament books. Shortly after the council we find him at Antioch (Gal. ii. 11; see sect. 162). This was probably in A. D. 51; and Paul's Epistle to the Romans (A. D. 57 or 58; sect. 232) forbids the supposition that Peter had then

been laboring in the capital, not only by its silence about him, but still more by Paul's declared principle not to enter on another's territory (II. Cor. x. 16 ; Rom. xv. 20–24). Paul, however, alludes to Peter as a missionary well known to the Corinthians (I. Cor. ix. 6). It is not probable, indeed, that Peter had then visited Corinth. True, Dionysius of Corinth (A. D. 160) mentions him, as well as Paul, as one who had planted Christianity in that city. But if his statement rested on fact, it is more probable that Peter did not visit Corinth until after Paul's epistles to that church had been written. The agreement between Paul and the leaders of the Jerusalem church (Gal. ii. 9) makes it certain that in the years immediately following the council Peter's work lay among the Jews, and, since James was at the head of affairs in Judea, among the Jews of the dispersion. If "Babylon," from which First Peter was written (v. 13), is to be understood literally, we infer that the apostle went to the far east ; and in any event that was a natural direction for him to take. The absence of his name also from the epistles written by Paul during his first Roman imprisonment makes it still further improbable that he had visited the capital as late as A. D. 63.

285. Yet the tradition that Peter finally suffered martyrdom at Rome is too early and constant to be rejected. His martydom itself is obviously attested by John xxi. 18, 19. His death is associated with Paul's by Clement of Rome (A. D. 96). Ignatius (A. D. 110) wrote to the Romans, "I do not command you as Peter and Paul." Dionysius of Corinth (A. D. 160) mentions the two apostles as having taught together in Italy and suffered martyrdom at (or about) the same

time; and thereafter the tradition appears universally accepted. Tradition, moreover, associated Mark's gospel with Peter's preaching, and assigned to that gospel a Roman origin. We must believe, therefore, that, after Paul's release, and hence after his establishment of Gentile Christianity, Peter turned to the west and finally went to the capital. This implies that the division of fields of labor ceased when the unity of Jew and Gentile in the church became an accomplished and recognized fact; and such is the intimation of Paul himself in the epistle to the Ephesians (ii. 14–22; iii. 5; iv. 1–16).

286. The exact date, however, of Peter's death is a matter of doubt. The prevalent belief of the early church was that he died under Nero in A. D. 67 or 68. The death under Nero is implied in the statement of Dionysius of Corinth, that he died at (or about) the same time as Paul; and this tradition became so fixed that in the fourth century the two apostles were said to have suffered on the same day. The later form of the report is, however, quite untrustworthy (*Harnack*, Chronologie, p. 201), and even the general fact, though well attested, has been disputed. Thus Professor Ramsay thinks (Ch. in Rom. Emp. p. 283) that, since one Roman tradition, preserved in Tertullian, declared that Peter ordained Clement as head of the Roman church, the earliest belief must have been that the apostle survived the reign of Nero. But this inference is precarious, since we do not know to what date that tradition assigned the ordination of Clement, and since the other tradition, assigning Peter's death to Nero's reign, was more prevalent. On the other hand, Harnack would date the death of both Peter and

Paul as early as A. D. 64, the year of the outbreak of
Nero's persecution (Chronologie, p. 243, note 1); but
the reasons for this date, so far as concerns Peter, are
not convincing, and are acknowledged to be inconsistent with the claims of First Peter to be the work of
the apostle (see Appendix). It is most probable,
therefore, that the common tradition is approximately
correct, and that Peter suffered in Rome toward the
close of Nero's reign. That he was crucified seems to
be implied, though not certainly, in John xxi. 18, 19.
This is all that history knows. Further particulars
about his death belong to the realm of legend.

287. His first epistle discloses in a lively way both
the teaching of the apostle and the condition of Christianity among the provinces of Asia Minor, to the
disciples in which it was addressed (i. 1). The apostle
implies that he himself had not evangelized his readers
(i. 12). They were for the most part of Gentile origin
(i. 14, 18, 21; ii. 10; iv. 3), and the description of
them as " the elect who are sojourners of the dispersion" (i. 1, R. V.) is due to the complete transfer of the
idea of Israel to the Christian community (see i. 17;
ii. 5, 9–11). Their situation was one of increasing
temptation and peril. Their faith in the risen Lord
was exposed to sore trial (i. 7). They needed to realize the duty of sober and steadfast hope of the glory to
come (i. 13). In particular did they need to refute by
their lives the charge of being evil-doers (ii. 12; iii.
16), to prove their loyalty to civil authority (ii. 13–15),
and to act well as members of society (ii. 16–18; iii.
7). They were evidently suspected by their pagan
neighbors, and were liable to suffer through gross misrepresentations (iii. 15). The writer warns them to

be willing to suffer, but that they must not give just occasion for it (iii. 17). In fact, they must prepare for a more fiery trial than any they had known (iv. 12). They might well rejoice, if called to suffer for being Christians (iv. 16), remembering the like sufferings of their brethren elsewhere (v. 9). But they must be careful not to be guilty of any real offence, lest they dishonor the cause for which they stand.

288. These exhortations point to a time when the prosecution of Christians by the civil authorities was a real possibility. Yet it is clear that other charges than their Christianity were likely to be made against them as the ground of the prosecution. This situation corresponds to what we know of the period which followed the outbreak of Nero's attack upon the Christians of Rome. At first they were punished ostensibly for alleged crimes against society. Soon, however, Christianity itself became a crime. The combination of the earlier and the later phase of the government's hostility is plainly the situation presented by the epistle (*Ramsay*, Ch. in the Emp. p. 282). We see no reason, however, to believe with Professor Ramsay that the proscription of "the Name" did not become the established policy of the Roman government till after the reign of Nero. Suetonius (Nero, 16) testifies that in Nero's police regulations Christians as such were classed with common criminals, and that implies that Christianity was already regarded as practically the proof of crime. Our epistle may, therefore, be placed shortly after the outbreak of Nero's persecution, in A. D. 65 or 66. We do not know, indeed, from other sources that the persecution extended to the provinces, neither do we know that it did not. Natu-

rally it would at least influence the attitude of provincial officers toward the sect which the emperor himself had denounced. The epistle, moreover, speaks of persecution rather as impending than as present. There can be little doubt that the hatred of the Roman populace against the Christians was echoed in the provinces; and that when once the imperial government had set the example, lower officials would be ready to listen to similar charges, and in some instances to initiate action.

289. Christianity, therefore, was, for the first time so far as our records show, called on to face the hostility of the empire and of Roman society. It was the beginning of the conflict which was to last for two and a half centuries. The first fierce outbreak, which the Roman historian (see sect. 1) records in condensed but clear language, had already occurred. Its echoes were being heard throughout the world. Christianity could only try to meet the emergency by following the exhortation of Peter to lives of such purity as would disarm enmity and prove the value to the state and to humanity of the new religion. With the rising danger, moreover, the Christian brotherhood in all lands was drawn more closely together and the common faith received fresh emphasis. Accordingly in Peter's epistle the influence of earlier Christian writings is plainly manifest. He betrays the influence upon him of both James (comp. *e. g.* i. 6 and Jas. i. 2, 3; i. 7 and Jas. i. 3; v. 5 and Jas. iv. 6; iv. 8 and Jas. v. 20) and Paul. Acquaintance with the epistle to the Ephesians is specially evident (comp. i. 3, 4 and Eph. i. 3; i. 5 and Eph. i. 19; i. 20 and Eph. i. 4; ii. 5, 6 and Eph. ii. 20–22; iii. 22 and Eph. i. 21; also v.

4 and Col. iii. 4; i. 1 and Rom. viii. 29; i. 14 and
Rom. xii. 2; ii. 10 and Rom. ix. 25, etc.). With apparent reference to the fact that his readers were mainly
Pauline Christians, he closes with the injunction, "this
is the true grace of God: stand ye fast therein" (v.
12, R. V.) The earlier division of labor had ceased.
The consciousness of a common faith in the face of
common perils had obliterated it. The apostle of the
circumcision united with the apostle of the Gentiles in
strengthening the disciples on the basis of their com
mon relationship to the one Lord and one church.

290. On the other hand Peter's teaching has an
individuality of its own. This epistle contains numerous reminiscences of his life with Jesus, and especially
of the Lord's sufferings (i. 3, 8, 21; ii. 21, 23; v. 1,
5). In it also, as in Peter's speeches in Acts, Christianity is notably the fulfilment of prophecy (i. 10–12,
25; ii. 6, 24; iii. 21); and what had been fulfilled
gave new eagerness to the writer's expectation of the
further glory to come (i. 3–9, 13; iv. 7, 13; v. 1, 4,
10), so that he has been well called "the apostle of
hope." For him also faith is the only condition of
salvation (i. 5, 8, 9, 21; ii. 4, 7; v. 9); but he lays
stress on the historic agencies by which Christian faith
had been created (i. 3, 21, 23). He represents it also,
like James, as faith in God revealed in Jesus Christ
(i. 21) and as manifested in obedience (i. 1, 14; ii. 1, 7,
15; iii. 12, 16; iv. 1, 2). He does not unfold, as Paul
had done, the nature of Christ; yet not only is God
"the God and Father of our Lord Jesus Christ" (i. 3),
but Christ is made the supreme object of love (i. 8, 9)
as well as of faith (i. 8, 9; ii. 7), the means of access
to God (ii. 5; iv. 11; v. 10), the corner-stone of the

spiritual temple (ii. 4), the sinless example (ii. 21, 22; iv. 1, 13), the head of the church (ii. 25; iv. 4), and the Lord of the universe (iii. 22), while reference is made to his activity through the Spirit before his incarnation (i. 11; iii. 19, 20). The work of Christ is represented as consisting fundamentally in his sacrificial death (i. 1, 11, 18, 19; ii. 24; iii. 18; iv. 1) and in his resurrection, whereby he has entered on the exercise of his saving power (i. 3, 11, 21; iii. 21). To Peter as to Paul all Christians are the true Israel, but Peter is specially fond of the thought (i. 1; ii. 5, 9, 10). The epistle, therefore, has a strong individuality of its own. Its leading motive, however, is hortatory rather than didactic. It is not concerned to preserve the faith from false teaching, but from the influences of trial and temptation. This corresponds with Peter's disposition; and just because of his solicitude that the Christians might honor by their lives the name of Christ, and might not flinch before the fierce trials which threatened them, does his epistle cast a peculiarly interesting light on the situation in which, after the outbreak of persecution by the Roman authorities, the new religion found itself.

291. There were, however, perils from within as well as from without, and these both practical and theoretical. Some idea of them may be gleaned from the Second Epistle of Peter and from the closely allied Epistle of Jude. Since the latter appears to have been written before the former, and presents much the same danger in a less developed form, it may be noticed first.

292. Of Jude himself we know nothing beyond what is implied in his being one of the Lord's brethren (sect. 276) and an evangelist (I. Cor. ix. 5). A story

was related by Hegesippus (*Eus.* HE. III. 20) that Jude's grandchildren were summoned for examination before the suspicious Domitian because they were descendants of David. They proved themselves, however, to be hard-working farmers, and declared that their faith taught them to expect only a heavenly kingdom at the end of the world. Thereupon the emperor dismissed them with contempt. If the story be true, it implies that in the reign of Domitian (A. D. 81–96) Jude himself was dead.

293. His epistle is an indignant invective against certain false disciples, and the churches into which they had intruded appear most probably to have been located in Asia (sect. 276). He describes them as immoral men, veritable antinomians, who turned grace into lasciviousness, and virtually denied "the only Master and Lord, Jesus Christ" (4, R. V.). Lewdness was their passion (5–8), and was defended under the plea of higher knowledge (8–10). They are reproved not for teaching error but for practising it. They mingled in the Christian feasts, and even dared to take conspicuous parts (12–16). They formed also exclusive coteries, claiming to possess the Spirit (19). With great variety of rhetorical figure Jude depicts the shameful folly of these sinful men (10, 12, 13, 16–23). He too, like Peter, wrote in the name of the common faith (3, 20). His Jewish training appears in his illustrations not only from Hebrew history (5, 7, 11), but also from tradition and extracanonical literature (6, 9, 14, 15). But he appealed especially to the teachings of the apostles as the recognized authority (17, 18). His brief letter thus discloses a new and unexpected danger to which Christianity was exposed. The doctrines of grace and liberty

were liable to be grossly abused. Against such carnal influences, as well as against Judaism and speculative philosophy, did the leaders have to strive. That they did so is another evidence of the clearness and completeness with which they apprehended the faith itself. On the other hand, these alien influences reveal the agitation of society produced by Christianity, and foreshadow the corruption to which in the following age some of the churches yielded.

294. In the Second Epistle of Peter the same class of perils against which Jude had warned reappear along with others. The errors, however, are now positively advanced by false teachers. The epistle was doubtless written from Rome not long before the apostle's death (i. 14), and was addressed to the same circle, or at least to a part of it, to which the first epistle had been sent (iii. 1). He had evidently read and used the Epistle of Jude (comp. ii. 1 and Jude 4 ; ii. 4 and Jude 6 ; ii. 10 and Jude 8; ii. 11 and Jude 9; ii. 12 and Jude 10 ; ii. 13 and Jude 12) and wrote to those familiar with the epistles of Paul (iii. 15, 16). He tells us also, besides his references to antinomians (ii. 1 to iii. 3), of some who had begun to question whether the Lord would indeed return (ii. 4). The apostle exhorts his readers to hold to the faith which they had been taught, denounces the wickedness and predicts the punishment of the false teachers, and solemnly affirms that the Lord will come, judgment will be issued, and the present world be destroyed by fire.

295. We thus see that Gentile Christianity had no sooner been established than it was threatened with internal and external perils of the most serious kinds. Alien teaching and practical immorality appeared

within; while the enmity of the empire and the sus·
picions of the populace loomed darkly without. There
is, indeed, no reason to doubt that the majority of the
disciples were everywhere witnessing to the holiness
and spiritual power of the new life which had been
begotten within them; yet the need shown by these
epistles of their being warned against the intrusions of
error proves that their condition was by no means an
ideal one, and forewarns us that the full establishment
of the Christianity taught by the apostles was destined
to be a slow and arduous process. It was in part the
perception of this fact that led the latter to realize the
importance for the future of their written instructions
(II. Pet. ii. 15; iii. 1, 2) and to bequeath an authori·
tative literature to the church.

III

THE FINAL TRANSITION FROM JUDAISM TO CHRISTIANITY

296. THE Epistle to the Hebrews turns our attention once more to Christianity in Palestine; not, however, merely to the condition of the Jewish disciples (sect. 172), but to the larger fact of the real transition which apostolic teaching effected from the religion of Moses to Christ. There can be little doubt that it was written shortly before the fall of Jerusalem (sect. 273), and that the increasing troubles of the Jewish nation, the evident approach of the crisis in her history (see Heb. x. 25), the widening separation of even the Jewish Christians from their former associations, together with the rapid growth of Gentile Christianity, suggested to the author his exposition.

297. The epistle presents Christianity as the legitimate and divinely intended result of the religion of Moses. It supplies a place in apostolic teaching the loss of which would have been irreparable. Judaic Christianity had hitherto presented the gospel as the true interpretation of the law, and remained devoted to the observance of the ritual. The apostle of the Gentiles had wrought out, by deed and word, the independence of the gospel both from Jewish ceremonialism and from the attendant disposition to rely for salvation upon works of all kinds. Yet it was assumed by all that the religion of Moses had been

divinely revealed. There was need, from the view-point both of the intellect and of practical necessity, that the independence of the new should be set forth on the basis of the old, that the former should be shown to be the goal for which the latter had been intended positively to prepare. Only thus could Judaism fully merge into Christianity. It was given to the author of the Epistle to the Hebrews to do this, and thus at once complete the transition for the Jew and preserve for the Gentile the permanent truths of Mosaism.

298. The bearing of this epistle on the actual condition of the Jewish Christians has already been pointed out (sect. 172). We are now concerned with it as a monument of apostolic thought, disclosing one phase of the truth which was destined to permeate the world. It is a brilliant exposition of Christianity as the intended result of Hebrew revelation and religion. It presents it as the completion of the revelations which God had spoken " by divers portions and in divers manners unto the fathers in the prophets " (i. 1, R. V.), and, therefore, as the perfect and permanent religion of mankind (vi. 1; xii. 28). The Christian's life of faith in invisible realities is also shown to be the perfect form of the true religious life (xi.). Christianity is thus the historical unfolding of Mosaism. The latter is contemplated as a revealed system of worship designed to disclose the way of entering into covenant relation with God. The point of departure for the argument, therefore, is the ritual, which was, according to our author, a direct embodiment of Christian truth in symbolic form. The new is simply the unveiling of the old. It is the reality implicated and

emblemized in the old. In it the Hebrew may see the spiritual truth of which the ritual was a picture, the real pattern of which Mosaism was a copy (viii. 5). Christianity is, therefore, the perfect and final religion of mankind. This presentation of the matter was evidently the needed complement of Paul's teaching, which represented the contrast between salvation by faith and by works, and the function of the law in creating the sense of guilt. Both representations were true, and necessary in order to complete the transition from the old to the new dispensation.

299. The argument of the epistle covers the whole ground. It begins by setting forth the divine dignity of Christ (i. to ii. 4), and meets the doubt of the Jew caused by the spectacle of the Crucified by showing that just in this way alone could Messiah fulfil the office of a saviour by being the true high-priest of his people (ii. 5–18). Jesus, therefore, occupies a far higher position than Moses, and faith in him is not only the supreme duty, but the only means of entering into the enjoyment of the promises of God (iii. 1 to iv. 13). This high-priestly work of Christ is then presented in detail (iv. 14 to vii. 28). It is shown that the Scripture foretold that such would be his office, then that by his experience on earth the Lord was fitted for it, and finally that his ideal priesthood surpasses and does away with the Levitical. The latter appears as merely the lingering shadow of a departed order, the type falling before the reality. The author, however, did not stop here. He went on to prove (viii. to x.) that the sacrifice which Christ offers in heaven before God is the only perfect one, and alone provides the basis for the new covenant which Jeremiah had predicted and under

which man attains actual fellowship with God. The
ritual did but emblemize his work. His offering is perfect and its effect is permanent. Christianity is the
final and perfect religion because of the divinity of him
who has revealed it, because of his ideal priestly office,
and because of the perfection of his priestly offering.
The condition, therefore, of enjoying the benefit of salvation is alone faith in him, and this the author presents in the light of all Hebrew history as the substance
and power of the true religious life (xi., xii.).

300. To the historian the value of this immortal
treatise lies in its disclosure of the completeness with
which the founders of Christianity apprehended the
relation of the new faith to its antecedents and so met
the problems which the transition from Judaism produced. Here the permanent religious truths of the
ritual — the necessity of sacrifice and of a priestly
mediation — were transferred to Christianity, while
showing that the forms of the ritual were not meant to
continue. We here see the new religion disentangling
itself from Judaism without losing the truth which the
latter contained. The epistle was written when the
ritual was about to be rendered forever impossible by
the destruction of the temple. It pointed out that in
its destruction the religion of revelation suffered no
loss. It thus completed the interpretation of past
revelation in the light of present history. In this
" word of exhortation " (xiii. 22) the religion of Moses
bloomed into the universal religion of mankind, of
which it had always contained the seed.

IV

RISE OF HISTORICAL NARRATIVES

301. DURING the whole period of the rise and prog·
ress of Christianity the apostolic reports of the career
and teaching of Jesus had been in constant circulation
among the churches. Apostolic teaching had never
been disassociated from the story of Christ's life, but
was regarded as only the inspired amplification of his
instruction and explanation of his mission. Hence by
" the gospel " was meant the glad tidings which God
had sent through Jesus and his apostles. Jesus had
himself begun by proclaiming " the gospel of the kingdom " (e. g. Matt. iv. 23 ; Mark i. 14, 15). Later he had
spoken of his entire message, including the report of
his life and acts, as " the gospel " (Mark viii. 35 ; x.
29 ; xiii. 10 ; xiv. 9 ; xiv. 15), and to Mark (i. 1) this was
" the gospel of Jesus Christ" which the Baptist's
ministry introduced. After Pentecost this was naturally the term used to describe the revelation contained
in the history and teaching of Jesus (Acts xv. 7 ; I.
Thess. i. 5 ; ii. 2, 4, 8, 9 ; iii. 2 ; II. Thess. i. 8 ; I. Cor.
iv. 15 ; ix. 12, 14, 18, 23, etc.) which the apostles pro·
claimed. It was mainly the recital of his works and
sayings, his death and resurrection (Acts i. 21, 22 ;
ii. 22–24 ; x. 37–43 ; I. Cor. xv. 1 ; Rom. i. 1–4). The
term, however, also came to include the apostolic ex·
planations of Christ's mission ; and this usage appears

frequently in Paul (Gal. i. 7, 11; ii. 2, 5, 7, 14; II. Cor. xi. 4; Rom. i. 16, 17; ii. 16; Acts xxvi. 24; Eph. i. 13; iii. 6; vi. 15, 19; Phil. i. 5, 7; Col. i. 5, 23; I. Tim. i. 11; II. Tim. i. 10). Yet even with Paul the doctrinal aspect was not confused with the historical (Rom. xvi. 25; I. Cor. xi. 23; xv. 1; I. Tim. vi. 3; II. Tim. i. 8; ii. 8); and when historical narratives of the Lord's life were composed, they were, at least in the age immediately succeeding the apostolic, called "gospels."

302. At first the circulation of the reports was oral. It is evident, however, from our synoptics that the reports tended to assume more and more fixity of form. This was the natural result of the desire to impress them on the disciples by repetition. There was not, indeed, at first any apparent intention to preserve them in documents. But the incidents were repeated and the words of Jesus were reported again and again, until a body of oral narrative existed which in much the same language was diffused throughout the churches; while at the same time some incidents did not attain the same wide circulation as others, and different apostles added special contributions to the common stock. This current narrative dealt mainly with Christ's public ministry, and particularly with that in Galilee, where Jesus had gathered most of his disciples and had founded his church, and with the last week of his life. It related both his works and words, selecting such incidents as were felt to be of special religious importance. There is no evidence that it dealt solely or mainly with his teaching. On the contrary, while his words were remembered, equal stress was laid on his miracles and his sufferings.

303. In time the need became apparent of putting the narrative into permanent, written form. The first reference to this is found in the opening verses of Luke's gospel, where we read that many had "taken in hand to draw up a narrative concerning those matters which have been fulfilled among us, even as they delivered them unto us which from the beginning were eye witnesses and ministers of the word" (I. 1, 2, R.V.). The earliest written accounts were thus the reproduction of the apostolic testimony. They appear from Luke's language to have been incomplete, since he emphasizes the relative completeness of his own work. Out of the same motives, however, considering them from the historical point of view, arose our first three gospels. They appear to have been accepted in the churches almost at once as possessing apostolic authority. We find them with John's, in the first half of the second century, the recognized gospels of the church. Oral tradition of course lingered by their side. Other gospels, usually affected by some peculiar motive, arose and were accepted for a while in limited localities (e. g. Gospel according to the Hebrews, according to the Egyptians, according to Peter, etc.). But these three, to which John's was afterwards joined, attained authority so rapidly in the churches that it is plain that they were regarded at once as the genuine embodiment of the apostolic reports. About the same time also Luke completed his gospel by the Acts (sect. 280).

304. The rise of this historical literature discloses another phase of apostolic history. It shows that primitive Christianity was not a mere ethical or theological movement, but was created by the career and

teaching of Jesus, and never lost its consciousness
of its historical origin. The large amount of matter
that the synoptic gospels have in common illustrates
the universal diffusion throughout the churches of
substantially the same narrative. Yet the story was
repeated with various, though harmonious, modifi-
cations. In Matthew's gospel Jesus is presented as
the royal Messiah who fulfilled the law and the
prophets, and established by his teaching and his
redeeming work the true kingdom of God, which em-
braces men of all nations. This is the gospel of the
Christianized Jew. In Mark's, Jesus appears rather
as the mighty conqueror, the Son of God, revealing
his power, and yet willingly submitting to death that he
might rise again. In Luke's, we have the Saviour of
the world, the gracious Son of man, wonderful in his
peerless character, whose message of redemption was
glad tidings to the nations; while in the Acts the
evangelist carried on the unfolding of Christianity to
its establishment as a non-Judaic, universal faith. The
point to be observed is that apostolic Christianity was
historically rooted in the life and work of Jesus, and
that his significance continued to be a subject of increasing interest and reflection. It was the message of
and about him that the apostles carried throughout the
world, on which the faith and hope of the primitive
disciples rested, and which appealed with triumphant
power to sinful, waiting humanity. It was further an
opportune fact that these historical books were produced at a time when most of the original witnesses
were still living and yet when their departure was near.
The future was thus provided with those facts, well
attested, on which it would ever need to rest its faith.

305. THE last third of the first century was in some respects a transitional period in the history of Christianity. The new religion had become firmly established. It was everywhere addressing itself to the task of maintaining the integrity of its belief and life against the hatred or seductions of the world, and of winning the world to its teachings. It had thus begun the struggle which was to last through the succeeding centuries. Within this period also appeared the beginnings of those sects which dissented from the established faith or sought to combine with it alien elements derived from Judaism or paganism; while, on the other hand, the organization of the churches, at least in some quarters, advanced toward greater centralization of authority and compactness of form. These features of the church's life continued to unfold in the post-apostolic age. Christianity, therefore, was already entering on the development and conflict to which as a world religion she was destined. At the same time the apostolic age had not closed. All the elements which historically lay at the foundation of subsequent Christianity had not yet been given. This is shown by the fact that during this period are to be located the last ministry of the apostle John and the writings which he issued. The latter entered so immediately into the

life and faith of the church that they plainly constituted part of its foundation, and, together with the
apostolic office of their author, require us to extend the
apostolic age practically to the close of the century.

306. During this period Christianity continued to
spread rapidly. Our information is scanty, but there
can be no doubt about the fact. We have already noted
its wide diffusion in the last years of Paul (sect. 262).
That it entered Egypt with much power is proved by the
remains of early Christian literature in that land from
early in the second century. There is also reason to
believe that it entered Arabia and Parthia, and possibly
India as well as, in the west, Germany and Gaul. It
touched Spain and perhaps Britain; while throughout
the central parts of the empire it had its adherents in
every country. The language of the Revelation (*e. g.*
vii. 9) implies that the new faith included representatives from all nations. Clement of Rome (A. D. 96) refers to the apostles as "preaching everywhere in city
and country." Ignatius (A. D. 110) writes of "bishops
settled in the farthest parts [of the earth]." Pliny,
governor of Bithynia and Pontus in A. D. 112, found the
Christians so numerous that the worship of the temples
had severely suffered. It is probable that by the close
of the century companies of believers existed in all the
larger cities and many of the smaller towns of the empire, and that the new religion was represented from
the Atlantic to the Indus, and from Germany to Egypt
and Arabia. Its strength lay in the cities. Early
Christianity is known to us mainly by the names of
city churches. The early post-apostolic letters, like
most of those of the New Testament, were addressed to
urban communities. In the Roman world the city was

the mistress of its surrounding district; and as Paul wisely chose cities for the sphere of his labors, so do they seem to have been generally the centres of the Christian evangelism. These facts enable us to imagine the activity of the disciples either in formal missionary work or in incidental labors. It is a reasonable estimate that by the close of the century they numbered a hundred thousand.

307. The Christians continued to attract also persons of very various positions in life. Undoubtedly most of them still belonged to the humbler classes ; but there are indications that people of wealth and occasionally some of high social standing had enrolled themselves among the followers of Jesus. Already Paul had found it necessary to warn the rich against the love of money (I. Tim. vi. 9, 10, 17–19); and, much later, the church at Laodicea was reproved for trust in riches (Rev. iii. 17). Toward the close of Domitian's reign, his own cousin, Flavius Clemens, was executed, and the latter's wife, Domitilla, banished, for " sacrilege ; " and the evidence is conclusive that they were really Christians (*Lightfoot*, Introd. to Clem. of R. ; *Ramsay*, Ch. in the Emp. p. 259, etc.). The *Cœmeterium Domitillœ* was one of the earliest Roman catacombs, and by its name confirms the inference, which may be drawn from the vague statements of secular historians, that Christianity had penetrated into the imperial family itself. Such instances, no doubt, were rare ; but they warn us against supposing that all of the believers were of the lower orders. The fact, also, that philosophic influences tended, as we shall see, to corrupt the faith indicates that many belonged to the educated class.

308. The worship of the Christians was still of the simplest kind. The first day of the week, already called " the Lord's day " (Rev. i. 10), was the one for formal gatherings. Early in the second century we find its observance, rather than the Jewish Sabbath, noted as the distinguishing mark of the Christian (*Ignatius*, ad Magn. 9). Justin Martyr's description of the simple service — the reading of " the memoirs of the apostles and the writings of the prophets," an exhortation by the presiding officer and the celebration of the Eucharist — will doubtless apply to the close of the first century as well as to fifty years later. Traces of the beginnings of liturgies and of Christian hymns may indeed be found in Clement of Rome (A. D. 96) and the Teaching of the Apostles (A. D. 100); the latter also in the Pauline epistles themselves (Eph. v. 19 ; Col. iv. 16 ; I. Tim. iii. 16); and we probably should conceive of the public worship of this period as in a state of transition from the spontaneous exercise of spiritual gifts, such as is described in Paul's epistle to the Corinthians, to the more formal service of later times. But it was still a simple service. The two rites of baptism and the Lord's supper were the only obligatory ceremonies. The latter was still connected with the *agape*, or love feast, and was usually celebrated in the evening. The meeting places must still have been commonly private houses.

309. There appears also to have been advancing, at least in some quarters, a decided modification of the organization of the churches. The Christian community in each locality had been governed originally by a body of equal presbyter-bishops after the model of the synagogue. But at the end of the century a single ruler appears in the churches of Asia called by pre-eminence " the bishop." Assisted by his corps of presbyters, he was in charge of the administrative and executive work of the church (comp. *Epp. of Ignatius*, and perhaps Rev. ii. 1, 8, etc.). Since in the earlier period "bishop" and "presbyter" denoted the same office, the later form of arrangement must have developed out of the former by the elevation of one to the position of permanent president. This centralizing process advanced, however, unequally in different places. It was more advanced in the east than in the west. At the close of the century it can be affirmed positively only of the churches of Asia. Yet the drift toward it must have been general. It was, in fact, a natural movement in the interest of efficiency of organization and unity of life. The church in each locality constituted one body, whether it had one meeting place or several. Over the whole the body of presbyters had presided; and when out of their number a permanent "bishop" was chosen, he still officiated as the head of the same local community. There is no evidence that these communities were united in an external organization, but only by their common faith and mutual love and the common recognition of apostolic authority (comp. III. John 10; Rev. i. 11). Neither had the priestly conception been attached to the governing officials; and while the local ministry of rulers and teachers and deacons existed everywhere, there were also travelling missionaries and evangelists, who went from place to place bearing the word of the Lord (III. John 6, 7; comp., too, The Teach. of the App. xi. – xiii.). The condition of affairs was thus transitional and varied; but a tendency toward increasing compactness of organization and toward the visible expression of the unity of the several churches in the person of a single chief ruler can be plainly discerned.

310. Of the causes which led to this, one of the most potent was the spread of false teaching among the churches. This was certainly the motive which led Ignatius (A. D. 110) to emphasize the duty of loyalty to the established officers and services of the churches which he addressed. The existence of this peril, which had already appeared in the time of Paul and Peter, is evidenced by the writings of John. The fourth gospel was written confessedly with an apologetic purpose (xx. 30, 31) ; and its prologue as well as its general contents indicate that the apostles felt forced to proclaim the true doctrine of the divine-human personality of Jesus. His epistles contain references to the same class of errorists (I. John ii. 18, 19, 22 ; iv. 1, 3 ; v. 6 ; II. John 7, 9–11 ; III. John 4). The "Revelation" denounces other false teachers (ii. 2, 6, 14, 15, 20–24), some of whom, as the Nicolaitans, appear to have combined gross immorality with their erroneous teaching. We know also from later writers that toward the close of the century a certain Cerinthus came from Alexandria to Asia. He combined a type of speculative Judaism with Christianity. To him Jesus was a man on whom the Spirit of the Christ descended at his baptism and left him before his death. His theology was controlled by the notion that God himself cannot come into immediate contact with matter. Hence intermediate beings were necessary to account for the origin and government of the world ; and the idea of a real incarnation and of redemption

by sacrifice vanished in the speculations of philosophy. This was one of the earliest forms of gnosticism; and it is not improbable that some of John's expressions were directed specifically against this teaching (*e. g.* I. John ii. 22; iv. 2 ; v. 6). On the other hand sections of the Jewish Christians who survived the fall of Jerusalem drifted into settled antagonism to the established Gentile Christianity. In some cases their Judaism was more potent than their Christianity, so that the latter became little more than nominal. They considered Jesus as only a man, and continued to regard the Mosaic law as necessary. They were afterwards known as Ebionites. Others of the Jewish Christians did not relapse so far, but still kept aloof from the established Gentile churches ; while still others strove to introduce eclectic combinations of Jewish or Christian ideas, or both of these, with philosophic elements. Thus Christianity was being seriously threatened in her beliefs, and the fact naturally led her leaders to emphasize the duty of fidelity to the existing organizations and to their authorized teachers.

311. On the other hand they felt with increasing force the universal enmity of the outside world. In fact the new religion now stood face to face with a hostile society and a frowning empire. Two great events had helped to produce this situation. The fall of Jerusalem (A. D. 70) had finally destroyed the cradle of the faith. There could no longer be a double Christianity, a Judaic and a Gentile. It was Gentile alone. Most of the Jewish Christians merged into the Gentile churches, while those who remained outside dwindled, as observed above, into dissenting and

heretical sects. Christianity thus became completely separated from Judaism, and, as a religion without a country, was forced to her world-mission. Then, further, Nero's persecution had placed the ban of the empire on the Christians in distinction from the Jews. His policy was continued by the Flavian emperors; and, though we have no record of further persecution until the reign of Domitian, there is little ground for doubt that Christianity was officially regarded as illegal (*Ramsay*, Ch. in the Emp. ch. xii.). In the later years of Domitian actual and violent persecution was waged. The emperor suspected that Christianity was a treasonable movement, and in both Rome and the provinces many were imprisoned or slain. The attitude of the government could indeed hardly have been different, so soon as Christianity was distinguished from Judaism. No religion was tolerated by Roman law which was not that of a subject nation; and, under the empire, societies of all kinds were regarded as dangerous to the state and allowed only under special licenses. Meanwhile popular hatred was increasing on account of the refusal of the Christians to recognize the pagan gods and to worship the emperor, a refusal which seemed sure proof of atheism and disloyalty. This gave plausibility also to the vulgar rumors that they were immoral and inhuman. Popular hatred thus supported governmental oppression. It was evident that Christianity had truly entered on a world-conflict. The fact at once intensified its consciousness of its mission and the need of unity for the struggle. This is illustrated by the antithesis between Christianity and the world which appears constantly in the writings of John.

312. Finally, with this widened environment, Christianity naturally felt as never before the influence of the intellectual, social, and political ideas which were current in the empire. As already remarked, heresies of an eclectic character began to appear. These, however, were but special manifestations of the larger fact that the new religion was exposed to the subtle operation of the forces dominant about her, and which threatened to impair her independence and integrity. It was pre-eminently an eclectic age; and Christianity was possessed of so much moral and intellectual vigor that she easily formed a new centre about which ideas gathered which were alien to her nature and detrimental to her proper progress. In the next century we find her heavily weighted by notions derived from pagan or Alexandrian systems, and affected by the institutions of Greek or Roman society. These influences doubtless began to operate before the apostolic age had closed. Many of the Gentile converts must have failed to understand the Hebrew presuppositions upon which the new religion rested. A new class of problems were necessarily suggested by contact and conflict with universal paganism. Current philosophical and social ideas had to be met and mastered. Christianity was now grappling with the whole world-problem, and needed to understand herself and her mission in the light of the enlarged sphere in which her subsequent history was to be enacted. It is this situation which gives historical interest to the writings of the apostle John.

313. Nothing is related in the New Testament of the life of John, after the council at Jerusalem (Gal. ii. 9), until we find him on the island of Patmos, an exile for

his faith (Rev. i. 9), and addressing the "Revelation" to the seven churches of Asia. So far as it goes, however, this evidence agrees with the tradition that he passed the last years of his life in Ephesus, was thence banished to Patmos by Domitian, returned to Ephesus after the emperor's death, and survived till the time of Trajan (A. D. 98). The tradition was early and widespread. It was also direct, for it is most explicitly stated by Irenæus, whose teacher, Polycarp of Smyrna, was a disciple of John. The banishment to Patmos was assigned by most other authorities also to the time of Domitian; and it is quite impossible to conceive of the advanced condition of the Asian churches, described in Revelation, as existing under an earlier emperor. We cannot say definitely when John left Jerusalem. It is perhaps the most probable view that he remained in Palestine until the approach of the war with Rome. It may be, however, that he had gone elsewhere before that time. Certainly he is not mentioned in connection with Paul's last visit to Jerusalem (Acts xxi. 18). Since, also, no reference to him occurs in the pastoral epistles nor in those of Peter, we may believe that he did not settle in Asia until after A. D. 70.

314. It is not surprising that John selected Ephesus for his last residence, in view of the importance of that city and the influence which the Ephesian church had exercised from the beginning of its history (sect. 211). There he was in the very centre of eastern Christianity. That he wielded great influence is attested not only by tradition, but by the authoritative tone of his writings (e. g. John xxi. 24; I. John i. 1–3; ii. 24; iv. 26; v. 13; Rev. i. 1–3) and their immediate circulation in the churches. He was not, indeed, the only one in that

region who had been a personal disciple of Jesus.
Early tradition relates that at one time Andrew was
there with him; and not far off, in Phrygian Hiera-
polis, lived Philip, though the notices of the latter seem
to confuse the apostle and the evangelist of that name.
There was also at Ephesus a certain Aristion, who appears to have been an aged and venerated disciple;
and around the apostle there seems to have gathered a
circle of prominent Christians, some of whom probably
had long been believers. But it was John who left the
chief mark on the place and time. Interesting stories
concerning his life and personality floated down the
stream of tradition. We are on sure ground, however,
only when we interpret his own writings.

315. The fourth gospel had for its avowed purpose
to prove " that Jesus is the Christ the Son of God; and
that believing ye may have life in his name " (xx. 31,
R. V.). It does this by giving certain discourses of Jesus
not found in the synoptics, in which the Lord bore witness to his unique relation to God, the world, and his
disciples. The apostle also gives a number of historical
incidents, bearing on the same theme, at most of which
he had himself been present. We are concerned, however, only to note the light thrown by this work on
the last years of the apostolic age. Its prologue gives
the key to the situation. Here Jesus is presented as
the incarnation of the divine Logos (Word) of God.
This indicates that the author was confronted by speculative theories concerning the person of Christ which
he felt it necessary to refute. The term "Logos"
had both a Hebrew and a Greek pedigree, and would be
recognized both by Jew and Gentile, and especially by
those touched by the eclecticism of Alexandria, as a

fit phrase by which to describe the founder of Christianity as the personal and perfect revelation of God (comp. art. *Logos*, Hastings' Dict. of B.). The apostle, however, did not subordinate his teaching to current philosophic notions. In his description of the Logos he only repeated ideas which had been taught in other terms by earlier Christian teachers (see *e. g.* Col. i. 13-20; ii. 9; Phil. ii. 5-11; Heb. i. 2-4). He united this teaching into one great representation, in which, starting with the eternal personality and divinity of the Logos, he traced his revelation of God in nature, in humanity, and finally in the incarnation. Of this theme the gospel which followed was intended to be the proof. Thus John showed that because of his real divinity Jesus was the perfect revelation of God; and further, that his incarnation was the crown of that manifestation of God which from the beginning of time he had been making throughout the universe. It was through him alone that men had ever known God at all; and in his coming in the flesh and in the religion which he had thus established, the final and complete disclosure of God, truth and duty had been effected. It must be evident that the publication of this conception of Christ and of Christianity marks the highest point possible in the claim which the new religion could make for itself; that thus it was prepared, as the only true religion, to demand acceptance by all mankind. Whatever of truth or duty might exist elsewhere found its synthesis in the personal revelation of the divine Word himself.

316. The First Epistle of John stands in close connection with his gospel. It is in fact intelligible only to readers of the gospel, and was probably issued with

or shortly after it. It is the application to Christian life of the conception of Christianity as the perfect revelation of God. It was written, the apostle says, on the basis of that manifestation of Life, contained in the incarnation of the Logos, which the apostles by their association with Jesus were qualified to declare (i. 1–4). In the revelation of God as light, *i. e.* as the embodiment of rational and moral truth, is to be found the determining factor of Christian knowledge and life (i. 5 to ii. 6), whereby the believer is necessarily separated from the world and error (ii. 7–27). Since, also, the fulness of this truth and life will be manifested at the second coming of Christ, it is necessary that the sons of God should show righteousness, which is the evidence of sonship, by obedience and love (ii. 28 to iii. 24); and the proof that they possess the divine Spirit is their true confession of Christ, adherence to revealed teaching, and the love which is the soul's response to Him who is in his own nature Love (iv.). We are next reminded that faith in the revealed Christ is the condition of the whole spiritual life wherein the world is overcome (v. 1–12); and the epistle closes with a statement of its purpose — " that ye may know that ye have eternal life, ye that believe in the name of the Son of God " (v. 13, R. V.; comp. John xx. 31) — and with a summary of the certitudes, given in Christian experience, whereby we may rest confidently in the faith which led to them. Even this general outline of the epistle shows that to John Christianity was the absolute revelation of God and the establishment in the soul of the genuine life in and with God. Thus its universality appeared in its absoluteness. With Paul its universality had appeared in its unlimited scope

and applicability ; in the Epistle to the Hebrews, in its being the final goal of Hebrew revelation ; with Peter, in its fulfilment of the prophetic hope of Israel ; but to John, in its being the perfect revelation of the religious realities, of the idea of religion itself. The apostle by no means resolved it into a speculative system. He remained true to the historial facts. But the profound significance of the facts had unfolded in accordance with the historical situation ; and when Christianity found itself confronted by the world, it asserted itself in the writings of John to be, from its very nature and because of the person of its Founder, the world's only real religion.

317. The Second and Third Epistles of John throw interesting light on the apostle's care of the churches. They are unmistakably Johannean, though the writer, quite in accord with his reserve in the gospel and first epistle, calls himself simply "the elder." The second epistle was addressed " to the elect lady and her children," by which we probably should understand a church rather than an individual, because of the following reference to " certain " of her children (4, R. V.) and to the directions against false doctrine (7–11). It is a brief note, perhaps carried back by some of the members of the church who had been at Ephesus (4), urging to a life of love and warning against the same class of false teachers mentioned in the first epistle (comp. II. John 7 and I. John ii. 18, 22 ; iv. 2). The true Christian, he says, will abide in the teaching of Christ (9), and the errorist should by no means be received to the church's hospitality (10). The third epistle is still more illustrative of the times. It was addressed to Gaius, a prominent member of some

church, commending certain missionaries on their way to another place, of whom Demetrius, who is specially commended (12), was probably one. We also learn that in the church to which Gaius belonged a certain Diotrephes had refused to receive missionaries sent by John with a previous letter, and had expelled those who did receive them. Diotrephes was doubtless a presbyter, possibly a presiding bishop; but his power was apparently more personal than official (9). In both letters John expressed the hope of visiting his correspondents shortly; and against Diotrephes he threatened the summary exercise of apostolic authority. We thus see the apostle's vigorous oversight of the churches, as well as the factious and false teaching against which he had to contend. The allusion to travelling mission aries shows also the efforts made to propagate the faith. In the Teaching of the Apostles (A. D. 100) we read of similar evangelists, there called apostles and prophets. The enthusiasm of missions was in fact so great that it was necessary to test the teaching and character of these itinerants, since false emissaries caught the zeal and divided the work. We can thus realize the practical difficulties of the times, even as John's larger works illustrate the greater problems of thought and life with which he dealt.

318. Finally, in the Revelation we are introduced to an entirely different kind of literature from any yet brought before us. Apocalyptic books were not strange in those days. Later Judaism, moved by the still earlier Book of Daniel, produced a number of such works. Their authors, however, generally imputed them, as in the case of the Book of Enoch and the Assumption of Moses, to some one of the older patri-

archs. These books excited a powerful influence on the thought and hopes of the Jewish people (see *Schürer*, HJP. II., III.; *Riggs*, Hist. of Jew. People, sects. 6, 157). Their characteristic was the representation of ideas or of future events by symbolic figures or actions. It was a favorite form of literature and adapted to times of storm and stress. The wonder is that Christianity did not produce more such works; and it is a testimony to the truly prophetic character of John that he did not, like the Jewish writers, attach his apocalypse to the name of an older prophet, but issued it in his own name.

319. This book describes itself as Christ's revelation of the future communicated symbolically to John (i. 1-3). It is addressed to seven churches of Asia (i. 4-6), and its general subject is the coming of Christ to judgment on the enemies of God and for the salvation of his people. It consists of seven visions or series of visions, which represent as many aspects of the triumph of the enthroned Lord. We are again concerned only to note its bearing on the mind and situation of the church. The opening messages to the churches furnish some interesting facts. Five of these churches are here mentioned for the first time; yet evidently they had all been long established. That of Ephesus still appears as the foremost in the whole province; and the references to various types of heresy (ii. 6, 14, 15, 20-24), to persecution (ii. 10, 13; iii. 10), to the enmity of the Jews (ii. 9; iii. 9), together with the careful discrimination of the spiritual conditions of the several communities, give a graphic picture of the situation which existed in Asia. Taking the book as a whole, it is evident that the return of Christ was

still the church's hope. It was not conceived, however, as an isolated event. It was, in fact, inclusive of a large and varied series of events which would lead up to it. All these were regarded as the appointed unfolding of God's decree, and over the whole process the enthroned Redeemer-King is himself presiding. That process would consist in Christ's progressive triumph, partly by proclamation of the gospel and partly by judgment on a wicked world. The latter aspect is very prominent, as was natural in a time of the church's feebleness and distress. The future was expected also to be a period of conflict. The power of evil would be arrayed against the church, and deadly apostasy would arise within her. Yet the redeemed people of God would be safe; their prayers for succor would be answered; their final salvation was secure. And this not only for them as individuals. The book contemplates the conflicts, perils, and final establishment of the church as a body. The seven churches of Asia were representative of the church universal, and the new Jerusalem was the visible embodiment of her ideal state. All this is depicted by means of symbols which denote principles and ideas rather than special individuals.

320. Thus in Revelation, as in John's gospel and first epistle, the consciousness of a world-conflict, a world-process, and a world-triumph is manifest. The return of Jesus is contemplated in relation to the enlarged environment in which Christianity stood. Revelation testifies to the persistence of the hope with which Christianity had begun, but also to the fact that into that hope had entered the fuller conception of Christ and his salvation which the apostles had

taught, and the broadened vision of the purpose of God which the history had made clear. Yet it was still the same hope, " Behold, he cometh " (Rev. i. 7) ; and the prayer was still the same, " Come, Lord Jesus " (Rev. xxii. 20).

321. With the Johannean literature the apostolic age closed. It is true, as already observed, that the last part of the century was transitional ; and we have at least one production, nearly contemporaneous with Revelation, which really belongs to the post-apostolic period. This is the epistle of Clement, written in the name of the church at Rome to that at Corinth (A. D. 96). The pseudo-epistle of Barnabas and the Teaching of the Apostles have also been dated by some scholars, but with less probability, in the first century. But the student of early Christian literature must recognize that these works are on a lower level, that their authors were sensible of dependence on those of the apostolic age, and that with them we pass out of the originative period of Christianity. In the writings of John the foundation of the new religion was completed. It would be erroneous, indeed, to imagine that all or even most of the converts fully appropriated the teachings of the founders of the church. The literary remains of the next generation show that the church failed to grasp many of the doctrines taught in the former age ; and the progress of subsequent Christianity, viewed internally, often reveals a slow and inadequate apprehension of the apostolic faith. This, however, only illustrates the unique and fundamental character of the apostolic instruction itself. On the other hand, the historian must perceive that the literature of

the apostolic period combines with the historical movement, in which the original faith in Jesus as Messiah
unfolded its content and expanded the area of its influence, to present an intellectual and moral unity which
was plainly the work of one Spirit, completing har-
moniously the presentation to men of the mission and
message of Jesus, and thus providing a foundation on
which subsequent Christianity was intended to build.
It is the fact of this unity which gives its supreme
importance to the history of the apostolic age, for it
certifies that apostolic Christianity was the normal and
authoritative exposition of the religion of Jesus.

APPENDIX

APPENDIX

CHRONOLOGY OF THE APOSTOLIC AGE

322. THE chronology of the apostolic age must be obtained chiefly from the book of Acts. While, however, that book makes clear the relative chronology of most of its events, there are but few of them whose absolute dates can be determined. We must obtain the fixed points which are ascertainable, compute other events from them, and always remember that the results in most cases are only approximate or probable.

323. The most certain date is that of the death of Herod Agrippa I. (Acts xii). Josephus (*B. J.*, II. xi. 6; *Antiq.*, xviii. iv. 6, vi. 10, vii. 2; xix. vi. 1, viii. 2) shows that Agrippa was appointed king of all Palestine on the accession of Claudius to the empire (Jan. A.D. 41), and that he reigned over this territory three years. The alleged existence of coins of his ninth year may be explained by the fact that he was given, with the title of king, the tetrarchy of Herod Philip by Caligula soon after the death of Tiberius (Mar. A.D. 37), and doubtless began to reckon the second year of his reign with Nisan of that year (Comp. *Turner*, Hast. D. of B. vol. I. p. 416). His death therefore may be assigned confidently to A.D. 44 and (Acts xii. 3) subsequent to the passover.

324. Again, the death of Christ, and hence the day of Pentecost on which Christianity was inaugurated, occurred in A.D. 29 or 30. The choice certainly lies between these two years (*Rhees*, L. J., sect. 50). For reasons which cannot be given here we accept A.D. 30; but, since Christ's

ministry may have been two and a quarter years in length, or may have begun in A.D. 26, the year 29 for his death cannot be positively excluded.

325. The date of the accession of Festus as procurator of Judea (Acts xxv. 1) is less certain. This event has commonly been assigned to A.D. 60 (see *Schürer*, HJP. Div. I., II. p. 182 note). Felix had been appointed procurator by Claudius on the deposition of Cumanus in A.D. 52 or 53 and was reappointed by Nero (*Jos.* B. J. II. xiii. 2). Josephus (B. J. II. xii. 8–xiv. 1) relates nearly all the events in which Felix was concerned as if they occurred under Nero, whose reign began Oct. 13, A.D. 54. Hence Felix must have been in office some years after A.D. 54. Since, moreover, Paul (Acts xxiv. 10, 27) refers to Felix as having been many years in office, the apostle's arrest can hardly have been before A.D. 58, which puts the accession of Festus, two years after, in A.D. 60. It cannot well be placed later, since Albinus, the successor of Festus, was already procurator in A.D. 62 (*Jos.* B. J. VI. v. 3), and the events recorded under Festus require more than a year. The probabilities therefore point to A.D. 60 as that of Festus' accession to office.

326. Every point of this calculation is indeed open to dispute, and the tendency of many recent scholars has been wholly to deny its result. Thus it is observed that Tacitus (Ann. xii. 54) states that Felix had previously ruled in Samaria while Cumanus ruled in Galilee, and though he does not say which of the two at that time ruled in Judea, his statement has been thought to prove that the residence of Felix in Palestine began so much earlier than has been commonly assumed that Paul's language might have been spoken several years before A.D. 58. But against this must be placed the narrative of Josephus, which, though consistent with the supposition that Felix had held a subordinate position in Samaria, knows nothing of a contemporaneous procuratorship of the two men, and assigns, as already noted, most of the

events under Felix to the reign of Nero. The Jewish historian on this point would seem more trustworthy than the Roman.

327. Again, the Chronicon of Eusebius dates the appointment of Felix in the 10th or 11th year of Claudius (= A.D. 50–51, or 51–52) and the accession of Festus in the second year of Nero (= A.D. 55–56). Harnack (*Chronol.* p. 235) and others think that the Chronicon was based on earlier chronologists and is fairly trustworthy. But these dates compel the assignment of events related in the former part of Acts to years which are certainly too early (see sects. 328, 334; also *Turner*, Hastings' D. of B. pp. 418, 419). The Eusebian date has indeed been supported by the statement of Josephus (Antiq., xx. viii. 9) that when Felix, after his recall to Rome, was accused by the Jews, he was acquitted through the influence of his brother Pallas, "who was at that time had in the greatest honor by (Nero)." Now Pallas was dismissed from office in Feb. A.D. 55. Hence it has been inferred that Felix was recalled soon after Nero's accession in A.D. 54. Yet this argument is vitiated by the difficulty of believing that, if Felix was recalled after Nero's accession in Oct. A.D. 54, he could have reached Rome and been acquitted before Feb. A.D. 55, and also by the fact that, while Pallas was dismissed from office in A.D. 55, he lived and retained great influence till A.D. 62. The language of Josephus, therefore, strong as it is, cannot be used to uphold the Eusebian date; nor would the recall of Felix in 54 be consistent with the assignment of the accession of Festus to 55–56. Josephus, moreover, explicitly states (B. J. ii. xiii. 2), that Nero reappointed Felix. Ramsay, on the other hand (St. Paul the Trav. p. 259), fixes the year of Paul's arrest as A.D. 57, and that of the accession of Festus as A.D. 59, by computing that the passover preceding the arrest (Acts xx. 6) fell on a Thursday, which it is said to have done in A.D. 57. This latter fact, however, is itself open to question, and Ramsay's

view further supposes that Luke's statement " we sailed away from Philippi after the days of unleavened bread " must be understood to mean on the very next day after. Finally, C. H. Turner (Hast. D. of B. *Chronology of the N. T.*) with much plausibility assigns the arrest of Paul to A.D. 56, and the accession of Festus to 58. The main difficulty with this scheme is that, while following Josephus rather than Eusebius, it fails to assign as much time as the Jewish historian would seem to require us to do to the administration of Felix under Nero. While, therefore, certainty is not possible, the year 60 still remains the most probable one for the accession of Festus.

328. Besides these principal dates, others have been sought with more or less success. The dominion of Aretas, king of the Nabatæans, over Damascus at the time of Paul's escape (II. Cor. xi. 32) cannot, from what we know of Damascus coins, and of the relation of Aretas to the Romans, have begun before A. D. 34, and probably not before A. D. 37 (see *Turner*, Hast. D. of B. *Chronology*). Again, the edict of Claudius on account of which Aquila and Priscilla had " lately " come from Rome to Corinth when Paul reached the latter city (Acts xviii. 2) is assigned by Orosius, a Christian historian of the fifth century, to the ninth year of Claudius (= A. D. 49). Orosius indeed was mistaken in citing Josephus for this date, and Ramsay (St. Paul the Trav. pp. 69, 254) may be right in the conjecture that the dates in Orosius are one year too early ; but his testimony accords better with the common than with the Eusebian chronology. Moreover we should not press Luke's expression "*lately* come from Italy " too far. In like manner the procuratorship of Gallio in Achaia could hardly have been earlier than A. D. 49, the year when his brother Seneca was recalled from exile, and may have been several years later.

329. The chronology of Acts is, then, to be constructed on the basis of these data. If the accession of Festus

was in A. D. 60, it was in the autumn of that year that Paul sailed from Cæsarea to Rome (Acts xxv. 1, 13; xxvii. 12). He arrived in the capital in the spring of 61 (Acts xxviii. 11, 12). The two years of his residence in Rome (Acts xxviii. 30) make the narrative of Acts close in A. D. 63. On the other hand, counting back from the accession of Festus, Paul's arrest, two years before (Acts xxiv. 27), was in 58. The preceding winter (A. D. 57, 58) he had spent in Greece (Acts xx. 3), after having, during the autumn of 57, travelled through Macedonia (Acts xx. 2). Before that he had spent three years in Ephesus (Acts xx. 31). This brings us to the summer or spring of A. D. 54 as the time of his departure from Syrian Antioch on what is usually called his third journey (Acts xviii. 23). That journey began after he had spent "some time" in Antioch, probably the winter, at the close of his second journey. On the latter he had passed eighteen months in Corinth (Acts xviii. 11), after having travelled through and labored in Galatia, Macedonia, Berea, and Athens. It is safe to assign therefore to the second journey two years and a half, which, counting back from the autumn of A. D. 53, must have begun in the spring of 51. The second journey began not long after the council at Jerusalem, which thus must be dated in A. D. 50, or possibly 51. The first journey of Barnabas and Paul (Acts xiii., xiv.) can only be assigned roughly to the period between A. D. 44 and 50. Neither can we say how long a time was consumed by it. We may assume for it the years 47, 48.

330. The date of Paul's conversion must be obtained from his statement in Gal. ii. 1: "Then fourteen years after I went up again to Jerusalem with Barnabas." Assuming this to have been the visit to the Council, the question arises, from what are the "fourteen years" to be counted? The most natural interpretation is to count them from the visit to Jerusalem mentioned in i. 18, which is there said to have been three years after his

conversion. Counting back from A. D. 50, and reckoning
the two periods of fourteen and three years inclusively as
was the common Jewish method, we have A. D. 37 for the
first visit to Jerusalem, and A. D. 35 for the conversion.
If the apostle reckoned exclusively, the dates would be
36 and 33 respectively.

331. For the events subsequent to the close of Acts we
are dependent on tradition and the dates assigned to the
later books of the New Testament. Paul's death under
Nero is placed by Eusebius in his Chronicon in A.D. 67, or,
according to Jerome (De vir. ill. 5), in 68. If the Eusebian dating of the accession of Festus be correct, Paul
reached Rome in 56 or 57, Acts closed with 58 or 59, and a
period of eight or nine years elapsed between the apostle's
release from the first imprisonment and his death. If the
common chronology be followed, he was released in 63,
and the remaining period was but four or five years.
Many insist, however (see *Harnack*, Chronol. p. 240,
Turner, Hast. D. of B. *Chronology*), that the apostle must
leave perished in the first outbreak, or at least in the first
year, of Nero's persecution, which took place according to
Tacitus in 64. It is noted that Eusebius places the persecution as well as the deaths of Peter and Paul in the same
year, thus assigning the latter to the year of the persecution though giving the wrong date. It is further argued
that the year 67 was fixed upon by the tradition which
Eusebius followed because of the legend that Peter was
twenty-five years in Rome, which years were calculated
in accordance with another tradition that the apostles
remained in Jerusalem for twelve years after Christ's
death. There is certainly force in these considerations.
But it may also be said that Eusebius, who knew nothing
of Tacitus, may have dated the persecution wrongly,
because, knowing on other grounds that the apostles lived
till near the close of Nero's reign, he fixed it to suit the
time of their death, having in mind, perhaps, not its first
outbreak, but its chief victims. Eusebius, though bringing

Peter to Rome during the time of Claudius, indicates no acquaintance with the legend of the apostle's twenty-five-year residence there; and in his history (II. 22, 25) represents the martyrdom of the apostles as the climax of Nero's increasing wickedness. The statement of the Chronicon, therefore, does not compel the belief that the apostles died in the first year of the persecution; and as reasons exist for believing that Peter lived till later, it may well be that Paul did also, in accordance with the tradition that the two apostles perished about the same time. While certainty is again unattainable, we may accept the year 67 as the approximate date of Paul's death.

332. Peter's death should be assigned to about the same time as Paul's, though probably a little later. Harnack (Chron. p. 243, note 1) dates it, like Paul's, in 64 on the ground (1) that Caius (A. D. 180-235) states that Peter died on the Vatican Hill, the locality which, according to Tacitus, witnessed the sufferings of the first martyrs in Nero's gardens; (2) that Nero's persecution did not last long; and (3) that the Roman lists of bishops, counting back from the death of Anicetus (A. D. 166) carries us back to 64 as the first year of Linus, Peter's successor. These arguments, however, are not convincing. The first is obviously insufficient. It is probable that persecution did continue more or less throughout Nero's reign (see sect. 288). The Roman lists of bishops are untrustworthy. In fact, Ramsay (Ch. in Emp. p. 283) finds a Roman tradition which, he thinks, justifies the supposition that Peter may have lived till even after Nero's death. Finally, the first epistle of Peter implies the existence of such a condition of things in the relation of the Christians to the government as can only be assigned to the years following the outbreak of Nero's persecution.

333. It was the steadfast tradition of the early Church. represented by Irenæus (adv. hær. II. 22, 5), that the apostle John lived till the times of Trajan. His death should be assigned, therefore, to A. D. 98 +.

334. These results may be tabulated as follows. Other schemes are presented for comparison.

		Lightfoot	Harnack	Turner	Ramsay
Crucifixion	30	[30]	29 or 30	29	30
Paul's conversion	35	34	30	35, 36	33
Paul's first visit to Jerusalem	37	37	33	38	35, 36
Death of Herod Agrippa	44	44	44	44	44
Paul's second visit to Jerusalem	44 or 45	45	[44]	46	46
First miss. journey	47, 48 ?	48	45	47	47–49
Jerusalem Council	50	51	47	49	50
Second miss. journey	51–53	51–54	47–50	49–52	50–53
Third miss. journey	54–58	54–58	50–54	52–56	53–57
Paul's arrest	58	58	54	56	57
Accession of Festus	60	60	56	58	59
Paul's arrival in Rome	61	61	57	59	60
Close of Acts	63	63	59	61	62
Paul's death	67 (68)	68 ?	64	64–65	65
Peter's death	67 (68)		64	64–65	
John's death	98 +				80 ?

SELECTED BIBLIOGRAPHY

THE student is referred to the admirable "List of Books" appended by Prof. J. H. Thayer to his little volume entitled *Books and their Use* (Houghton, Mifflin and Co., 1893); also to Prof. M. R. Vincent's *Students N. T. Handbook* (Chas. Scribner's Sons, 1893). The following bibliography is intended to include only works specially representative of various schools of investigation.

I

GENERAL WORKS ON THE APOSTOLIC AGE

A. Neander's *History of the Planting and Training of the Christian Church* (4th ed. 1847) really began the modern literature on this subject, and is still of the highest value. F. C. Baur's *Church History of the First Three Centuries* (Eng. trans. 1878, 9) represents in most complete form the reconstruction of the history of Primitive Christianity by the Tübingen School. A representative reply to the latter, and still perhaps the best book in this department, is G. V. Lechler's *The apostolic and post apostolic Times* (Eng. trans. 1886). A. Ritschl's *Die Entstehung der altkatholischen Kirche* (2d ed. 1857) broke with the Tübingen scheme, represented the Christianity of the second century as the result of the union of degenerate Paulinism with Hellenism, and started a new and fruitful line of investigation. Philip Schaff's *History of the Apostolic Church* (1853) is readable, popular, and still valuable; while O. Pfleiderer's *Das Urchristenthum* (1887) represents a later modification of the Tübingen views, especially emphasizing the influence of Alexandrian philosophy on early Christianity. C. Von Weizäcker's *The Apostolic Age of the Christian Church* (Eng. trans. 1894, 5) is an able work, written in the spirit of free, independent criticism; while J. I. Döllinger's *The First Age of the Church* (1867) is from the Roman Catholic point of view. W. M. Ramsay's *The Church in the Roman Em-*

pire before A.D. 170 (1893) is a work of high value, which none
should fail to study.   O. J. Thatcher's *Sketch of the History of
the Apostolic Age* (1893) is a brief outline, somewhat influenced
by the Ritschlian conception of the history.   Most recent of all
are A. C. McGiffert's *The Apostolic Age* (1898) and Jas. Vernon
Bartlet's work with the same title (1899).

II

LIVES OF THE APOSTLES

(1) PAUL. Conybeare and Howson's *The Life and Epistles
of St. Paul* (revised ed. 1875); Thos. Lewin's work with the
same title (4th ed. 1878); F. W. Farrar's *The Life and Work
of St. Paul* (1879) ; and W. M. Ramsay's *St. Paul the Traveller
and the Roman Citizen* (1896) are the most important British
productions on this subject. F. C. Baur's *Paul the Apostle of
Jesus Christ* (Eng. trans. 1873–5) represents the Tübingen school.
A. Sabatier's *The Apostle Paul* (Eng. trans. 1891) is an interesting and able work, freely critical but very suggestive. G. A.
Gilbert's *The Student's Life of Paul* (1899) is brief, but to be
commended to younger students. Three works, connected with
phases of the apostle's life, should be particularly mentioned;
namely, James Smith's *Voyage and Shipwreck of St. Paul* (4th
ed. 1880), George Matheson's *Spiritual Development of St. Paul*
(1891), and R. Steinmetz's *Die Zweite römische Gefangenshaft
des Apostels Paulus* (1897).

(2) PETER. S. G. Green's *The Apostle Peter, his Life and
Letters* (1873); Henriot's *Saint Pierre* (1891) ; to which may be
added E. Scharfe's *Die Petrinische Strömung der Neutestamentlichen
Literatur* (1893).

(3) JOHN. J. M. Macdonald's *Life and Writings of St. John*
(1877).

III

WORKS BEARING ON THE RELATION OF CHRISTIANITY TO
JUDAISM AND PAGANISM

E. Schürer's *History of the Jewish People in the Time of Jesus
Christ* (Eng. trans. 5 vols. 1896) is invaluable. Briefer is O.
Holtzmann's *Neutestamentliche Zeitgeschichte* (1895). A. Haus-

rath's *A History of the New Testament Times* (Eng. trans. 4 vols. 1895) is less to be commended. J. S. Riggs' *A History of the Jewish People during the Maccabœan and Roman Periods* is the best succinct account of the external environment of Jewish Christianity. F. Weber's *System der altsynagogalen Palästinischen Theologie* (1880); J. Drummond's *The Jewish Messiah* (1877); V. H. Stanton's *The Jewish and Christian Messiah* (1886); and J. B. Lightfoot's *Dissertations on the Apostolic Age* (1892) illustrate the subject from important points of view. A popular work is C. Geike's *New Testament Hours; The Apostles, their Lives and Letters* (1895).

For the pagan environment of apostolic Christianity reference should be made to Th. Keim's *Rom und das Christenthum* (1881); Th. Mommsen's *The Provinces of the Roman Empire* (Eng. trans. 1887); L. Friedländer's *Darstellungen aus der Sittengeschichte Roms in der Zeit von August bis zum Ausgang der Antonine* (6th ed. 1888–90); J. Marquart's *Römische Staatsverwaltung; 3te Band, Das Sacralwesen* (1885); C. F. Arnold's *Die Neronische Christenverfolgung* (1888); P. Allard's *Histoire des Persécutions pendant les deux premiers siècles* (1885); A. Aube's *Histoire des Persécutions de l'Église jusqu'à la fin des Antonins* (1875); Ramsay's *Church in the Empire*, already mentioned; E. Hicks' *Traces of Greek Philosophy and Roman Law in the N. T.* (1896) · S. R. Forbes' *The Footsteps of St. Paul in Rome* (1889); H. Cox's *The First Century of Christianity* (1886); Northcote and Brownlow's *Roma Sotterranea*, pp. 1–110 (1879); W. M. Ramsay's *Historical Geography of Asia Minor* (1890).

IV

CHRISTIAN INSTITUTIONS

W. Cave's *Primitive Christianity* (1840); E. Hatch's *The Organization of the Early Christian Churches* (Bampton Lectt. for 1880); J. B. Lightfoot's *Essay on the Christian Ministry* (Com. on Philippians); J. Réville's *Les Origines de l'épiscopat* (1894); Jas. Cunningham's *The Growth of the Church in its Organization and Institutions* (Croal Lectt. for 1886); F. J. A. Hort's *The Christian Ecclesia* (1897); A. V. G. Allen's *Christian Institutions*, chaps. ii. and iii. (1897).

V

CHRONOLOGY OF THE APOSTOLIC AGE

Wieseler's *Chronologie der Apostolischen Zeitalters* (1848); J. B. Lightfoot's *Chronology of St. Paul's Life and Epistles* (Biblical Essays); Schürer's Hist. of Jew People, etc. I. ii. pp. 163, 182; A. Harnack's *Die Chronologie der Altchristlichen Literatur bis Eusebius;* Erster Band (1897), especially the sections on *Chronologie des Paulus* (p. 233) and *Das Todesjahr des Petrus und Paulus* (p. 240); C. H. Turner's article on *The Chronology of the N. T.* in Hastings' Dictionary of the Bible; W. M. Ramsay's *St. Paul the Trav.* pp. 45, 49, 51, 58, 128, 174, 189, 226, 234, 254, 258, 264, 265, 275, 286, 289, 313, 351, 363; Th. Zahn's *Einleitung in das N. T.*, vol. ii. p. 626 (1899); Blass' *Acta Apostolorum*, pp. 21–24 (1895); B. W. Bacon in *The Expositor*, 1898 p. 123, 1899, p. 351; G. H. Gilbert's *Student's Life of Paul*, Append. ii. (1899).

VI

INTRODUCTIONS TO THE NEW TESTAMENT

Those of G. Salmon (1889), B. Weiss (Eng. trans. 1888), A. Jülicher (1894), H. J. Holtzmann (1885), Th. Zahn (1897–9), and F. Godet (Eng. trans. 1894, 1899) are the representative ones. To them may be added P. Gloag's Introductions to the Pauline Epp. (1874), to the Catholic Epp. (1887), and to the Johannine Writings (1891); also J. R. Lumby's *Popular Introduction to the N. T.* (1883).

VII

THE THEOLOGY OF THE APOSTLES

A. Neander's *Planting and Training, etc.* (see above); A. Immer's *Theologie des N. T.* (1877); O. Pfleiderer's *Paulinism* (Eng. trans. 1877); C. F. Schmid's *Biblical Theology of tne N. T.* (Eng. trans. 1870); B. Weiss' *Biblical Theology of the N. T.* (Eng. trans. 1882); W. Beyschlag's *N. T. Theology* (Eng-

trans. 1895); **W.** Alexander's *System of Bib. Theology* (1888);
G. B. Stevens' *Pauline* (1894), *Johannine* (1895), *and N. T. Theology* (1899); W. Milligan's *Lectures on the Apocalypse* (1892);
G. Milligan's *Theology of the Ep. to the Hebrews* (1899); J. J.
Lias' *Doctrinal System of St. John* (1875); C. A. Briggs' *Messiah of the Apostles* (1895).

VIII

SPECIAL TREATISES

The following are mentioned, out of the vast mass of similar
literature, because bearing on a few points of special interest.

F. C. Baur's *Die Christuspartei in der Korinthischen Gemeinde*
(Tüb. Zeitschr. f. Theol. 1831. Heft iv.), with which compare
K. Wieseler's *Zur Geschichte der Neutestamentlichen Schrift und
der Urchristenthum* (1880); B. B. Warfield's articles on the *Canonicity and Genuineness of Second Peter* (Presbyterian Review,
Jan. 1882 and Apr. 1883); W. K. Hobart's *The Medical Language
of St. Luke* (1882); J. B. Lightfoot's *Dissertations on the Ap. Age*
(1892); F. J. A. Hort's *Judaistic Christianity* (1894); W. R.
Sorley's *Jewish Christians and Judaism* (1881); G. P. Fisher's
Supernatural Origin of Christianity (3d ed. 1870); R. J. Knowling's *The Witness of the Epistles* (1892).

The following works, pertaining to particular books of the
New Testament, are also worthy of special notice. The commentaries on *The Epistle of James* by J. B. Mayor and W.
Beyschlag; on *Romans* by Sanday and Headlam, to which should
be added the *Analysis of the Ep. to the Rom.* by the late Canon
Liddon; on the *Pastoral Epistles* by B. Weiss, to which add the
Appendix on the Epp. to Tim. and Titus, by Geo. G. Findlay, in
the Eng. trans. of Sabatier's *St. Paul.* Recent attempts to analyze into its sources the Book of Acts have been made by F.
Spitta (*Die Apostelgeschichte,* 1891), C. Clemen (*Chronologie der
paul. Briefe,* 1893), Joh. Jungst (*Die Quelen der Apostelg.* 1895),
but they do not commend themselves either by their processes or
their results. Hackett's *Commentary on Acts* (revised by A. Hovey,
1882) is still standard, though it does not include the most
recent archæological investigations. These latter are included
in the small but excellent *People's Com. on Acts,* by E. W. Rice
(1896). Blass' *Acta Apostolorum* (1895) is very interesting from

the critical and philological points of view. The " Revelation "
has also of late years received much attention. The history of
attempts to analyze it into sources may be read in an article by
Geo. A. Barton in the Amer. Journ. of Theology (Oct. 1898)
entitled *The Apoc. and recent criticism.* See also on the same
subject Briggs' *Messiah of the Apostles,* chh. ix–xv. But for the
best treatment of the Apocalypse, we refer to W. Milligan's
Revelation of St. John (Baird Lectt. for 1885) and the same
author's *Discussions on the Apocalypse* (1893).

INDEXES

INDEX OF NAMES AND SUBJECTS

[References are to pages. Names of modern authors are in italics.]

INDEX OF BIBLICAL REFERENCES